W9-CTU-248

Castles and Fortifications of Britain and Europe

Dobroslav Líbal

Hamlyn

ACKNOWLEDGMENTS

The Publishers would like to thank the following photographers and institutions for having put their pictorial materials at their disposal:
Pavel Vácha: 1, 3, 5, 9, 10, 15—18, 30—35, 37—39, 42, 55, 64—67, 70, 73, 74, 78, 81, 83, 85—87, 100, 104, 113—115, 117, 119, 120—124, 126—131, 133, 135, 138—140, 142, 143, 145—147, 149, 150, 161—163, 171—175, 177, 179, 180, 183, 186—188, 242, 244, 264, 271, 272, 274—276, 278, 279, 281; Vladimír Uher: 22, 41, 43, 45, 53, 71, 75, 79, 89, 103, 107, 108, 125, 154, 157, 158, 167, 178, 181, 201, 203, 204, 207, 208, 232, 234, 245, 247, 250, 251, 253, 255—258, 263, 265, 267, 269, 277, 282; Ondřej Kavan: 7, 11, 19, 21, 47, 49, 52, 102, 105, 106, 262; Miroslav Vlček: 88, 151—153, 156, 170; Vítězslav Motl: 237, 249; Jaroslav Major: 246
© Istituto geografico De Agostini, Novara: 90, 92, 94, 96, 98, 137, 160, 166, 194, 195, 198, 199, 239, 241, 243, 248 (from the publication *Monumenti d'Italia, Castelli,* Novara 1978)
© Newnes Books, London: 4, 8, 13, 14, 24—29, 56, 58—61, 63, 109, 110, 112, 210 (from the publication *Castles and Houses in Britain,* London 1986)
© KLM Aerocarto-Schiphol: 116, 214, 270 (with the kind permission of Vestingmuseum, Naarden)
© SPADEM: 252, 254, 259, 261, 266, 268 (the pictures were furnished by Le Musée des plans et reliefs, Paris)
The engravings from Schedel's Chronicle (121, 205) were photographed with the kind permission of the National Museum in Prague; the model of the fort in Hradec Králové (279) was photographed with the kind permission of the Regional Museum in Hradec Králové.

Designed and produced by
Aventinum for
The Hamlyn Publishing Group
Limited, a Division of The Octopus
Publishing Group,
Michelin House, 81 Fulham Road,
London SW3 6RB

Copyright © Aventinum, Prague 1992
Translated by Slavoš Kadečka
Photographs by Pavel Vácha et al.
Drawings by Jarmila Líbalová
Graphic design by Aleš Krejča

All rights reserved. No part of this
publication may be reproduced,
stored in a retrieval system, or
transmitted, in any form or by any
means, electronic, mechanical,
photocopying or otherwise, without
the permission of The Hamlyn
Publishing Group Limited and the
copyright holder.

ISBN 0 600 57310 9

Printed in Czechoslovakia by
Spektrum, Brno
2/99/81/51-01

Castles and Fortifications of Britain and Europe

Contents

The Legacy of Rome

Fortifications are almost as old as human society, and surprisingly complex and formidable defensive systems were devised by prehistoric societies and the earliest civilizations. However, the main European tradition stems from the fortifications built by the Romans throughout their vast empire, and these will be taken as the starting point of this book.

In this, as in other fields, Roman influence persisted despite the collapse of the West Roman Empire in the 5th century AD, which was followed by centuries of turmoil sometimes called the Dark Ages. Then, slowly, the culture of the Middle Ages took shape in Western and Central Europe. In the east, meanwhile, the East Roman or Byzantine Empire survived with its capital at Constantinople (modern Istanbul). However, its gradual disintegration under the impact of Islam, along with later disasters such as the disintegration of Kievan Russia under the impact of the Tartars, meant that Eastern Europe underwent its own separate development —architectural among many other things—over the centuries.

Culturally the rest of Europe developed in a different way. Deeply rooted in its Roman heritage, Romanesque and Gothic culture gradually spread over an ever-increasing number of countries, ultimately reaching from Portugal to Finland, from Scotland to the eastern boundary of Poland, to the Carpathians, the Danube and Dalmatia. For a time two islands in the eastern Mediterranean, Rhodes and Cyprus, also formed part of the 'West', as did the Holy Land.

Medieval fortifications were of two main types: castles and fortified cities. Castles had two military functions: they formed part of a kingdom's defences, but they also served as power bases for the powerful feudal lords who mainly occupied them.

The two functions were often mutually contradictory, and this was largely responsible for the struggles between monarchs and feudal barons for the control of castles that played so great a part in medieval history.

By contrast, the Romans knew no such conflict. Their entire fortification system was intended for collective security: a city or region was defended not as an isolated unit but as part of the Roman Empire. This difference in function makes it difficult to believe that there were significant elements of continuity between Roman and medieval methods of fortification; but, as we shall see, they existed nonetheless.

The fortifications of Rome itself date back to the 6th century BC, when the earliest wall was built. A second wall was added after the Gauls sacked the city in the 4th century BC. The rampart, almost 10 metres high and up to 3.6 metres wide, was surrounded by a ditch almost 9 metres wide.

One of the oldest city walls in Europe is to be found in Spain, in the Catalonian city of Tarragona. It surrounds the old city, which is situated on top of a hill rising to 160 metres above sea level. The earliest part of the wall, up to 10 metres high, is pre-Roman and dates from about the 6th century BC; it consists of huge blocks of stone, some at least 4 metres long. The Roman wall was erected at two different periods, and continued to function during the Middle Ages.

Another example of early Roman fortification is the city wall of Pompeii in Southern Italy, which was destroyed in AD 79 by an eruption of Mount Vesuvius. The wall originated in about the 2nd century BC. It was punctuated at irregular intervals of at least 50 metres by towers which protruded slightly from its outer face. A number of its gateways were

1
Cologne, Germany. Remains of the Roman fortifications of Colonia Agrippina, built in about AD 50. The tower and wall shown in the picture are modern restorations.

2
Constantinople (now Istanbul, Turkey). Fortifications in depth on the west and north-west sides of the city, built in the reign of Theodosius II (408-50). After Ebersolt.

built as simple passages, without protective towers on each side.

Forum Iulii, the present-day town of Fréjus in Provence, is of considerable importance in the history of Roman fortifications. It was founded by Caesar in 44 BC and became a thriving Roman port. At present it is possible to see only fractions of the wall, which comprises a complicated trace. (The trace, or *enceinte*, is the outline of a fortification.) The wall was strengthened with semicircular towers. The west gate, known as the Porte des Gaules, opened in a curved sector of the wall flanked by a round tower on each side. The most remarkable feature of all is the citadel facing south, which soared high above what was then sea level. The angles of the walls have three round towers placed close to one another, in a fashion that heralds the layout of medieval castles. (The Roman fortifications of another famous city, Cologne, were erected somewhat later, shortly after the middle of the lst century AD.)

The defence of the Roman Empire was organized on its frontiers, the *limes*, and it was there that the principles of Roman fortification were fully developed. The fortified places there were of three main types: the legionary fortresses (*castra*), the forts (*castella*), and the watchtowers (*burgi*).

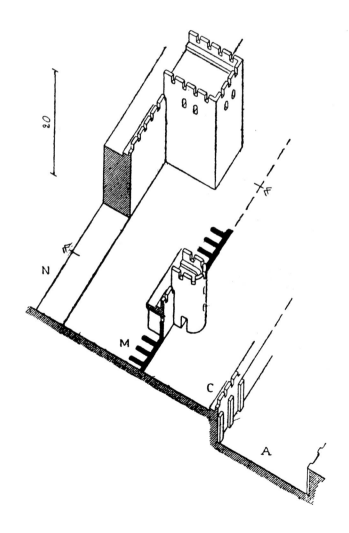

Once the *limes* were stabilized, the temporary materials used to fortify Roman military camps were replaced by durable and incombustible materials such as stone and brick. The characteristic gateway system developed, comprising a central passageway flanked with a tower on each side. The towers also served to strengthen the trace of the masonry wall, which was shielded by a ditch and a rampart on the outside.

The gates and towers of forts and fortresses resembled those subsequently built in the Middle Ages not only in shape, but also in their relationship to the wall. This was because their system of fortification was applied to Roman towns, which later provided models for medieval engineers. The first stage in the process can be seen at Augusta Praetoria Salassorum (present-day Aosta), founded by the

Emperor Augustus about 25 BC. Here the walls, initially 10 to 13 metres high, imposed a rectangular contour on the town. The fortifications were copied directly from those of Roman fortresses. The four gateways were flanked with rectangular towers, and other rectangular towers were placed astride the walls at regular intervals.

The legionary fortress of Carnuntum, above the southern bank of the Danube near Petronelle in Lower Austria, was also protected by fortifications with gateways flanked by towers straddling the wall; additional strength was provided by placing towers at relatively short intervals inside the wall. It is beyond doubt that Carnuntum was completely laid out by the 2nd century AD. Unfortunately, after the Second World War archaeological investigation of the city ended and the excavations were filled in.

In many respects the great palace of the Emperor Diocletian at Split in Yugoslavia retained the character of a legionary fortress. Completed by AD 305, it was almost square in plan, and had three axially oriented gateways, each of them guarded by two octagonal towers standing against the outer face of the walls. The four corners were reinforced by

3
Saalburg, Germany. Restored Roman frontier fort to the north-west of Bad Homburg. View of the south gate (Porta decumana), beginning of the 3rd century.

square towers meeting the wall only at the adjacent corners. The long curtains (outer walls, not part of the building) were punctuated at regular intervals by small square towers.

At the height of Roman power, life seemed so secure that the Empire's cities were not fortified at all. However, from the late 2nd century AD destructive incursions by Germanic tribes showed that the frontier defences were no longer impenetrable. The consequence was an increase in the number of fortified cities, of which Rome itself was an outstanding example. In 272 the warlike Emperor Aurelian (270-75), the conqueror of Palmyra, decided to fortify the city with a 19 kilometre wall of layered concrete faced with tiles, 3.5 to 4 metres thick and almost 8 metres high. The top of the wall was provided with interior walkways protected by battlements with wide merlons. (Merlons are the raised portions of battlements, broken by gaps—crenels—through which the defenders can fire at the enemy.) The curtains were some 30 metres long. The wall was strengthened by 380 rectangular towers which projected slightly from its face and were substantially higher than the wall itself. The wall was later heightened, and the design of the gates was modified at the beginning of the 5th century, just before the city was captured and sacked by Alaric the Goth.

A number of towns and cities that once formed part of the Roman Empire still possess the fortifications that were built during the late Imperial period. The old part of the French town of Senlis (Oise) is enclosed by a Gallo-Roman wall, one of the best preserved in the country. In plan it comprises an irregular oval. The average height of the wall is 7 metres, and it is as much as 4 metres thick. There were 28 semicircular towers—most of them still in existence—separated by curtains averaging 27 metres in length. Senlis is a remarkable example of medieval fortifications.

Another good example is found in the far south of France. At the northern foot of the Pyrenees lies the little town of St Lizier (Ariège), once Lugdunum Consoranorum, where the surviving Roman fortifications include 12 towers, 6 semicircular and 6 rectangular.

These two examples must stand for many others that cannot be described here. From England and Spain to Hungary, medieval cities existed that relied for protection on fortifications that had originated in Roman times.

Roman towers were extremely varied in plan. As well as rectangular, semicircular and U-shaped plans, they could also be circular, triangular, hexagonal, heptagonal or octagonal.

After the conversion of the Roman Empire to Christianity, Constantinople (modern Istanbul) became at least as important as Rome. The celebrated

4
Lindau, Germany. The Roman *burgi* (watch towers) of what subsequently became the town of Lindau.

10

5
Portchester Castle, England, from the south-west. Roman fort above the sea near Portsmouth, accessible through two gateways, from the west and from the east. On the west, land side it was protected by a rampart and a ditch. A Norman castle was built in the north-west corner in about 1120.

major Byzantine cities, most notably the walls of the famous city of Nicaea (present-day İznik).

The qualitative difference between the fortifications of the two capital cities of the Roman Empire, Rome and Constantinople, is hard to understand. It is also of some historical interest that Constantinople's fortification system remained unknown in Western and Central Europe until the time of the Crusades, while the principles on which it was based were not fully applied there until much later still. This fact testifies more eloquently than religious and cultural schisms to the gap that opened up between the two halves of the initially united classical world.

The commonest elements in the Roman defence system were not the legionary fortresses, some 660×660 metres in area, but the smaller forts that clustered thickly along the *limes* but are also found in other areas. The important restored fort of Saalburg in the Taunus, to the north-west of Bad Homburg, represents a scaled-down version of the fortress. It had a rectangular layout with rounded corners, and covered an area of 225×150 metres. The stone wall was punctuated by four gateways, each flanked by two towers projecting into the inner space of the fort. The wall was partly surrounded by a double ditch. The main building, erected in its final form at the beginning of the 3rd century AD, was not defensive in character.

The small strongpoint in the Gallo-Roman town of Noviodunum (present-day Jublains), in the north-west of France, disappeared as early as the second half of the 3rd century. The building in its centre, 30×20 metres in area, had four square corner towers and was protected by an earth rampart. Further protection was afforded by a square surrounding wall 4.7 metres thick and 4 to 5 metres high, with U-shaped towers projecting from it.

The Roman fort at Portchester (portus castra) in Hampshire is laid out in a similar fashion. It has an almost square plan (183×196 metres). There are closely spaced U-shaped towers situated obliquely in three corners of the walls; the fourth corner is occupied by the tower of a Norman castle subsequently built on the site.

However, a number of Roman forts do not adhere to the orthodox plan, their defences being adjusted to local conditions. One example is Pevensey Castle in Sussex, which dates from the 3rd century and was converted into a Norman castle after the Conquest. The Roman walls, still 6 metres high in places, were strengthened by regularly spaced U-shaped towers and enclose an unusually large oval ward. The west gateway is flanked by two towers.

The smallest components of the Roman defence

system of fortifications on its west and north-west sides, facing the land, was built in the first half of the 5th century AD, under the Emperor Theodosius II (408-50). This was significantly different from Rome's defences, and vastly more powerful. The fortifications were not only monumental, but consisted of several lines of defence. The battlemented main wall was 4.5 metres thick, with 50 metre long curtains between 20 metre high towers. These projected in their entirety from the external wall face into a bailey, 20 metres wide. This was surrounded by another, lower wall with slightly higher semicircular towers sited opposite the midspan of the main wall curtains. Some of the towers were six-, seven- or eight-sided. At the foot of the outer wall there was another, outermost bailey 16 metres wide, and beyond this a deep ditch 20 metres wide. The whole superb system is usually attributed to the reign of Theodosius in the scientific literature (Ebersolt). Assuming that this dating is correct, the city walls of Constantinople were already in the 5th century on a par with the fully developed fortification systems of the High Middle Ages. And indeed they in turn became the models for the fortifications of

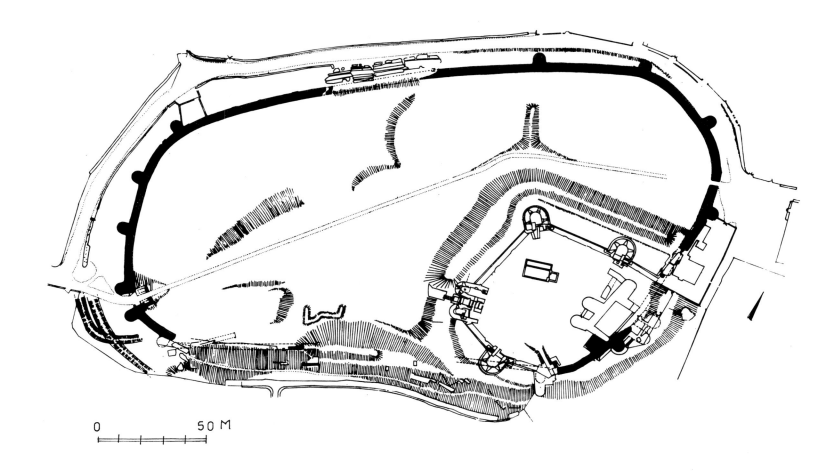

0   50 M

6
Pevensey Castle, England.
Plan of a late 3rd century
Roman fort, converted to a
Norman castle after the
Conquest. The Roman walls
and towers were protected by
a ditch. After Peers.

system were the watchtowers, or *burgi*. These were
initially made of timber, which was later replaced by
masonry, and are of the most varied dimensions in
plan, for example from 10×10 to 16×16 metres.
Apart from tower-shaped structures there were also
large rectangular or square *burgi* (32.6×32.6 metres) surrounding an inner courtyard. One such
burgus has been preserved in the historic centre of
Lindau in Germany, which stands on an island in
Lake Constance.

In the 5th century AD the West Roman Empire
collapsed, and for a long period the Roman tradition of fortification was in abeyance. During the
Dark Ages, fortifications were used by tribes and
kingdoms but, apart from the selection of the site
and the principal means of defence (ditches and
ramparts), they had little connection with the dramatic developments that took place in the early
Middle Ages.

Despite the elapse of centuries, these were based
on the techniques devised by the Romans. But by
contrast with the universality of Roman practice,
the new development was scattered and fragmen-
ted, eventually giving rise to different fortification systems in different states and societies. To
synthesize and present all this is a formidable task,
requiring a profound knowledge of different countries and periods, and the ability to trace the inter-
actions between various individual developments.

Further difficulties are caused by the fact that
specific areas have often not been studied as fully as
possible. On the national level, a comprehensive
treatment of fortifications exists only for Italy and
Hungary. Generally speaking, by far the greatest
attention has been paid to castles. But in some circumstances the conclusions drawn from a study of
castle architecture can be misleading, especially
when such studies are selective, concentrating on
the most important areas of a country. By contrast,
the study of city fortifications is still in its early
stages, and there are serious gaps in our knowledge
of the bastion system.

This book therefore represents the first attempt at
a general survey of this important field. Its results
will have a bearing on the historic struggles of na-
tions and states for survival and the preservation of
their cultural, economic and political identities.

The Beginnings of Medieval Fortification

At the end of the Dark Ages, new types of fortified structures appeared with the growth of early feudalism. To be the lord of a fortified place became necessary to a leader's prestige, while on a practical level the predatory activities of the Vikings, Normans and Magyars must have stimulated the adoption of defensive counter-measures. The new fortified places, or castles, had important points of resemblance to the late Roman *burgi*. The nucleus consisted at first of a residential timber tower that was erected on top of a motte, or artificial mound, and surrounded by an area enclosed by a palisade and a ditch. The basic or ideal plan of such a fortified place was circular, but numerous variations evolved, for example, the oval mound with a bailey or basecourt at its foot. The economic significance of the basecourt is reflected in one of the meanings of its French equivalent, *basse-cour*, a poultry yard. Normally the tower was not situated in the very centre of the mound but at its edge, although here too there were many variations in layout. As a rule there was no way into the ground floor from outside, a ladder providing access to an entrance at first floor level; later, an annexe-like forebuilding containing stairs would serve this function.

The type of castle with a tower as its nucleus rapidly spread all over Europe. The artificial mound was not, however, a universal feature, since towers were often set up on natural elevations. The commonest feature of the type was its compact layout, optimally expressed by a circular plan including a ditch, often filled with water, and a rampart.

It became apparent quite early on that timber—the most widely used building material in the post-classical world—was unsuitable because of the danger of fire. Consequently towers soon began to be built of stone, although timber remained in use and did not actually disappear until the beginning of the 12th century. In time the palisade too was replaced by a stone or brick wall strengthened with towers.

The size of the nucleic stone tower, built on a rectangular or square plan, also helped to determine future developments. In Western Europe the basic dimension—the length of the side of the square, or of the shortest side of the rectangle—stabilized at about 20 metres. Elsewhere, smaller towers, with sides about 10 metres long, prevailed. The first type developed into the powerful donjon, or keep, whereas the second gave rise to lesser strongholds or towers.

Stone keeps, quite frequently found in the 11th century, became very common in the 12th century. Both towers and keeps were residences as well as fortresses. As early as the 990s the ambitious Foulques Nerra, Count of Anjou, had a stone keep built at Langeais (Indre et Loire); although in ruins, it still

stands with three sides partly preserved. The keep
was oblong in plan. There are shallow buttresses, or
pilasters, at intervals along the outside walls, a
technique, used here for the first time, that subsequently became common in keeps on both sides of
the Channel. Unfortunately the original height of
Foulques's castle is not known.

The monumental keep at Beaugency (Loiret), on
the Loire, is rectangular in plan (23 × 20 metres)
and austere in appearance, with buttressed corners;
it is generally held to have originated in the 11th
century. There was no forebuilding containing
stairs, the first floor being accessible only by ladder.
Inside the keep there were wooden floors.
Beaugency was probably erected before the Norman conquest of 1066. The windows were certainly
made to be used by archers.

A further stage of development is represented by
the magnificent keep at Loches (Indre et Loire).
The rectangular tower, 25 × 14 metres in plan and
40 metres high, is provided with a lower forebuilding housing the stairs. The exterior wall faces were
broken by pilasters with adjoining semicircular half-
columns. The battlements were equipped with a
brattice—a projecting wooden hoarding—which
enabled the defenders to throw stones at their as-
sailants or pour boiling water and pitch down on to
them.

The keep at Loches is regarded as one of the most
effective of the early donjons. Opinions concerning
its dating fluctuate; in seems most likely to have
been built in the second third of the 11th century,
but a number of scholars are prepared to date it to
the following century. Another French castle, at
Chauvigny (Vienne), is dated to the end of the 11th
century. The ruins of its monumental donjon survive; the façade is divided by shallow buttresses.

★

7
Loches, France. View of the castle from the south-west, with the massive keep in the centre; it probably dates from the second third of the 11th century. In the foreground is the wall from the reign of Henry II of England (1154-89); to the right are high towers with loopholes for crossbows, added to the wall in the later 13th century.

8
The Tower of London. Aerial view from the north-east. In the foreground is the ditch from which rises the outer wall, dating from the reign of Edward I (1272-1307); the bastion in the north-east corner was probably built under Henry III (1216-72). The Norman keep with the chapel (1066-1100) is in the centre; to the left, at the rear, are the Wakefield Tower and the adjoining Bloody Tower with the 13th century gateway.

9
Gnandstein, Germany. South façade of the Romanesque castle hall dating from 1180-90, heightened in the late Gothic period. To the north there is a circular tower in the inner courtyard, dating from about 1100, which is protected in the north and east by a massive wall.

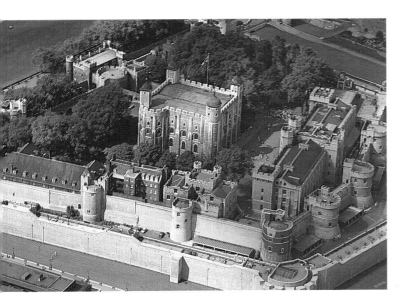

The keep was taken across the Channel by the Normans after their conquest of England in 1066. The first was at Windsor, where a large circular keep was erected in about 1075; it was later substantially rebuilt. Initially it was probably a shell keep, with no buildings inside.

At the end of the 1070s work began on a massive keep that was intended to serve as a symbol of Norman power. This was the White Tower, the nucleus of the present Tower of London, which was completed by the end of the 11th century. The keep is an irregular oblong in plan, its longest (south) side measuring almost 36 metres. The semicircular apse of the Romanesque chapel forms the projecting south-east corner, while the north-east corner is occupied by a circular staircase. The walls vary in thickness from 3.3 to 4.5 metres. The inside of the White Tower is divided into two by a cross-wall running north-south. Its exterior design, with slender turrets in the corners and shallow buttresses

along the walls, became the model for subsequent Norman towers built on English soil. The outer defences consisted of the River Thames, the old Roman wall of London, and a wall with a ditch on the two remaining sides.

The biggest Norman keep of all was built in about 1080 at Colchester in Essex by the King's steward Eudo. It covers an area of 50 × 38 metres and is notable for its extremely thick walls and general

10
Ávila, Spain. Panoramic view of the city from the south, showing the wall and its towers. End of the 11th century.

monumentality. Colchester Castle in its entirety, including the bailey, outer walls and ditch, was probably completed by 1101.

★

Eleventh century French and English castles, mostly still extant, are monumental structures. In Germany, where stone castles were mostly built on the sites of former natural strongholds, the situation was rather different.

An example of an 11th century German castle uncovered by archaeological excavation is Todenman, to the north of Rinteln in Lower Saxony, which was destroyed by fire as early as 1080. It has an almost regular layout consisting of a circular area in which the tower had been situated (not uncovered by the excavators) and an oval nucleus enclosed by a massive wall; adjoining the wall were the tower of the hall and a chapel. The layout shows a consistent differentiation of functions which directly determined the development of Central European castles, so different from those of England and France.

The earliest parts of Todenman probably date back to about AD 1000. It provides very early evidence of the tendency of German castle plans to become elongated.

★

By chance, examples of 11th century German castle architecture have been particularly well preserved in the area between the Weser and the Elbe, in the former duchies of Saxony and Thuringia. The most striking characteristics of the new stone castles were massive circular towers as much as 15 metres in diameter.

Within the complex layout of one of the biggest German castles, Querfurt (Halle) it is possible to identify a Romanesque nucleus, parabolic in plan, culminating at its west end in a massive circular tower called Der Dicke Heinrich (Stout Henry), which dates from about 1070. It stands on the site of a slightly larger oblong building erected during the Carolingian period.

The castle of Seeburg (Halle) was trapezoidal in plan. Here too there is a circular tower, originally some 30 metres high and with walls almost 6 metres thick, which rises above the ditch to the south-east. By contrast, Neuenburg Castle in Freyburg has a compressed oval plan, but in the south-east corner there used to be a massive circular tower which was destroyed in the 13th century. Mention should also be made of the circular watchtower (Mantelturm) of the castle of Altenburg (Leipzig) and the tower of the castle of Gnandstein (Leipzig), about 35 metres high, which dates from about 1100. The imperial castle of Lauenburg (Halle) is still bigger. The western lower castle is compact in plan, with a residential tower. The nucleus of the castle to the east is divided into three parts; the eastern and western parts are guarded by watchtowers.

Bohemia also played a part in the development of medieval fortifications. According to the archaeological evidence, the unique fortifications of Prague Castle were begun during the reign of Prince Břetislav I, in the 1040s. If so, Prague Castle must rank among the outstanding fortresses of the period. However, the historical data are in conflict with the archaeological testimony, which is currently under question. The principal period during which the construction of the fortifications took place was the second third of the 12th century.

The most important early example of castles in Italy can be found in the south of the peninsula, where the builders were—as in England—the Normans. At some point after the mid-11th century, the Norman ruler of Southern Italy, Robert Guiscard, had a castle built at Melfi. With its keep and its four towers, two of which were almost free-standing, Melfi is an example of a very early castle layout.

Early medieval Spain is best represented by the magnificent fortifications of the Castilian city of Ávila. This is one of the oldest walled cities of the feudal period. The battlemented wall was strengthened by a crowded line of semicircular towers; the curtains were about 30 metres long. Entrance to the city was afforded by eight gateways. The hilltop site of Ávila made a ditch unnecessary.

As we shall now see, the European achievement of the 11th century laid the basis for the dynamic changes in the art of fortification that occurred in the centuries that followed.

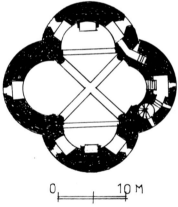

11
Provins, France. The Tower of Caesar, a keep from the early 12th century, erected on an artificial mound. The circular wall was built by the English captain Thomas Guerand after the fall of the town in 1432.

12
Étampes, France. Plan of the Tour Guinette, the keep of a royal castle to the north-west of the city. Before the middle of the 12th century. After C. Enlart.

13 ▶
Rochester Castle, England. View from the east. The peripheral wall, reinforced with towers, dates from about 1190; the keep was erected in the 1130s.

The Early Twelfth Century

In 1095 the first Crusade was proclaimed, and in 1099 the Crusaders took Jerusalem. In the course of their passage through the Byzantine Empire, Asia Minor, Syria and Palestine, they encountered far more mature and complex fortification systems than anything they had known in their own homelands. Consequently the experience of the Crusades exerted a gradual, but deep and decisive, influence on the development of European fortifications. Another factor was the further development of the feudal system, which stimulated ever more intensive castle-building and, later, the fortification of cities.

The experience of the Crusades was particularly important in reviving study of the technology and tactics of siegecraft, which had been mastered by the Romans but had subsequently declined. The besieging forces used various 'engines' including catapults, mobile towers and battering rams. The undermining of walls was also an important technique.

The besieged used missile-throwing engines for their defence.

By comparison with the preceding periods, our knowledge of 12th century fortifications is much more detailed. Surveying the century by roughly fifty-year periods will clarify matters, although such surveys cannot of course be exhaustive.

The keep at Gisors (Eure) in Normandy was built on a motte (artificial mound) by the great landowner Robert de Bellême for the King of England, William Rufus (William II). It has a slightly irregular octagonal plan. In 1123-24 King Henry I greatly strengthened its defences by fortifying the castle ward with a wall 7-8 metres high and 1.5 metres thick, with rectangular towers projecting out of the wall face and opening into the enclosure.

In the Paris region, radical changes in keep design soon took place. At Houdan (Seine et Oise), the 30-metre-high keep dates from the first third of the 12th century and is a circular structure with four U-shaped towers. The interior is square, with slightly chamfered corners and stairs in the thickness of the wall. There are loopholes rather than windows.

West of the collegiate church in the ancient city of Provins (Seine et Marne) lies the Tower of Caesar, which stands on a walled motte. This is one of the finest early feudal keeps in France, built some time before the middle of the 12th century. Although rectangular in plan, the central part has emphatically bevelled corners from which spring semicircular turrets. Between these and the tapering upper Romanesque part there are flying buttresses.

The transition from the rounded, heavy forms of Romanesque to the Gothic style first took place in the Paris region, and had a significant impact on the design of keeps. The culmination of this development is represented by the keep known as the Tour Guinette, which dominates the city of Étampes

(Seine et Oise). The austere walls of this curious ruined tower are 4 metres thick and reach a height of 27 metres. The keep dates from before the mid-12th century. During its reconstruction under Philip II Augustus, each of the storeys was vaulted. Small by comparison, the keep at Château Chervix is 9×13 metres in rectangular plan and 30 metres high. On its outside walls, sets of double and triple pilasters are linked with blind semicircular arcades.

In England castle construction was somewhat different in character. Around 1100 a Norman castle was built within the walls of a Roman fort at Pevensey in Sussex. The rectangular keep is built into the old wall, from which six U-shaped bastions project strongly, one of them being a feature of the original Roman fort. The castle was surrounded by a moat. The western gateway was situated between two baileys on the moat side.

A typical example from the reign of King Henry I (1100-35) is Rochester Castle in Kent, which domi-

14
Castle Rising, England. View through the Romanesque gateway of the keep, built in about 1138. The Norman fortifications of the castle, with ramparts and ditches, are very well preserved.

15
Lenzburg, Switzerland. The
ground floor of the big square
tower and the adjoining hall
date from the 11th-12th
centuries. Intensive
construction went on in the
14th-15th centuries.

16
Chillon, Switzerland. View of
the famous castle from the
south-east. In the foreground
is the tower, originally
Romanesque, which was
strengthened in the 13th
century. The Romanesque
wall on the land side was
supplemented by three towers
erected from 1255 onwards.

nated the point at which Wattling Street crossed the River Medway. It has a square plan with four slender angle turrets rising above the level of the parapet. The south-east angle and turret, which project emphatically from the wall face, are round. On the north side there is a lower forebuilding, constructed at the same time as the keep, which protected its first-floor entrance. The verticality of the building is imposing. The turrets, a storey higher than the mass of the castle, rise to some 35 metres. The entire castle is battlemented. An internal cross-wall divides the keep from top to bottom. The artistic decoration of the interiors is of a high standard. The castle was built by William de Corbeil, Archbishop of Canterbury. Its general appearance is Norman,

17
Saaleck and Rudelsburg,
Germany. Two castles of
Romanesque origin: the
lower, on the left, is Saaleck,
the higher, on the right,
Rudelsburg.

18 ►
Prague Castle,
Czechoslovakia. The towers
on the south façade of the
hall. After 1135.

with no visible influence from other kinds of Continental architecture. In about 1190 stone walls were built around it.

In the mid-12th century William de Albino, who married Henry I's widow, built Castle Rising in Norfolk. Although 24×21 metres in plan, the keep is only 12 metres high. In the corners there are square, slightly projecting turrets. The walls are divided by blind arcades or pilasters. The very wide stairs in the forebuilding on the eastern side give access to an oblong minor wing adjoining the north-east corner of the keep. The main floor is divided into several rooms. The keep was protected by an external fortification system.

Castles built outside northern France and England were entirely different in character. The origins of the Swiss castle of Lenzburg (Aargau) go back to the 11th century. The cigar-shaped nucleus of the famous Swiss castle of Chillon (Vaud) was built in the mid-12th century on a rocky island in Lake Geneva, with an oblong tower in the centre.

In Germany a heavy monumentality characterized castle construction during the first half of the 12th century. The enormous imperial castle of Kyffhausen (Halle), overall 600 metres in length, was built for the Emperor Lothair (1125-37). Its layout, determined by the configuration of the ground, was oblong. The castle consisted of three parts, the central one of which has largely been destroyed. The eastern lower castle has an irregular trapezoidal plan, the southern side of which is rounded. The western entrance is guarded by a circular watch-tower, on the northern side of which stands a tower-shaped residential building 10 metres high. The north-south wall divided the enclosure of the lower castle into two unequal parts, the easternmost containing the Romanesque chapel.

The more compact upper castle is divided by two interior walls running north-south. The highest point of the ridge is controlled by the Barbarossa Tower, a residential tower clad with rusticated blocks which was built later than the rest, in the second half of the 12th century. There was a hall on its southern side.

The interesting castle of Saaleck (Halle), dating from the early 12th century, has an oblong layout with a pair of circular towers some 11 metres in diameter at either end. The eastern tower merges with the outside wall. The visual outline of the castle is highly impressive.

22

In the castle of Cheb (Eger, now in Czecho-slovakia) archaeologists discovered part of the wall with two circular towers, built in the first half of the 12th century.

Early castle building in Austria is represented by Rauheneck, a notable example of the oblong layout in its developed form. It originally consisted of an upper and lower castle. The plan of the upper castle is an irregular trapezium extended in a north-south direction; the rhomboidal plan of the lower castle projects slightly westwards beyond the general contour of the castle. The short south side of the upper castle consists of a thick wall with a massive tower. The hall is situated along the east side of the upper castle. The lower castle adjoins the upper in the north. There is a Romanesque chapel in the north-west corner of the lower castle.

The first mention of Rauheneck dates from 1137, but some authorities believe it was actually built in the late 11th century. The shape of the big southern tower and the way it projects beyond the wall are surprising features.

In the Bohemian capital, Prague, an oblong tower-shaped hall was built in the early 12th century or earlier; it stood at the eastern end of the palatial High Romanesque residence of the Bohemian princes. According to one chronicler, in 1135 the Czech prince Soběslav I began 'to restore Prague, the metropolis of Bohemia, after the fashion of Roman cities'. This refers to Prague's magnificent stone fortifications as well as to the new hall of Prague Castle.

The fortifications were most probably linked with those dating frome the time of Břetislav I. The castle, 425 metres long and some 140 metres across at its widest point, was enclosed by a stone wall 2 to 2.5 metres thick and up to 14 metres high, clad with carefully dressed stone blocks. The west side of the castle was defended by a ditch. Each of the tall towers of the south and east gateways had a vaulted passage at ground level. The tower of the west gateway is situated on the north side of the passage. The towers are inside the wall.

The fortifications of the long south side of the castle, facing the Lesser Town below, were quite remarkable. The wall was strengthened in the Roman way with solid towers the same height as the wall; they were variously rectangular, pentagonal and semicircular. On the west side of the castle a high tower projects from the wall face in its centre. Another, stronger tower stands in the north-west corner. A tower is concealed in the burgrave building near the east end of the castle's north side.

The fortifications have in large part been preserved. No doubt this represents one of the most extensive fortification systems of the early feudal age in Europe. As the quotation from the chronicler suggests, the fortifications of Prague Castle were inspired by Roman precedents. Rectangular and semicircular towers were very frequently used; more unusual were pentagonal towers, which can, however, be found for example among the fortifications of the Roman town of Venta Silurum, present-day Caerwent in Monmouthshire. The result is that Prague Castle represents the oldest large-scale application of Roman methods of fortification outside the *limes* of the empire.

In about 1125 Soběslav I built the castle of Přimda on the frontier between Bohemia and the Palatinate. The castle consists of a sturdy two-storey residential tower with a small forebuilding.

There is not enough reliable evidence concerning early 12th century castle-building in Italy, Spain and Portugal for any coherent description to be attempted.

To sum up, the oblong layout of German castles was clearly the most important development in the art of fortification during the early 12th century, although the fortifications devised for Prague Castle are also of great importance.

19
Niort, France. The double-
keep castle. About 1160.

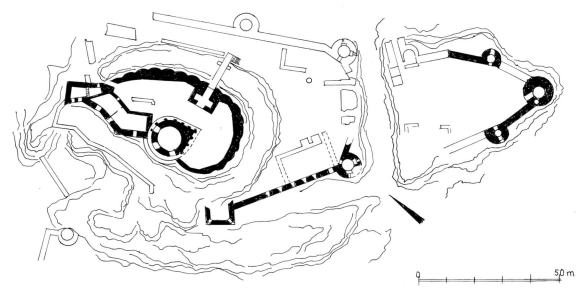

20
Château Gaillard des Andelys,
France. Plan of the castle.
After C. L. Salch.

0   50 m

24

The Later Twelfth Century

The second half of the 12th century was one of dramatic conflicts. Battles raged in the Holy Land, and also in Italy and the Iberian peninsula. A huge area of France came under the control of the Angevin Henry (Plantagenet), who as Henry II was also king of England, and this led to protracted struggles between the Angevins and the kings of France. Thus the entire European situation stimulated the development of fortification systems from their still somewhat primitive forms.

The first major area of development was the part of France dominated by the Angevin kings of England, as the following examples demonstrate.

The castle of Niort (Deux Sèvres) dates from about 1160. It consists of two keeps, slightly different in mass, which controlled a courtyard protected by a lower connecting wall. At the angles of the keeps are three-quarter-circular towers of equal height, each with a round turret in the centre of the wall face. There are similar turrets along the connecting wall. The sides of each keep are decorated with blind arcades. The entire structure is battlemented.

The keep at Chambois is a pure Norman type, common in England but unusual on royal French soil; significantly, Chambois is in the department of Orne, which forms part of historic Normandy. The turrets of this circular keep are slightly higher than

21
Château Gaillard des Andelys, France. An overall view of this famous fortress. There is an outer bailey with a circular tower at the top on the left; top right is the upper castle with a massive wall 'corrugated' on the outside. Above it rises a great tower with small buttresses. 1196-97.

22
Ghent, Belgium.
S'Gravensteen, the castle of
the counts of Flanders.
Behind the outer wall (with
heavily restored upper parts)
rises the massive keep. The
castle was built in 1180.

23
Kenilworth Castle, England.
Plan of the keep. Built
between 1155 and 1170. After
Reynolds.

the battlements. The entrance is situated on the first
floor of the southern forebuilding, which is square in
plan. The walls are crowned with machicolations on
stone corbels and battlements. The keep at Chambois dates from the end of the 12th century.

At Ambleny (Aisne) the keep, with its sturdy
U-shaped turrets, was probably built by the French
King Philip II Augustus at the end of the 12th
century.

Of great significance were the new fortifications
ordered for the powerful keep at Loches (Indre et
Loire) by Henry II of England (1154—89). The
castle area was enclosed by a wall strengthened with
solid semicircular towers of equal height. This is in
fact analogous to the fortifications constructed
somewhat earlier at Prague Castle.

In the course of the major reconstruction of
Henry's castle of Chinon (Indre et Loire) the walls
were strengthened by the addition of rectangular,
semicircular and U-shaped towers.

The important Norman castle at Gisors (Eure)

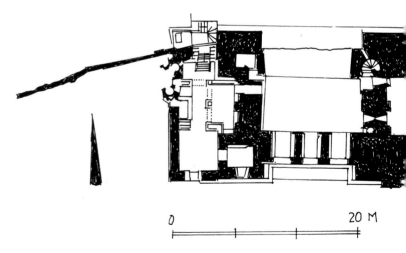

0   20 M

was also reconstructed under Henry II. Its existing keep was enclosed in a hexagonal wall, and a chapel consecrated to St Thomas of Canterbury was built in the narrow ward between the wall and the keep (1184). The mound was surrounded with a ditch.

The outer wall, 7-8 metres high and 1.5 metres thick, was strengthened with towers that were semicircular or *en bec* (pointed towards the enemy).

At Issoudun (Indre) the White Tower, 27 metres in height, stands on a high motte. It was built

24
Arundel Castle, England. Aerial view of the castle, which has been converted into a mansion. In the centre, on top of a motte, is a shell keep. On its north and south sides there are large baileys, their walls reinforced with towers; they were built as early as the 12th century.

late in the 12th century by Henry II's son, Richard Coeur de Lion. The tower at La Roche Guyon (Seine et Oise), also late 12th century, is similar.

Angevin fortifications in the eastern borderlands of Normandy culminated in the castle of Château Gaillard des Andelys (Eure) which soars above the right bank of the River Seine. It was built by Richard Coeur de Lion in 1196, the work being executed at a tremendous pace and completed within 14 months. An irregular oval in plan, the upper castle was situated on the top of a cliff, its keep (circular, but drawn out to a point on its east side) standing on the edge of the precipice. Shallow pilasters connected by arches run along part of its outer face. On the rocky slope the keep broadens out into a massive scarp (4.5 metres thick at the foot). Its curtain wall, extending from the keep on either side, is vertically 'corrugated' in the most vulnerable sector to facilitate enfilades—raking fire from the side, a very important resource for defenders confronted with a direct assault. The huge lower castle, separated from the upper castle by a moat, was protected by a peripheral wall (only partly preserved) with circular towers projecting from the wall face. In the lower

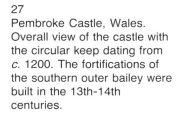

27
Pembroke Castle, Wales.
Overall view of the castle with the circular keep dating from c. 1200. The fortifications of the southern outer bailey were built in the 13th-14th centuries.

◄ 25

Richmond Castle, England. Ruins of the castle, built in the late 11th century. The keep was built later, by Henry II.

28

Dover Castle, England. View of part of the castle including the massive keep built by Henry II. The inner wall was built at the same time. In the foreground there is a section of the outer wall, construction of which probably began at the end of the 12th century.

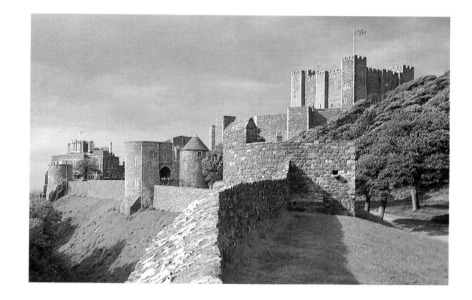

◄ 26

Conisbrough Castle, England. Ruins of the castle with an outer bailey in the foreground, its walls reinforced with towers. On the right is the keep, of unusual circular plan with six buttresses. About 1180.

29

Framlingham Castle, England. View of part of the castle, protected by a wall with rectangular towers. Late 12th century.

castle extensive caves were cut into the rock adjoining the ditch.

The corrugated curtain wall of the inner bailey was imitated from Islamic fortifications. The experience of the Crusades also certainly influenced the concentric system of outer walls used at Château Gaillard. At the time of its construction the castle was regarded as impregnable.

S'Gravensteen is a well-known castle in the capital of Flanders, Ghent. Various modifications and reconstructions of later date have obscured its initial character—that of an early feudal fortress, consisting of a bulky rectangular keep in an oval enclosure. The castle was erected in 1180 on the site of an earlier fortification.

In England, the construction of the monumental keep of Kenilworth Castle in Warwickshire was accomplished between 1155 and 1170. Kenilworth has

a rectangular plan with massive walls up to 5 metres thick and square corner turrets. A rectangular forebuilding, somewhat later in date, stands against the west wall; it houses the stairs to the first floor. On the south-west side there was an oval bailey.

Of the other castles built during the reign of Henry II, mention should be made of Hedingham Castle in Essex, which is notable for its slender dimensions. Only two of the keep's four corner turrets survive.

The Norman castle at Newcastle controlled the crossing of the River Tyne. Its keep, built in 1172-77, has been preserved in good condition. It is 26 metres high and stands on an artificial mound. The corners of the building, with walls up to 5.5 metres thick, have rectangular turrets. Pilasters run down the middle of each curtain wall. The stairs are housed in a lower forebuilding.

30
Hohenklingen Castle,
Switzerland. The oldest parts
of the castle with the
rectangular tower were built in
the 12th century.

31
Landeck, Germany. The
castle ruins dating from
c. 1200. The outer wall with
one rectangular and four
U-shaped towers dates from
1416

In the centre of imposing Arundel Castle, in Sussex, stands a motte 23 metres high supporting a typical circular shell keep with flat buttresses on the outside. Its outer wall is 3 metres thick. Around the motte there is a large bailey, the massive walls of which are strengthened with towers. Both the keep and the bailey date from the 12th century.

The monumental keep of Richmond Castle in Yorkshire, with corner turrets and pilasters along the outer faces of the walls, was also built under Henry II. The castle is situated in a dominant position on a rocky promontory above the River Swale. Its massive stone walls are earlier than the keep, dating from the late 11th century.

A tendency to replace rectangular keep plans with polygonal or circular plans appeared in England as early as the 12th century. Probably the oldest example (about 1180) is Conisbrough Castle in South Yorkshire, the circular keep of which is reinforced with rectangular buttresses.

The ruins of Pembroke Castle in Dyfed, Wales, are also monumental. A mighty round keep from about 1200 stands at its heart; it is almost 27 metres high, with walls over 6 metres thick at the base. The south side of the upper castle was strengthened with two semicircular towers. The wall of the large 13th century outer bailey was protected by five projecting round angle towers, a gateway and a barbican. The castle was never captured during the medieval period.

The most ambitious project of Henry II's reign was the construction of 'the key to England', the royal castle of Dover overlooking the Channel. The massive 28-metre-high keep has outside walls of extraordinary thickness. Four corner turrets rise above the level of the parapet, and the keep is approached by way of a triple-towered forebuilding. It is surrounded by a polygonal wall from which rectangular towers project at intervals, and a second, outer wall was added later, mainly in the reigns of King John and Henry III.

This advanced fortification was not unique in England. Framlingham Castle in Suffolk was probably built at the same time. It has no keep, its oval enclosure being surrounded by a wall reinforced with thirteen towers.

The fortification system that evolved during the reigns of Henry II and his son Richard Coeur de Lion exemplifies an important phase in the development of medieval fortifications, one emphasizing the defence of curtains by means of enfilades directed from towers projecting from the wall face. The fortifications of Château Gaillard represent the culmination of contemporary techniques. In England's poorer neighbour, Scotland, the first stone castle, Sween in Argyll, was not built until the mid-12th century, when its builders took the Norman keep as their model.

In Switzerland, the castle of Thun was begun by the Duke of Zähringen after 1190. The massive rectangular tower is one of the few examples of a pure French donjon built on Germanic territory during the early feudal period. The circular corner towers tapering to a point were additions of a later date, as was the fortification of the outer bailey. The castle of Hohenklingen, dominating the city of Stein am Rhein (Schaffhausen), was also built in the 12th century.

The Holy Roman Emperor Frederick I Barbarossa (1152-90), a direct contemporary of Henry II of England, was the first of the great Hohenstaufen rulers of Germany. With vast family domains in south-west and parts of central Germany, the Hohenstaufens were extraordinarily active as castle builders in both Germany and Italy down to the mid-13th century.

Hohenstaufen castle architecture soon dominated large areas of Germany. Its principal features consisted in accentuating the strength of the buildings—frequently by the use of rusticated stone blocks—and simultaneously decorating them to a high artistic standard. In the course of time this gave rise to the specific Hohenstaufen late Romanesque and early Gothic style.

Alsace was a major Hohenstaufen base. Landsberg (now Bas-Rhin, France) is considered one of the outstanding examples of Hohenstaufen castle building. Fully clad with rusticated stone blocks, the

32
Thurandt, Germany. The castle stands above the town of Alken in the valley of the River Mosel. About 1200.

main buildings consisted of a watchtower and a more architecturally sophisticated hall (second half of the 12th century). The outer defence system and the outer bailey date from the early 13th century.

The construction of the older St Ulrich's Castle, at Rappoltsweiler (Ribeauvillé, Haut-Rhin), was also quite remarkable. Its watchtower is square in plan and is clad with rusticated stone blocks.

The late 12th century castle of Landeck in the former Lower Palatinate has a polygonal plan with a sturdy rusticated tower inside the north-eastern part of the reinforced curtain wall.

In 1174-84 Barbarossa built the castle of Kaiserwerth on the right bank of the Rhine. Only the ruins of the monumental oblong hall now remain, but adjacent to the rear of the hall stood a powerful tower, square in plan. The layout of the main building was unusually compact.

The fortified town of Nideggen lay outside the Hohenstaufen domains, in Jülich, to the south-east of Aachen. At its western end are the ruins of a castle of compact, irregular trapezoidal plan with a bulky oblong residential tower from the 12th cen-

tury on its east side and a chapel on the ground floor. Despite such examples, however, residential towers never attained the importance in Germany that they enjoyed in Western Europe.

The valley of the River Mosel near the town of Alken is dominated by the castle of Thurandt, which has two circular towers. It was built in about 1200.

The imperial halls of the early feudal period were not at first intended to serve as fortresses. An exception to this rule was the biggest Hohenstaufen hall, at Wimpfen on the Neckar, which dates from about the 1160s. It was some 215 metres long and almost 90 metres wide. Inside the peripheral wall lie the Red Tower in the east and the Blue Tower in the west, both square in plan and clad with rusticated stone blocks.

The imperial hall at Gelnhausen (Hesse) was also fortified. It was founded after 1180 by Frederick Barbarossa on an island in the River Kinzig, to the south of the town. The outline of the hall, defined by a wall 2 metres thick and clad with rusticated stone block on both sides, is an irregular polygon. Initially the wall was provided with a walkway and

◄ 33
Gelnhausen, Germany. Interior of an imperial castle founded after 1180, showing the ruins of a Romanesque hall with the Torhalle (the entrance building at the gateway) in the background.

34
Münzenberg, Germany. Panoramic view of the castle, which dates from before 1175. The east tower is Romanesque in origin whereas the west tower was added much later, in the mid-13th century. The ruins of a Romanesque hall can be seen between them. The outer fortification system, later in date, is concealed by greenery.

35
Querfurt, Germany. View of part of the castle from the south. One of the outer fortification roundels (1461-79) is in the foreground; behind it stands a late 12th century residential tower, the Merterturm. In the background are the circular tower known as Dicker Heinrich (Stout Henry, 1070) on the left and the Pariser Turm (Paris Tower, 1200) on the right.

battlements. In its west side there is the only gateway, guarded by a substantial tower. The hall beyond the gateway, with a chapel on the first floor, is partly the result of change of plan. The eastern part of the ward contains the foundations of a circular tower, 16 metres in diameter, which, however, was never built. The outer bailey to the west is contemporaneous with the hall, but the bailey wall was not put up until the 15th century.

Not far from Gelnhausen stands the bizarre castle

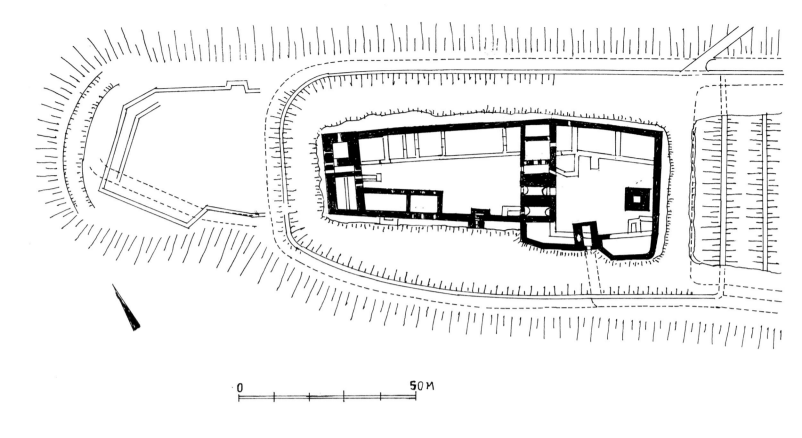

36
Eckartsberga, Germany. Plan
of the castle. After Dehio.

37
Eckartsberga, Germany. View
of the castle with, on the left,
the mid-12th century
Romanesque residential
tower with a Gothic
superstructure, and, on the
right, the slender early Gothic
watchtower.

of Büdingen (Hesse), completed before the end of
the 12th century. It has a compact polygonal plan
and is enclosed by a rusticated wall 2 metres thick
and some 7 metres high. The original watchtower
(subsequently destroyed) was round outside and
hexagonal inside; it formerly stood in the eastern
part of the polygonal inner ward. On the northern
side of the ward there was a Romanesque hall. The
castle was surrounded by a ditch.

The concentric layout of the castle is remarkable
by comparison with such Hohenstaufen castles as
the small one at Egisheim (now Eugisheim, France)

34

or the famous Castel del Monte in Southern Italy.

One of the most impressive early Hohenstaufen castle ruins stands above the town of Münzenberg in Hesse. Its dating is uncertain. The first major phase of castle construction ended before 1175 at the latest. In area it was a compressed oval 120 metres long and up to 40 metres wide. The peripheral wall of

rusticated stone blocks was crowned with battlements. Near the eastern end of the castle there was a circular watchtower to which access was by ladder to the first floor. The monumental three-storey hall with rows of Romanesque windows was adjacent to the southern part of the peripheral wall. On its east side the hall met the chapel, which stood near the southern gateway. The architectural details of the hall recall the imperial hall at Gelnhausen. The west tower that so effectively completes the castle skyline was not built until about the middle of the 13th century.

Münzenberg ranks among the most attractive examples of Romanesque fortification architecture in Europe. A comparison with contemporary Western European castles convincingly illustrates the differences between medieval fortifications west and east of the Vosges.

The most impressive feature of the castle of Rieneck, dating from about 1170, is its extraordinarily massive northern tower, in the shape of an irregular polygon outside and an octagon on the inside. On the third storey a chapel is built into the thickness of the wall. There is a residential Romanesque tower in the northern corner with walls 2.7 metres thick. The gateway on the south-east side connects the upper castle with the almost square

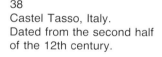
38
Castel Tasso, Italy.
Dated from the second half
of the 12th century.

39
Bruck, Austria. Castle near
Lienz in East Tirol, with a
Romanesque tower.

40
Landštejn, Czechoslovakia.
The late 12th century castle,
with two Romanesque towers
and a lower Gothic tower on
the left; in the foreground is
the outer wall with a small late
Gothic bastion tower.

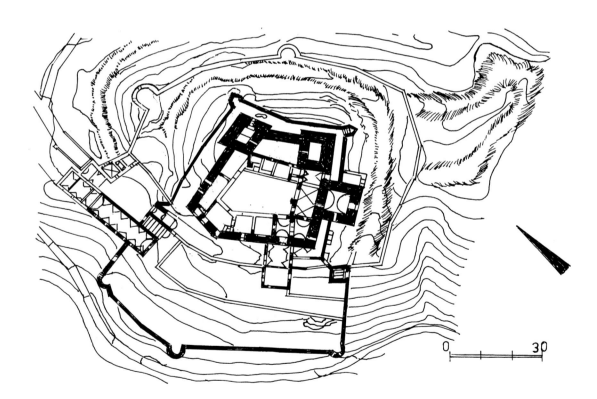

41 ▶
Landštejn, Czechoslovakia.
Plan of the castle with a
Romanesque nucleus and a
complex Gothic fortification
system.

outer bailey, which was entered from the south-east
by a tower gate. Just beyond the south-east side of
the outer bailey a slender watchtower was erected at
a later date; it is now 27 metres high, with an entrance 9 metres above ground level.

The castle is surrounded by a ditch 20 metres
wide with a rampart. A small outer bailey was added
along the south-west side of the lower castle. The
plan of the castle represents an interesting com-
promise between the more or less square layout of

42
San Gimignano, Italy. Group
of towers in the town.

Western Europe and the elongated, oblong Central European type.

There were also important developments in the Duchy of Saxony and in Thuringia.

In the course of the 12th century, building continued at Querfurt (Halle). The casle church and the second hall were erected during this period, and an outer bailey was added on the east side and to a lesser extent to the south. Two towers were built as part of this extension, the north-east tower being protected by a wall.

Among the most important medieval forts of the Landgrave of Thuringia was the castle above the town of Eckartsberga, near Naumburg. Its principal features still proclaim its origin in the second half of the 12th century. The upper castle has an elongated trapezoidal plan.

The construction of the castle of Rudelsburg (Halle) began in the second half of the 12th century. It has a compact trapezoidal plan with a sturdy south-east tower and a thick east wall.

Gnandstein (Leipzig) in Saxony was very similar, with an almost square plan and a circular watchtower. It was bounded on the south and west sides by town houses. Its western outer bailey is almost rectangular in plan. The Romanesque construction of the castle ended in the late 12th century.

A characteristic example of a Romanesque lowland castle is Burgsteinfurt in Westphalia, near Germany's border with the Netherlands. Built in the last third of the 12th century on an artificial mound on an island in the River Aa, it is oval in plan, with a Romanesque entrance tower with living quarters. A strong circular watchtower was built at the northern end. The late Romanesque two-storey chapel has also been preserved. The outer bailey, also oval, is situated on another island.

At the end of this brief survey of the most important early feudal castles in Germany, mention must be made of the Hohenstaufen castle at Cheb (formerly Eger) in Czechoslovakia, which occupies the north-west corner of the subsequently enlarged site. A watchtower, clad with rusticated stone blocks, overlooks the southern ditch. The north side of the enclosure is defined by the ruins of a big rectangular hall with a line of first storey windows. The Hohenstaufen castle at Cheb was built in the 1180s.

Of town fortifications in Germany, the walls of Korbach in Hesse are particularly worth mentioning. Dated to the end of the 12th century, they are reinforced with semicircular towers.

A considerable number of Romanesque castles were also erected further south, especially in Lower Austria and Tirol. A good many of them have since been drastically remodelled. Powerful rectangular towers were most common (for example at Bruck, near Lienz in East Tirol), but pentagonal watch-towers were also built.

The castle of Rauhenstein, near Baden, is a Romanesque structure with a tower, a hall and a chapel. The tower of the large castle of Reifenstein (Castel Tasso), near Sterzing (now Vipiteno, Italy) dates from the second half of the 12th century.

At Drosendorf, a town on the river Dyje near the Austrian border with Moravia, the fortifications date from the end of the 12th century. The walls are provided with semicircular towers which are quite sparse, leaving very long stretches of curtain wall. A ditch was dug only along the most vulnerable east and south-east sides. The Horn Gate is guarded by a pair of towers.

Since early feudal keeps were essentially Norman structures, erected in northern France and England, it is remarkable that they should have appeared at an early date in Bohemia. The episcopal castle at Roudnice, sited on a rock above the River Elbe, is of particular significance in this respect. Only a few remains of the original castle survive, but a late 17th century drawing gives an almost complete idea of its appearance. Its characteristic feature was its distinctly oblong plan. The keep was about 40 metres long and about 14.5 metres wide. Its corners were reinforced with three-quarter-circular towers. Along the north side ran three semicircular towers placed at regular intervals, while each of the shorter sides was divided by a single tower. The walls were clad with carefully dressed blocks of stone. The sturdier south-west tower is the result of a later modification, distinguished by ashlar cladding. We do not know what the south side of the keep was like, or its original height. At present the walls are 10 metres high. Semicircular towers are very rare in France, the nearest comparable instance being at Niort. The ground floor at Roudnice housed a vaulted Romanesque hall.

The keep at Roudnice dates from the late 12th century and is unique in Central Europe east of the Vosges. It is undoubtedly related in some way to French castle-building, but it is not merely an imitation, for it also reflects the influence of Prague Castle's fortifications.

Also very interesting is the monumental castle of Landštejn, in the Czech-Moravian borderland near the frontier with Lower Austria. It is pentagonal in plan. The east corner is occupied by an almost square tower, originally timber floored, which was accessible from the south by ladder; but there is also a slightly lower and smaller residential tower in the north corner. The first storey houses a vaulted Romanesque chapel. On the wall parapet between the towers there was a defence gallery on corbels. The castle was built in the second half of the 12th century. Its two-tower layout is unique.

At San Gimignano, near Siena in Italy, the surviving 13 tall towers (there were originally 72) seem to fall outside the main line of development of fortification architecture. Most of them were built in the 12th century, but the building of castles proper in Italy was concentrated in the 13th and subsequent centuries.

In the Iberian peninsula, post-classical castle construction was stimulated by the Reconquest, the long struggle that culminated in the expulsion of the Moors. The absence of a comprehensive survey makes it difficult to generalize about Spanish and Portuguese castles, of which there is a great variety of types. In Catalonia the Romanesque castle of Solsona had an irregular trapezoidal layout with a circular tower and three other towers in the corners. The castle in the Catalonian town of Peratallada underwent a complex development. Its Roman-

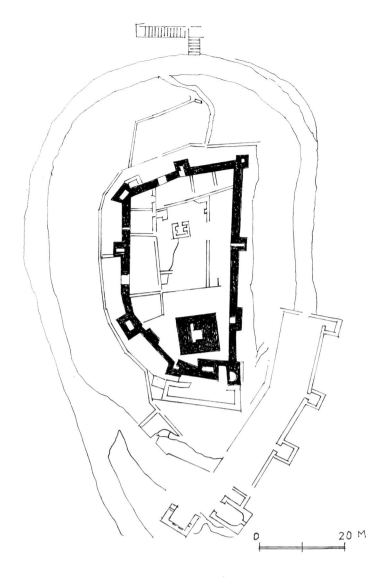

esque nucleus, compact but irregular in plan, is enclosed by a high peripheral wall. In the centre of the enclosure there is a large battlemented rectangular tower. The nucleus is situated in the north-western part of the castle area, with other buildings on its south side. It has a rather complex configuration, with an irregular trapezoidal courtyard mostly surrounded by Romanesque buildings dating from various periods. Of particular interest are also the Romanesque architectural details, notably the windows with mullions.

Also 12th century is the splendid castle of Loarre, not far from Huesca in Aragon. With its dominating tower, it stands on a rocky hill; the large outer bailey to the west is reached through a gateway flanked by semicircular towers that project from the outer wall face. The peripheral wall of the outer bailey is strengthened by nine circular towers. Another monumental Aragonese castle is Alcaniz, which has a rectangular main tower and a Romanesque hall. The construction of the castle began in 1179, when Alfonso II gave it to the Order of the Knights of Calatrava.

Finally there is the three-storey Romanesque fortress at Aledo, near Murcia in the south-east of Spain. It is a tower roughly 13×13 metres in plan, and its vaulted interior is reminiscent of the Romanesque residential towers of Central Europe.

The continuing struggle with the Moors increased

44
Pomba, Portugal. Plan of the castle, 1171. After B. Ebhardt.

◄ 43
Peratallada, Spain. Large Romanesque tower of the Catalonian castle, with the wall in the foreground.

45
Obidos, Portugal. The Romanesque nucleus of the castle, with the outer fortification system in the foreground.

the importance of Spanish cities' fortifications. In the majority of cases these fortifications were built in conjunction with the late Roman walls. The walls were reinforced with closely spaced semicircular towers called *cubos* in Spanish.

The Roman walls of the town of Segovia in Castile were renewed in the 11th and 12th centuries and reinforced with 86 towers. The walls of the town of Plasencia (Estremadura), founded in 1189 by Alfonso VIII, are reinforced with 68 semicircular towers.

The characteristic features of Romanesque castles in neighbouring Portugal are the slender towers rising higher than the curtain wall and projecting from its outer face, and the rectangular form of the principal towers.

The plan of the castle at Guimarães, not far from Porto, is sharply pointed on one side. The principal tower has walls 2 metres thick and is 27 metres high. On both long sides of the castle wall there are gateways, each guarded by two towers of the same height as the walls; the other towers are higher. The Moorish-style battlemented masonry is clad with dressed stone blocks.

One of the most impressive early medieval Portuguese castles is Almourol, on an island in the River Tajo, close to the town of Abrantes. In plan the castle is an irregular polygon. The principal wall is strengthened by slender towers rising above it; in the corners of the trace they are U-shaped. Both walls and towers are battlemented, and so is the tall principal tower.

The island on which Almourol stands was fortified even in Roman and Moorish times. The castle was built in 1160 by Gualdim Paes, Grand Master of the Knights Templar, who took part in the struggle against the Moors. In 1171 the Order and its Grand Master also built the important castle of Pombal, to the south-west of Coimbra. In plan it is roughly semi-oval. The peripheral wall is strengthened by rectangular towers rising above it. The massy principal tower is over the gateway to the castle.

The castle overlooking the fortified town of Obidos, to the north of Lisbon, makes an extraordinarily picturesque impression. It has a rectangular principal tower and slender U-shaped towers in the peripheral wall. There is another rectangular tower near one of the corners.

Twelfth century Portuguese castles form an independent group, unrelated to castles in Spain. A typical feature is the dense distribution of towers along the peripheral wall, probably influenced by the architecture of Crusader castles in the Holy Land.

To sum up, the art of fortification was greatly enriched and diversified in the late 12th century. In France and England, notable improvements were introduced during the reigns of Henry II and Richard Coeur de Lion. East of the Vosges the monumental castle architecture of the Hohenstaufen dynasty indicated that castles in Western and Central Europe served distinctly different functions, while castle architecture in the Iberian peninsula was entirely separate and independent. The late 12th century can be seen as a preparation for the 13th century efflorescence in which medieval fortifications spread over most of Europe in the form of both castles and fortified cities.

46
Fère en Tardenois, France.
Plan of the castle. After Salch.

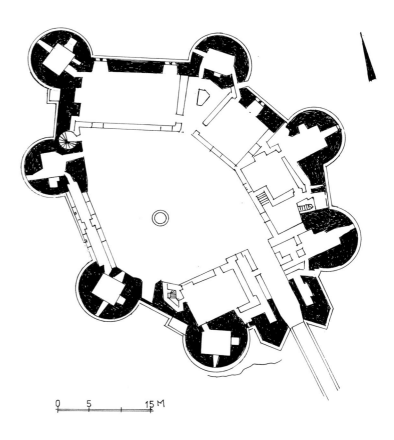

0   5   15 M

40

The Thirteenth Century

The 13th century was one of the crucial phases in the development of European society. Feudalism now extended far beyond Western Europe. In the course of the century its supreme artistic manifestation, the Gothic style, gradually prevailed over a vast area. On the military plane, there was an extraordinary increase in the number of castles, to which must be added strongholds of other kinds and urban fortifications. Only from the 13th century is it possible to trace and interrelate developments in various parts of Europe, thus greatly extending the scope of our study.

The relationship between fortifications and the Gothic style of architecture is also a question of some moment. There is a great difference between this period and the 12th century, when only the Hohenstaufen castle builders made any consistent attempts to achieve a high artistic standard. The architecture of the 13th century fortifications was not only functional, but gradually became a creative element in the overall development of European art.

In France the long reign of King Philip II Augustus lasted from 1180 to 1223. A bitter enemy of the Plantagenets, he ultimately succeeded in greatly reducing their continental possessions. The wars (conveniently if misleadingly described as Anglo-French) were characterized by hard struggles for Plantagenet castles, which fell into French hands one after another, sometimes only following a tenaciously protracted siege. These struggles inevitably exerted an influence on fortification techniques and siege tactics which was soon reflected in changed methods of castle construction. Philip himself responded to the situation by organizing a corps of military engineers.

47
Fère en Tardenois, France. Ruins of the castle (built from 1206 onwards), with the gateway on the right and several towers in the background.

During the reign of St Louis—Louis IX (1226-70) —tremendous developments took place in the fortification of cities. Across the Channel, castle architecture became increasingly sophisticated, a process culminating in the Welsh castles built by Edward I (1272-1307).

The Hohenstaufen castle tradition developed in two directions. In Germany it led straight to the castle-building of the later 12th century. But in Southern Italy and Sicily it culminated in a famous group of castles built by the Emperor Frederick II in the early 13th century.

Royal castles were also built in Bohemia during the late 13th century, while at the end of the century a growing number of castles were built by the Order of the Teutonic Knights of the Cross in Prussia.

In all the above examples of 13th century castle construction an application of the principles of Gothic art is visible, albeit in widely differing degrees of creative intensity and formal rigour.

The cities provided new fields for the art of Gothic fortification. In France the first phase in the development of city fortifications coincides with the reign of Philip II, while the second took place under Louis IX. Italy was also important in the development of urban fortifications, as too was the Bohemian state under King Přemysl Otakar II (1253-78).

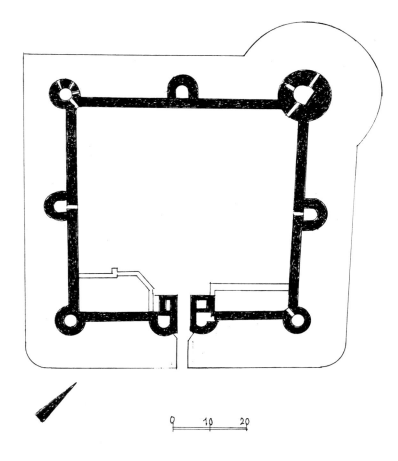

48
Dourdan, France. Plan of the castle. After Salch.

49
Dourdan, France. City castle from the east, with the donjon on the extreme right, one of the gate towers on the left and the east tower in the foreground. About 1220.

42

The bitter Anglo-French struggle for fortified castles led to improved methods of both attack and defence. Castle walls, often erected without proper foundations, could be undermined by sappers, a technique used in the 12th century. In the castles built by Philip II, therefore, great stress was laid on deep, strong foundations and thick walls as well as powerful scarps and vaulted interiors. Arrangements for flanking fire became extremely efficient, and keeps took on an extraordinary monumentality.

Defence had previously been concentrated in the parapet walks or in the upper storeys of the towers; but experience showed that they could not resist for long when the castle ditch was filled up with soil and powerful mobile attacking towers were hauled right up to the walls. Therefore the number of loopholes was increased in the exterior faces of the curtain walls and the different storeys of the towers. Brattices and machicolations, supported by stone corbels, were also installed to harry the enemy from the battlements.

The 'castle reform' initiated by Philip II went much further than this, effecting radical changes in the entire layout of castles.

Chronologically the first of the few examples we have selected seems to be the castle at Fère en Tardenois (Aisne). This has a compressed oval plan enclosed by a peripheral wall; the wall is reinforced by seven tall, strong, U-shaped towers, closed on their interior faces and provided with embrasures. The castle was built on an artificial mound paved with ashlar. The inner courtyard is entered from the south-east through a gateway protected by two small towers. The castle, lacking a keep and outer fortifications, was built from 1206 onwards. Its fortification values gradually increased. The absence of a keep—until then the main centre of defence—is surprising; however, the new arrangements brought the weight of the defensive capability closer to the enemy, to the emphatically projecting towers.

The castle of Bouillancourt (Somme), with its regular hexagonal plan and circular towers at all its angles, is also dated to the early 13th century. Today only the western part of the castle, with a couple of towers, remains. It was at the beginning of the 13th century, too, that the huge, long-vanished keep of the Louvre in Paris was built.

An outstanding example of the new trend in French castle architecture is the royal castle of Dourdan (S. et O.), situated in the western part of the fortified town. It has a rectangular plan with an inner courtyard. In the northern corner there is a

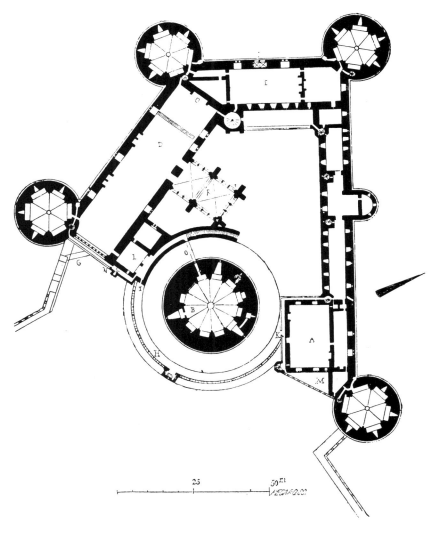

50
Coucy le Château, France.
Plan of the early 13th century
castle before its demolition.
After Enlart.

circular keep 25 metres high. The remaining three corners are also reinforced with strong semicircular or circular towers. The entrance to the castle is situated in the middle of the south-east side, between two large semicircular towers. There is a smaller, semicircular closed tower in the middle of each of three curtain walls. The castle was protected by a deep ditch.

Dourdan was built in about 1220 by Philip II. Its keep was later converted into a circular watchtower and, because of its position at the corner, was integrated into the defences. The castle is an early example of the French type of rectangular castle.

The importance of Philip II as besieger and builder also appears in his programme for strengthening the castles he had won from the English. At Chinon

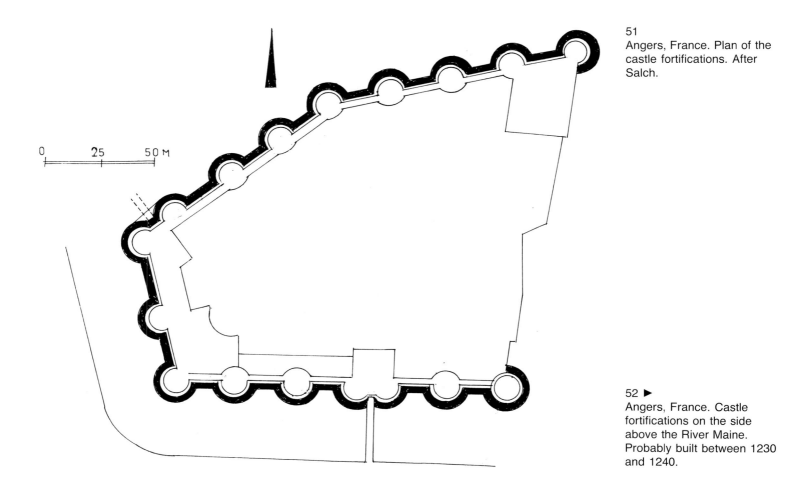

51
Angers, France. Plan of the castle fortifications. After Salch.

0   25   50 M

52 ►
Angers, France. Castle fortifications on the side above the River Maine. Probably built between 1230 and 1240.

and Gisors, for example, he had powerfully vaulted circular keeps built.

The culmination of early 13th century French castle-building was Coucy le Château (Aisne), which was tragically destroyed during the First World War. The main part of the castle occupied the north-western end of the fortified area, which also included the townlet of Coucy. The upper castle has a quadrangular, very irregular trapezoidal plan enclosed by walls, with a courtyard with buildings around it—the typical French rectangular castle layout. In the four angles there were vaulted circular towers, over 20 metres in diameter, with loopholes cut almost tangentially to the walls. In the middle of the south-east side of the castle was a circular vaulted keep; at 31.25 metres in diameter and 55 metres in height, it was, according to Viollet-le-Duc, the biggest tower built for military purposes in Europe. It was defended by a moat more than 6 metres wide with a revetment wall. The wall of the rather irregularly shaped outer bailey was strengthened by U-shaped and circular towers, closed on their inner faces, vaulted and with loopholes; each

end of the wall ran up to the south-east angle towers of the main structure. The gateway between the town and the outer bailey of the castle was guarded by a pair of three-quarter-circular towers.

The outer bailey was directly adjacent to the fortified townlet, with the monumental Laon gateway hemmed in by two massive semicircular towers closed on the inside. On the outer side of the ditch there was a U-shaped barbican with two entrances.

The keep at Coucy represents the culmination of two centuries of development. However, the possibilities of the keep had been exhausted, and it was soon practically obsolete. By contrast, the circular angle towers anticipated the future development of fortifications along the lines of the walls.

The citadel of the walled city of Carcassonne (Aude) in the South of France consists of a number of closely spaced circular towers around the walls. After 1226 it was rebuilt into a rectangular castle of northern French type.

The first castle at Angers (Maine et Loire) was the stronghold of Henry II of England. The present castle was built early in the reign of Louis IX (St

Louis, 1226-70), between 1230 and 1240. It stands above the south-east bank of the River Mayenne, and is an irregular pentagon in plan. With the exception of the precipitous river side, the high walls of the castle are defended by closely spaced drum towers with loopholes. Mostly closed on the inside, the towers were lowered to the wall level in 1588, but initially they were 40 metres high, standing one to two storeys above the parapet of the wall. In the peripheral wall there are now 17 towers. The now vanished southern gateway was guarded by a pair of circular towers. The stunning visual effect of the towers, with their huge battered (that is, gently widening) plinths, is enhanced by the banded strata of slate, sandstone and granite. At the foot of the wall there was a ditch 30 metres wide and 11 metres deep. There was no separate keep in the courtyard.

In 1231 the medieval fortifications of the upper city of Boulogne sur Mer (Pas de Calais) were built on the remains of the city's Roman fortifications. Along the north and south sides in particular, there are very closely spaced, 17 metre high semicircular towers along the walls, and four gateways with typical semicircular towers flanking their central passageways.

In the eastern angle of the city wall stands the castle built at the same time as the city fortifications. In the context of French castle architecture its layout is quite remarkable and exceptional. In plan the castle is an irregular octagon. Buildings line the inner courtyard, but there is no keep. The angles of the walls are reinforced by U-shaped towers. The castle was entirely surrounded by a ditch. In many respects the castle at Boulogne resembles the basic design already used at the beginning of the 13th century at Fère en Tardenois.

A major reconstruction of the castle of Najac (Aveyron), in the South of France, took place in 1253. The castle is a slightly irregular rectangle in plan. The rectangular south-west angle is occupied by a square Romanesque tower; in the south-east angle stands a circular keep, 40 metres high with vaulted ceilings. The peripheral wall 26 metres high is lined with U-shaped towers of different sizes.

Outstanding among many examples of the same type is the castle at Billy (Allier), which was com-

53
Carcassonne, France. The castle of the old city, built after 1226.

pleted in about 1247. It has an oval plan and walls with four closed semicircular towers. The narrow gateway is dominated by two towers. On the opposite side a much stronger tower functioning as a keep adjoins the outer face of the walls.

A new element is represented by the pointed towers which were built in the late 13th century to strengthen the wall of the famous castle of Loches (Indre et Loire).

It was in the 13th century that city fortifications assumed a major role. At Provins (Seine et Marne) the fortifications of the Upper Town were begun in the 12th century, although they were mainly built in the 13th. The town wall, 2.5 to 3 metres thick, is strengthened with square, semicircular, and a few polygonal towers, 12 to 20 metres high, with curtain walls 25 to 30 metres long between them. The wall is battlemented. Visually most effective is the area on the south-west side of the city, with the St Jean gate guarded by two pointed towers and clad with rusticated blocks. The wall is articulated with closely spaced semicircular and rectangular towers, closed on the inside, and circular towers at the angles.

Between 1191 and 1221 Philip II Augustus refortified his capital, Paris. The walls were reinforced with semicircular towers closed on the inside.

Viewed from a distance, the old city, 'La Cité', of Carcassonne on the right bank of the Aude, seems like a miraculously untampered with survival from the High Middle Ages; and indeed the city's medieval fortifications are authentic and famous enough to have been intensively studied since the 19th century. So it is all the more surprising that many facts about it are still in dispute. A complicating factor has certainly been the 19th century reconstruction carried out by Viollet-le-Duc, a

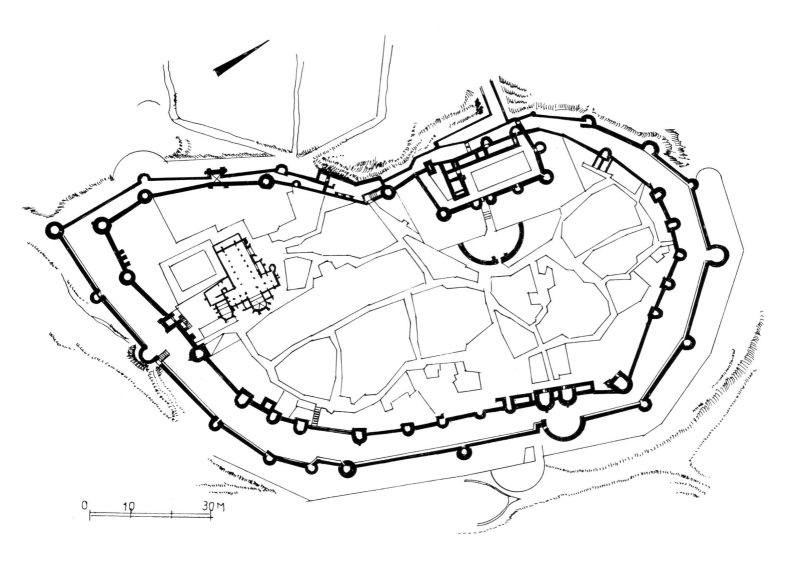

54
Carcassonne, France.
Schematic plan of the upper
city fortifications. After Morel.

55
Carcassonne, France.
Fortifications on the north-
west side of the city, with the
Porte d'Aude in the
foreground; the main entrance
was from the west. The
photograph shows the inner
and outer walls, with the city
castle in the background. Mid
to late 13th century.

magnificent achievement which, however, has made it more difficult to trace the course of some important historical developments.

The prevailing theory concerning the gradual construction of the fortification system assumes that, in the first phase, the old Visigothic inner wall remained unchanged, and that a new wall was built in front of it, at a distance of 10 metres at most (and often rather less) to enclose a small bailey. This outer wall is relatively low, with towers that are as high or higher than it is. The towers are mostly U-shaped, although some are circular or semicircular, with loopholes and battlements which were certainly rebuilt or modified on many later occasions. The towers are partly open at the rear.

The first major phase of construction of the castle at Carcassonne—a relatively small fortress within the walled city—is generally dated to 1240-60. The barbicans in front of the gateways were built during the same period.

In the second phase of construction, from the third quarter of the 13th century, the work was concentrated on the old Visigothic main wall, in which the towers put up are mostly semicicular, closed at the rear and partly set into the wall. Several towers are provided with pointed 'beaks' on the outer face; however, there are also circular and U-shaped towers and one of rectangular plan.

Five of the original Visigothic towers, dating from the 5th century, survive in a group on the north side of the wall. Here the curtain walls were very short (5-6 metres). It can be assumed that the spacing of the towers elsewhere along the wall was at least partly determined by the siting of their Visigothic predecessors.

The monumental Narbonne Gateway is framed by two towers in the usual way. With a few exceptions, the towers of the inner wall are more archaic in character than those of the outer wall. The exceptions obviously indicate the existence of some undocumented later phase of work on this wall. Several towers in both walls, generally provided with vaulted interiors, were equipped to withstand a prolonged onslaught in isolation, even if cut off from the rest of the defensive system.

In the preceding paragraphs we have described the presumed development of the fortifications at Carcassonne. Visually, however, the city gives quite a different impression, especially thanks to the lowness of the outer wall. At present one can only express the feeling that the suggested sequence of construction may not be entirely correct.

There is a perfectly preserved late 13th century wall with gateways and towers at Aigues Mortes

56
Kenilworth Castle, England. View of part of the castle ruins, with the 16th century Leicester Buildings in the foreground.

(Gard) in the South of France. Once a coastal town, it was newly laid out in 1248. It has an almost rectangular plan with a recessed north-west corner where the wall bypasses an earlier free-standing keep. This is known as the Tour de Constance and dates from before the mid-13th century; its ground floor and upper storey are rib vaulted.

The single wall of Aigues Mortes is 2.5 metres thick and 11 metres high. Three corners (not the corner with the Tour de Constance) are reinforced with higher three-quarter-circular towers. Towers punctuate the walls at regular intervals, linking up with the grid-plan of the streets and the tower-guarded gateways. At first sight the disproportionately large number of gateways is surprising, since gateways were always the most vulnerable defensive points of a castle or city. On the long north-west side of the city there are two main gateways, each with a passage flanked by a pair of typical semicircular towers; the gateways alternate with two semicircular towers whose mass, closed at the rear, projects into the enclosure. On the south-east side there is a gateway with two towers in the middle, while on the north-east side there is only a postern in a shallow tower. On the side facing the sea, two major gateways alternate with three oblong posterns. Shallow polygonal bartizans (projecting corner turrets) rise from their outer corners.

The towers and gateways are higher than the walls. Their interiors are vaulted, and there are loops in the walls for archers to fire through. Each gateway was protected by a portcullis. Both the gateways and the curtain walls had brattices.

There is no outer fortification system at Aigues Mortes.The defences consist of only a single wall, which was enfeebled by the many gateways and posterns; these did enable the besieged forces to sally out from many points, but the drawback in terms of creating numerous weaknesses was far more serious.

The construction of the fortifications at Aigues Mortes dates from 1272-75. Technically, by comparison with contemporary developments in European city fortifications, they are not of high quality.

On the other hand, the appearance of the whole city is impressive, and the state of preservation of the walls, towers and gateways is unequalled anywhere in Europe.

The 13th century was the golden age of English castle-building. It was characterized by an extraordinary variety of layouts and a sensitivity to architectural values as well as defensive capability. The technique of strengthening the outer fortifications developed apace, drawing on the traditions of Henry II and Richard Coeur de Lion. In line with this tendency, gateways in particular became monumental structures.

Kenilworth Castle in Warwickshire expanded splendidly in the early 13th century under King John and his son Henry III. A new wall was built

57
The Tower of London. Plan after Nitschen.

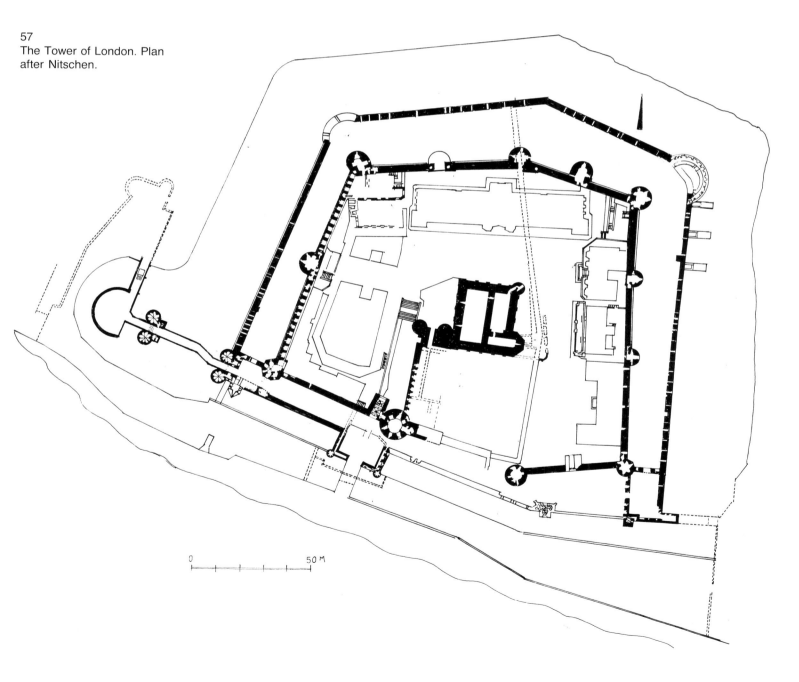

0   50 M

49

around the castle to enclose the outer bailey; its northern part was destroyed in the late 16th century, but the rest survives. The wall was strengthened with towers, three of which are still in existence. The area is entered from the southwest through a gateway protected by two semicircular towers.

Henry III built part of what is now the wall of the Inmost Ward at the Tower of London, pierced with a great many loopholes. The surviving section of Henry's wall adjoins the very powerful Wakefield Tower, on the Thames side of the castle. Near the Norman keep a gateway guarded by two towers was built.

Rather unusual for England was the layout of Chepstow Castle, overlooking the River Wye not far from its confluence with the Severn. Its pronounced oblong shape, with four courts standing in a row on an elongated ridge, is reminiscent of the castles of Central Europe. The remains of a Norman keep, the Great Tower, stand in the upper bailey. Towers of various types reinforce the peripheral wall. The construction of the castle was completed in about 1246.

The inner bailey of a castle that has been discussed earlier, Pevensey in Sussex, was surrounded by a wall in the early 13th century. It was equipped with three large U-shaped towers with numerous loopholes for archers.

By the late 13th century, Restormel Castle in Cornwall was technically rather old-fashioned. A shell keep, it comprised a low circular wall built on the sloping scarp of a ditch; the residential buildings stood against the inner face of the wall. On the outside, the ruins of a gateway and of a small, almost square building can be observed.

The most important British castles of the late 13th century were built in Wales; several of them are concentric (wall-within-wall) structures, and all are equipped with monumental and complex defences intended to perpetuate the English domination of Wales. The oldest is Caerphilly Castle in Mid Glamorgan, dating from 1271. It was an almost square castle comprising an inner wall with two twin-towered gateways and massive drum towers in the corners. The battlemented outer wall was equally formidable, with an artificial lake, moats and outworks strengthening the castle's defences still further.

Caerphilly Castle was a great baronial fortress built by Gilbert de Clare, Earl of Gloucester, but all the other great English strongholds were erected on the orders of the warrior-king Edward I (1272-1307).

58
Caerphilly Castle, Wales. The castle, with its mostly circular towers, is protected by a lower outer wall and a surrounding artificial lake. The corners are reinforced with early roundels. The castle dates from 1268; even the outer fortifications were constructed before 1300.

Flint in North Wales is the second oldest, built for the King between 1277 and 1280. It has a trapezoidal plan with three circular corner towers; just beyond the fourth corner is a huge circular keep surrounded by a moat. 'The Flint' was built by James of St George, the Master of the Royal Works, who seems to have been the chief architect of the great Edwardian castles.

Those that followed Flint form a group that represents an extraordinary advance, both technically and aesthetically, in the art of fortification. Conwy Castle in Gwynedd is situated on top of a rock on the south-west bank of the River Conwy, close to its estuary. Its layout was divided functionally into an upper and a lower castle with wards or baileys, initially separated by a wall. The whole plan is of irregular oblong shape. It is not concentric, but the extraordinarily thick wall (up to 4.5 metres) is strengthened by eight relatively low but very powerful drum towers built into it and projecting well into the interior of the castle layout.

Among the remarkable features of Edward's Welsh castles are the narrow turrets (bartizans) rising from, and surpisingly far above, the massive towers. Only four are left in Conwy, where they are round. Both the towers and the walls are battlemented, with narrow loopholes. There were buildings all round the baileys. The castle was partly protected with a ditch.

Conwy Castle was built in 1283-88. The town wall, integrated with that of the castle in a single defensive system, has 3 gateways and 21 towers.

The construction of Caernarfon Castle, at the southern end of the Menai Strait, began in 1283; the structure was completed under Edward III. The principles on which it was built were identical with those applied at Conwy Castle. In plan, Caernarfon is roughly oval. The trace of its battlemented walls is interrupted by bulky, polygonal, relatively low tow-

59
Conwy Castle, Wales. Interior of the ruins of the castle (built in 1283-88), with the main wall, inner buildings and towers in a massive peripheral wall.

ers, varying in design but with slender turrets, as at Conwy. The most massive of the towers is the Eagle Tower in the west corner, which has three bartizans. The main twin-towered gateway (the King's Gate) leads into the castle from the north; a second gateway (the Queen's Gate) no longer exists. To the west the castle is linked to the walled city of Caernarfon. The other sides of the castle are protected by the sea and the estuary of the Seiont. Caernarfon,

especially when viewed from the sea, is a fascinating sight, with its distinctive banded masonry, its articulated mass, and its turret-broken skyline.

The third and final castle of the group is Beaumaris Castle on the island of Anglesey. It was built from 1295, in the initial stages by James of St George. The layout is roughly similar to that of Caerphilly Castle. The walls of the square inner bailey are defended by drum towers in the corners, semicircular towers in the middle of the east and west sides, and a twin-towered gatehouse in the north and the south wall. The outer bailey is surrounded by a polygonal wall. In the four main corners circular towers are placed tangentially against the wall. The longer (east and west) sides of the outer wall are also defended by three smaller semicircular towers. The wall of the outer bailey rises from the surrounding ditch. Although never completely finished, Beaumaris Castle represents one of the peaks of Gothic fortification; it has been described as the most perfect of all concentric castles.

Earlier in his reign Edward I also built Harlech Castle (1283-90) in North Wales, close to the coast from which it could be supplied in the event of a Welsh rising. It has a rectangular layout with drum towers in the corners with bartizans like those of Conwy and Caernarfon. The narrow middle bailey is surrounded by a low outer wall that was originally battlemented. The twin-towered gatehouse is particularly impressive.

The Edwardian type of castle is also found in Scotland, where the ruins of Caerlaverock in Dumfriesshire are particularly attractive. It is triangular in plan, with a great twin-towered gatehouse at the apex and a large drum tower at each angle of the wall. The basic layout is that of a French rectangular castle with an inner courtyard. The towers terminate in a line of stone corbels designed to support the brattice. The date of the castle has not been definitely determined, although it probably falls in the last quarter of the 13th century.

The Scottish castle of Rothesay, on the island of Bute, originated as a large shell keep in the late 11th century, but was modernized in the 13th century by the addition of four huge, symmetrically arranged drum towers, a gatehouse and a drawbridge across the wide pentagonal moat.

Back in England, important urban fortifications survive at Canterbury in Kent. The south-eastern and eastern sides of the city are surrounded by a stone wall (now quite low), whose semicircular towers, closed on the inside, are laid out at short, not entirely regular intervals. The wall is linked to the trace of the fortifications of Roman Canterbury

(Durovernum). In the north-west only the West Gate remains, with a semicircular tower on each side of the passageway. Above the central part of the gate there are machicolations supported on stone corbels. Both the gate and some towers terminate in restored battlements. The walls of Canterbury were probably rebuilt in the early 13th century. In the 15th century the masonry of the towers and gate was pierced with loopholes.

At the end of the 12th century, Anglo-Norman or Plantagenet fortification techniques were undoubtedly superior to those of France. This situation was reversed by the reforms of Philip Augustus, and the development of the Gothic style emphasized France's creative supremacy. But the castle-building of Edward I of England not only re-reversed the situation but produced fortified structures of great splendour that had no peers anywhere in contemporary Europe.

★

The Holy Roman Empire shared a common border with the Kingdom of France all the way from the lower Rhône to the North Sea; and this border separated them into two entirely different cultures as far as castle architecture was concerned. It is interesting to note in this connection that oblong layouts reminiscent of Central European castles occur in the French departments of Jura and Doubs —and that in the Middle Ages these departments formed part of the Holy Roman Empire.

One example is the castle of St Denis at Chassagne, near Ornans (Doubs). This consists of an oblong upper castle occupying the narrow top of the hill, with a tower built beside the oblong hall. Towards the top of the castle hill there were two further rectangular towers. A neck ditch separates the upper castle from an extensive outer bailey, which is in turn protected by another neck ditch. The entire layout of the castle has a pronounced Central European character.

From 1255 onwards the architect Master Pierre Mainier improved the defences of the famous Swiss castle of Chillon (Vaud) on Lake Geneva. In particular he erected three semicircular wall towers, closed on the inside, on the eastern, landward side of the castle.

The castle of Tarasp (Graubünden), on a rocky eminence, dates back to the early feudal period. On the top of the castle rock stands a large residential tower protected by the adjacent high shell wall. The outer bailey dates from the 16th century. The castle

60
Caernarfon Castle, Wales. Aerial view of part of the castle. In the foreground stands the most powerful of the castle's towers, with three bartizans, situated in the west corner of the castle plan. There are a surprisingly large number of loopholes for archers, even in the merlons of the battlements. 1283-1320.

was restored at great expense in the early years of the present century.

The Swiss town of Sion, in the Rhône Valley, is dominated by the ruined castle of Tourbillon, built at the close of the 13th century. The castle of Chenaux, in the town of Estavayer (Fribourg), also dates from the 13th century.

Luxembourg was another important castle-building area. The largest castle in the country—and one of the largest in Europe—is Vianden, the oblong nucleus of which probably dates from the first third of the 13th century. It has a rather unusual layout, its east end consisting of a two-storey chapel with a central polygonal nave in refined early Gothic style. The lower storey of the chapel is surrounded with massy walls. The western area of the

61
Beaumaris Castle, Wales. View of the outer defence system. The wall, with its numerous towers, rises up from the moat. The slightly projecting parapet walk is supported by small, closely spaced corbels. Built from 1295.

upper castle contains the ruined Knights' Hall, also executed in the earliest Central European version of the Gothic style. On the outside the walls of the hall are reinforced with rounded towers.

The flat terrain of Belgium, the Netherlands and northern Germany created very different conditions for castle-building.

The moated castle of Beersel (Brabant) has been rebuilt. In spite of this, it is possible to visualize its original, more or less circular layout, with three tall U-shaped towers from the 15th century. The castle was built of brick in the 13th century and later on adapted for artillery. Its hewn architectural elements are of stone.

The nature of the terrain influenced the somewhat monotonous architecture of Dutch castles, which are mostly of the lowland moated type. It also had another important consequence. Whereas castles built on top of hills and mountains, mostly on remote, inaccessible sites, fell into ruins once their defensive function had become obsolete, lowland castles were often remodelled into residences. As a result, there are very few ruined medieval castles in the Netherlands. One is the large castle of Valkenburg near Maastricht, in the province of Limburg, which was sited on a wooded hill. The castle originated in the 13th century and had a compact rectangular plan.

One of the best preserved Dutch castles is the moated castle of Hernen. It is rectangular in plan,

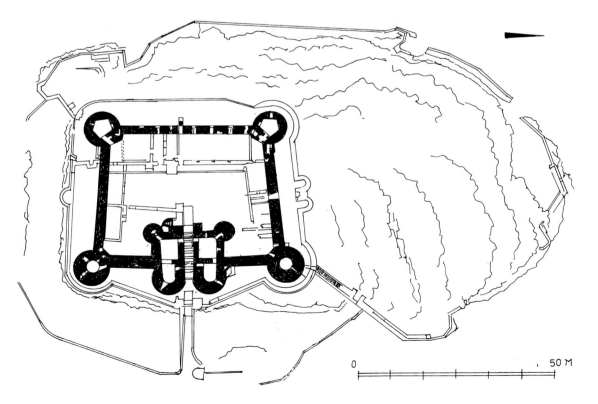

62
Harlech Castle, Wales. Plan.

63 ►
Harlech Castle, Wales. Aerial view of the castle with a fully developed bailey and a lower outer wall whose outline follows that of the main castle. The castle was built in 1286-90.

0   50 M

54

and has round and polygonal corner towers of different sizes, partly supported by corbels.

The origins of these rectangular plans have not been identified with any certainty. They may well reflect the influence of Roman tradition. In the centre of neighbouring Westphalia the moated castle of Rheda was built on an island in the 1220s. Erected on an artificial mound, it is oval in plan. The most important element is the massive four-storey keep, roughly 18×11 metres, which is unique in this part of Europe. The top storey was used as a residence. The architect of this mysterious tower, which dates from about 1230, was probably influenced by the building workshop of the nearby Cistercian monastery of Marienfeld. Ideas brought back from the Crusades may also have played some

part. The Hohenstaufen style is represented by the rusticated pilasters on the keep.

The moated castle of Vischering was begun before 1271 on the eastern outskirts of Lüdinghausen in Westphalia, to the south of Münster. The shell keep, roughly circular in plan, and the trapezoidal outer bailey stand on two islands in a pool.

Unusual in Central Europe is a group of castles, rectangular in plan, that are to be found in the former Duchy of Saxony in the region of Halberstadt. One of these, the 13th century castle of Zilly, is almost square in plan, with a tower in the north-east corner. Within the west wall there is an oblong hall; the remaining buildings surrounding the square inner courtyard are of later date. The castle was adjacent to a circular structure of earlier origin. So far it has proved impossible to discover the stylistic source of these Saxon castles.

The hereditary domains of the Hohenstaufen family, in what were then western and south-western Germany, comprised a quite different environment for building. Alsace in particular is rich in castles. Among the foremost is Guirbaden, or Girbaden (Bas Rhin), a notable example of the oblong layout, right on the edge of the quite separate Anglo-French castle-building area. On the highest, eastern end of the site stands the upper castle, compactly polygonal in plan, with an ashlar-clad watchtower. The lower castle, with its ruined

hall, meets the upper castle on its west side. West of a wide ditch there is an outer bailey, and in its western corner stands a tower in its own enclosure. The masonry consists mostly of rusticated blocks in the Hohenstaufen style.

A document of 1226 refers to the castle as newly built, including its sumptuous late Romanesque hall. Its architectural details put it among the most important hall buildings of the Hohenstaufen period.

A very impressive example of a Vosges castle is Hohandlau (Bas Rhin), with an irregular polygonal plan. The peripheral walls have survived, and two tall, slender watchtowers stand in the east and west corners. The main buildings belong to the mid-13th century. To the east there was a wide ditch, in the south an outer bailey of later date.

The most dramatic-looking castle ruins in Alsace are at Ortenberg (Bas Rhin). The castle was built on a rocky hill, on the top of which stands a pentagonal watchtower, surrounded by a pentagonal shell rising to about 16 metres and equipped with narrow, extraordinarily high loopholes. Like the tower, it is battlemented. To the south it adjoins an upper castle (also pentagonal) containing the hall, while the large outer bailey extends to the east and south. The architectural details of the castle are executed in the late Romanesque and early Gothic styles. The masonry is clad with granite blocks. The latest research

65
Tourbillon, Switzerland. Castle controlling the town of Sion. Construction began in 1294.

◄ 64
Tarasp, Switzerland. Castle on a dominating site. Some building was done in the 12th century, most in the 13th century; the outer fortifications date from the 16th century.

dates the construction of the castle to the mid-13th century.

A number of similar examples could be quoted from Alsace, and also from the neighbouring Palatinate (Pfalz). Among the latter is one of the most important castles in the Holy Roman Empire, Trifels, in which the imperial crown jewels were kept from 1126 onwards. The surviving parts date mainly from the early 13th century. Trifels stands on a rocky hill 160 metres long and 8-60 metres wide at the top. A conspicuous residential tower 24 metres high was built at its highest point. It was fully clad with rusticated blocks, had a vaulted ground floor and upper storeys, and also housed a rib-vaulted chapel with a decorative oriel in its east façade. The adjoining hall has disappeared, leaving almost no trace of its presence. The castle was protected by a

buildings along the inner wall face were subsequently altered. The splendid rusticated wall cladding of the Hohenstaufen parts of the castle is particularly impressive.

Neuleiningen, on the northern border of the Palatinate, was built in 1238-41. The upper castle is laid out as a rectangle of 45 × 48 metres, with four circular towers in the corners and the hall (now in ruins) along its west side. There is an outer bailey on the eastern side of the castle. This rectangular layout of the French type is found nowhere else in the Palatinate. It is assumed that it reflects French influence, perhaps resulting from comings and goings during the Crusades.

Only a fragment of masonry with rusticated cladding remains of the moated castle at Lahr in Baden. It too was rectangular in layout, with four circular

wall encompassing an outer bailey that widens out to the east.

Trifels is typical of the oblong castle built on a rocky eminence. Another excellent example of the early 13th century Hohenstaufen castle is Steinsberg near Heidelberg, with an ovoid polygonal plan and a massive octagonal watchtower in the centre. The tower is accessible through a pointed entrance some 12 metres above ground level. The original

corner towers and a higher tower in the centre. The castle dates from 1218.

One of the most visually effective ruins in Germany is the castle of Runkel, built on a crag over the River Lahn. Its panoramic effect is accentuated by its three towers, each dating from a different period. The development of the castle seems to have been a very complex process. The mainly rectangular central tower seems to be the oldest part of the castle. It is provided with a 'beak' on its east side, which was more exposed to enemy attack than the river side. This is one of the oldest examples in Germany of a rectangular tower with a beak. The original early 13th century castle on top of the crag obviously had an oblong layout with the tower in the centre. The massive shell wall protecting it from the south-west also formed part of the original layout. But its southern part, about 6 metres thick, is of late Gothic origin. The massive pentagonal towers to the north date from about the mid-14th century, whereas the southern tower is believed to have originated late in the 15th century. The narrow bailey in the south-east was supplemented in the 14th century with a new bailey in the north-west, accessible from the south through a gateway. In the final phase the south-west bailey was added.

The castle of Wildenberg near Preunschen stands in the wooded, mountainous Odenwald in Franconia. It is oblong in plan, with a typical rectangular corner on its south-east side with a tower gateway housing a chapel on the upper floor. Along the short southwest side runs a massive wall, the inner face of which meets the angle of the obliquely placed watchtower, as at Cheb. In its immediate vicinity, closing off the north-eastern side of the castle, stands the magnificent late Romanesque hall with architectural details in the earliest Gothic style. The majority of the buildings and walls are clad with rusticated stone blocks. The beginnings of this interesting castle reach back to the early 13th century. The hall was completed just before the mid-13th century.

The magnificent castle of Salzburg was built in an

◀ 66
Chenaux, Switzerland. Castle in the town of Estavayer. The circular towers date from the 13th century, the gateway from the 15th century.

67
Beersel, Belgium. Moated castle, built in the 13th century; the U-shaped towers are 15th century. The castle has been considerably restored.

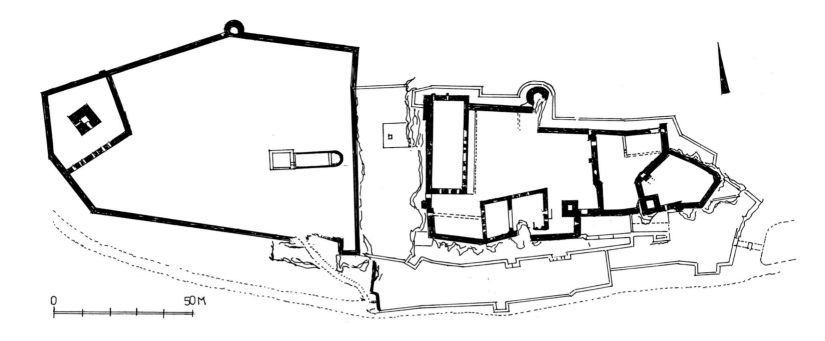

elevated position near Bad Neustadt an der Saale in Franconia. Initially the fortified seat of the Bishops of Würzburg, in the 13th century it became a castle of the 'Ganerbenburg' type (that is, divided between several families). The polygonal castle area is enclosed by a wall and further protected by a ditch to the north-east and east. There are four square wall towers, one of them (facing north-east) a gate-tower; it is clad with rusticated stone blocks and has a late Romanesque portal with a sawtooth decorative motif influenced by Norman architecture. The towers inside the castle area are also partly of Romanesque origin: one, the 'Münze palace', is remarkable for its extraordinarily attractive details in very early Gothic style. The castle may be characterized as Romanesque-Gothic, its construction having proceeded from the early to the mid-13th century. The towers straddling the north-east and east walls represent an example of towers used to strengthen a peripheral wall that was unique in Germany at that time.

The finest early 13th century castle in Thuringia was Wartburg above Eisenach; however, subsequent reconstructions have largely obscured its character as a medieval fortification.

The fortifications of 13th century German cities pose some as yet unsolved problems. Unlike castles, urban fortifications have received only marginal attention in scholarly writings, where the general tendency has been to date them later rather than earlier. Interest has concentrated on gateways as architectural works (particularly in the Baltic) rather than as integral parts of a fortification system. And whereas the often magnificent urban works of the 14th century and later have been thoroughly

68
Guirbaden, France. Plan of the castle, built between about 1215 and 1226. After W. Hotz.

69
Hohandlau, France. Plan. Dating from the middle of the 13th century, the castle was extended in the 14th century and reconstructed in the 16th. After Salch.

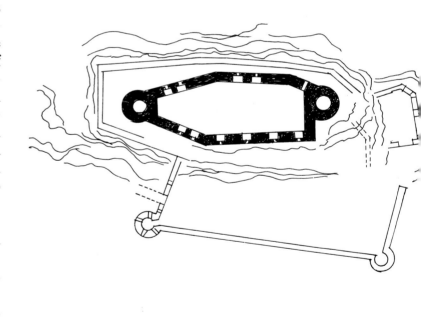

70 ►
Trifels, Germany. The castle was mainly built in the early 13th century, but was extended in the 14th.

documented, the medieval beginnings of German city fortifications in the 13th century have been left relatively obscure and unstudied.

The best preserved medieval city fortification in the Rhine valley is that of Münstereifel, which has a very irregular oblong layout. There are circular towers at the angles of the wall, but in other parts of it rather shallow rectangular towers appear at intervals on the relatively long curtain walls. At the north gate, called Werthertor (Werther's Gate), a tower with a passage through it is flanked by a pair of strong semicircular towers which reflect West European influence. The fortification dates from the 13th-14th centuries.

Castles of the most varied types and sizes are to be found in the Alpine countries, although a study of their riches is greatly hindered by the radical remodelling of many of them over the centuries.

South Tirol is an area of extraordinary importance. Of the many possible examples that might be given, mention must be made of the castle of Boimont between Bolzano (Bozen) and Merano (Meran). It is rectangular in layout, with a pair of residential towers in the northern corners, and dates from the early 13th century. Its refined architectural details are late Romanesque in style.

The tower of the large castle of Sprechenstein (Castel Pietra), near Vipiteno (Sterzing), was built just before the middle of the 13th century, but work on it continued down to the 16th century.

The centre of the strong castle of Roggendorf, in Pöggstall (Lower Austria), is occupied by a bulky residential tower. A similar, early 13th century tower has been preserved in the middle of the former frontier castle of Hainburg, on the south bank of the Danube.

Probably as late as the reign of Přemysl Otakar II (1253-78), King of Bohemia and Duke of Austria, a number of moated castles were built in Lower Austria with regular rectangular plans. Pottendorf had a pair of towers, one in each east corner, and a third tower outside the west wall, clad with rusticated stone blocks. Under Otakar II the rectangular layout was also used in the oldest part of Vienna's castle, which had four corner towers.

The ruins of Kollmitzgraben, overlooking the Dyje on the Austro-Czech border, are a remarkable sight. The skyline of the upper castle consists of two circular towers of unequal height, undoubtedly influenced by the castle architecture of neighbouring Moravia.

Schlaining in the Burgenland has an oval plan. In its south-east section there is a small irregular area with a semicircular corner tower. The Romanesque hall dates from the first half of the 13th century. The strong south-west gateway rises from a

century, and was most probably built by Otakar II in about 1260, when Hainburg was a key strategic point in his defences against the Hungarians.

In 1268 Otakar II founded the town of Marchegg, which was then close to the Hungarian border. Its rectangular plan was remarkably large (720 × 860 metres). Before its building had been completed, the town was enclosed with a wall, without towers at first but with two gates, the Vienna Gate and the Hungarian Gate, each designed in the Czech manner as a passageway with a circular tower on one side. The fortification system also included an outer bailey, a ditch and a rampart. The city's castle has a rectangular plan. Together with the large city of Uherský Brod, founded in the borderlands of Eastern Moravia, Marchegg represented a point of departure for expeditions against the Hungarians, whom Otakar then regarded as the greatest danger to his Central European domains.

Bohemia constituted a strong natural fortress, surrounded on all sides by mountains covered with

71
Salzburg, Austria. Tower of the castle's Romanesque gate; early 13th century.

72
Boimont, Italy. Plan of the castle from the early 13th century. After J. Weingartner.

wide ditch, beyond which there is an outer bailey with a slender tower in the south-west corner. The ditch also surrounds the castle on its west and north-west sides. The fortifications of Schlaining were strengthened substantially in the 16th and 17th centuries.

The medieval fortifications of the city of Hainburg, below Babenberg Castle, have remained almost intact. The walls are laid out as an irregular trapezium, with three rather concave sides; only the south-west wall has an almost straight trace. The only wall with battlements also has massive mural towers, rectangular, pentagonal or octagonal in plan, with narrow loopholes.

The gateways have also been preserved. The most important is the Vienna Gate (Wienertor), whose pointed arched passageway is protected by a portcullis and projecting, semicircular rusticated towers on each side of it. The unifying stone superstructure is of a later date.

The history of Hainburg's fortifications is not documented. It is generally dated to the late 13th

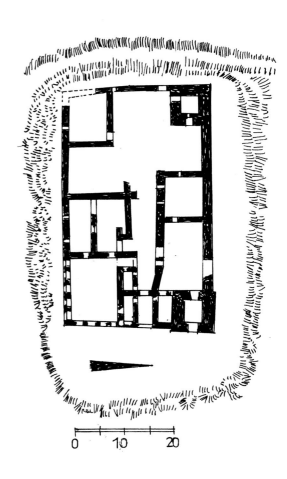

0   10   20

deep, almost impenetrable forests. The only vulnerable point was on the southern border of Moravia, which was defined politically rather than naturally in the 11th century. Hence the early interest of Bohemian rulers in defence systems, culminating in the extraordinary and thoroughgoing efforts made in the 13th century to build castles and fortify cities. Stimulated at first by outside influences, these efforts soon also manifested a distinctive national creativity.

The most remarkable early 13th century castle in Central Europe was the royal castle of Týřov (Rakovník district), overlooking the River Berounka, which was built by King Wenceslas I (1230-53) in about 1240. Týřov represents a rather unusual synthesis of different types of castle-building. Its oblong layout on the top of a hill is in the Central European tradition. The west end of the castle consists of an almost square residential tower, obviously built in the second phase of construction. The courtyard of the upper castle was entered from the east through a passage in a small hall guarded to the north by a tall circular watchtower at the junction of the upper and the lower castles. The fact that the lower castle has a rectangular layout of the French type is of great interest, and the combination of this with the Central European oblong plan suggests that the castle of Týřov was the work of Czech builders welding two outside traditions together.

Wenceslas' son and successor, Přemysl Otakar II (1253-78), was one of the most remarkable medieval builders of castles and fortified towns. His systematic construction of castles and cities is probably without parallel in the history of medieval fortification, and indicates the excellence of the Bohemian administration.

As early as the 1250s a royal castle was built at the newly founded town of Písek in southern Bohemia. Sited above the River Otava, the main castle area was slightly trapezoidal in plan, with a large inner courtyard. Only the west wing and some remains of the north and south wings survive. An arcaded corridor ran round the courtyard at the ground and first floor levels. A tower stood on each side of the west wing above the river. The south tower was rectangular; the north tower is shown as circular in an 18th century picture. A third tower was located by archaeologists above the central part of the east wing. The chapel was situated on the first floor of the south wing. The castle was also fortified against the town.

The castle of Zvíkov was founded during the reign of Wenceslas I in the 1240s; it lies north-east of Písek, on a spur above the confluence of the rivers

73
Hainburg, Austria. The Vienna Gate, about 1260.

Vltava and Otava. Zvíkov has a powerful tower, with rusticated cladding of stone blocks, adjoined by two wings. Wenceslas' son, Otakar II, gave the castle its monumental grandeur, building a royal hall of an irregularly pentagonal plan determined by the position of the earlier buildings and the nature of the terrain. A passage in the west wing gives access to the hall courtyard which, like Písek, is arcaded at the ground and first floor levels. In spite of an inadequate restoration in the 1880s, the arcaded courtyard of Zvíkov Castle creates an impression of lofty medieval splendour. Most of the rooms overlooking the courtyard on the firs floor were rib vaulted. The chapel, on the first floor of the south wing, is of the highest architectural standard.

Zvíkov Castle was thoroughly fortified. In the early Gothic phase of its construction the northern outer bailey was fortified with a wall some 3 metres thick and circular towers at the northern angles. This bailey was separated from the courtyard by a wall affording access to the hall. The southern outer bailey was controlled by a slender wedge-shaped watchtower, situated near the southern entrance and with its edge towards the enemy.

Zvíkov Castle, undoubtedly one of the most attractive of medieval fortresses, was built by the Písek building workshop from the 1250s onwards. The chapel was completed in the last phase of construction, about 1270.

Investigations have ascertained the layout of a castle in the town of Kadaň (Chomutov district), above the River Ohře. In plan it was an almost regular square, with four corner towers of which only one survives. Founded before 1261, Kadaň is closer in style to contemporary Italian castles than Písek and Zvíkov. However, many more of Otakar's castles were rectangular in plan.

An important non-royal dwelling is the episcopal castle in the city of Horšovský Týn in western Bohemia. Built in the 1250s, it has a regular trapezoidal plan with a hall in its west wing and two towers. The first floor of the southern tower houses the episcopal chapel, with an interior in the early Gothic style. The second chapel, incorporated into the south-east of the building, is of earlier origin.

The diversity of Otakar's royal castles is revealed by Bezděz (Česká Lípa district), which stands, visible from far and wide, on a hill in the Central Highlands of Bohemia. It was constructed from the 1250s to the 1270s, its elongated plan being completely at variance with the compact layouts elsewhere. At the summit of the rock stands a tall circular watchtower guarding the entrance to the oblong courtyard of the upper castle, originally with the wing of the royal hall and a chapel added during the early years of the reign of Otakar's son, Wenceslas II (1283-1305). The area of the lower castle, which slopes away to the west, was initially much narrower than at present. The part of the wall which slopes down to the much smaller and lower Devil's Tower formed part of the original fortifications. Along the south side there was an extensive fortified ward with three gates.

Within sight of Bezděz the same builders erected another royal castle, Houska (Česká Lípa district), with a three-wing rectangular layout and a watchtower (no longer extant) on a high rock. Construction went on until about 1270. The three wings surround the courtyard, which is enclosed by a high wall to the south. An interesting feature of the castle is the low, early Gothic second floor built on top of the original first floor. Here and there Houska has architectural details that are older than those at Bezděz or contemporary with it.

One of Otakar's most interesting castles is Křivoklát (Rakovník district). The upper castle has

74
Marchegg, Austria. The tower of the destroyed Vienna Gate, built after 1260.

le is protected by a complex system of walls without towers.

The above examples constitute only a selection of the major 13th century Bohemian, Moravian and Silesian castles, which were of European significance. Moreover Otakar II was also a great founder of cities, acting for political, economic and—perhaps above all—strategic reasons. Hence he created a remarkable system of fortified cities along Bohemia's border with the Holy Roman Empire and Hungary. An undated royal order has been preserved concerning the provision of fortifications for the royal city of Kolín. Within four years the citizens were obliged to dig a ditch 12 metres wide, face it with masonry on both sides, and build a wall 12 metres high above the ditch. The order does not mention a gateway with towers, which is rather surprising. However, these do appear in an order (also undated) to the town of Čáslav, which expressly mentions rounded towers ('turres obrotundae'); three of these were to be placed in the vicinity of the gates. An order concerning the town of Ústí nad Labem mentions walls, towers and an outer bailey.

75
Týřov, Czechoslovakia. Circular watchtower (*c.* 1240) at the junction of the upper and the lower castles.

76
Písek, Czechoslovakia. A reconstruction of the castle's plan as it was in the 1250s. After Durdík.

a triangular plan with a circular watchtower in the east corner. The nucleus of the three-wing hall is Romanesque. The first floor of the main wing houses a monumental hall. The extensive lower castle to the west, irregularly trapezoidal in plan, is of early Gothic origin. There are the foundations of an early Gothic building along its north side.

Osek (Teplice district) in northern Bohemia is an important, though ruinous, example of a royal frontier castle from the reign of Otakar II. Its residential tower is built on the highest point of the hill. The upper castle area slopes down, widening towards the south. In its south-west corner there is a lower tower with an adjoining chapel. The complicated route into the upper castle was guarded by a circular tower. The lower castle has an irregular trapezoidal plan. Further east stands the castle's second major tower, a circular watchtower that controls the southern outworks and its gateway. The entire cast-

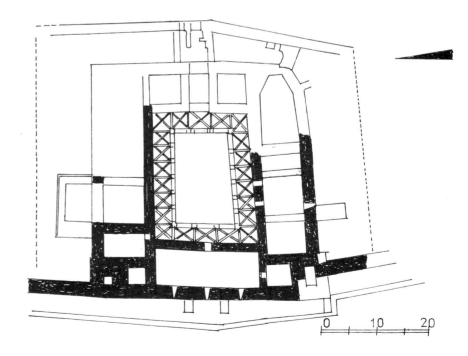

77
Zvíkov, Czechoslovakia. Plan
of the first floor of the royal
hall. The tower and parts of
the adjoining wings were built
about 1240, the entire project
being completed in about
1270.

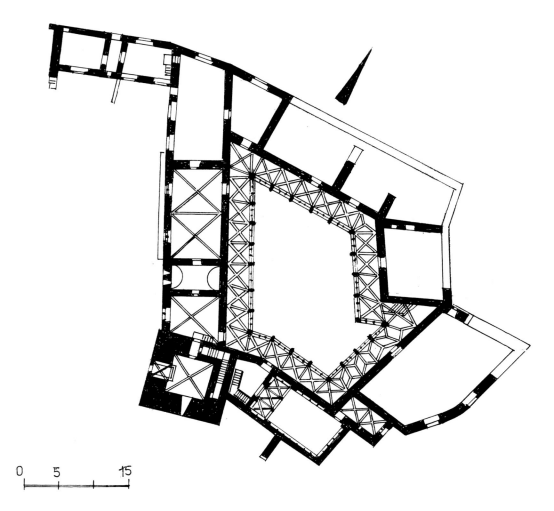

78
Zvíkov, Czechoslovakia. View
through the arcades on the
first floor of the royal hall.
About 1260; drastically
reconstructed in the 1880s.

0   5   15

79 ▶
Zvíkov, Czechoslovakia. View
from the south, with the Písek
Gate in the foreground and
the watchtower behind it.
About 1270.

80
Bezděz, Czechoslovakia.
View of the castle (1250s-
1270s) from the south-east,
showing the royal hall and the
adjacent chapel (c. 1285) on
the right of the big tower, with
the lower Devil's Tower to the
left.

81
Bezděz, Czechoslovakia. Plan
of the castle, built in the third
quarter of the 13th century.

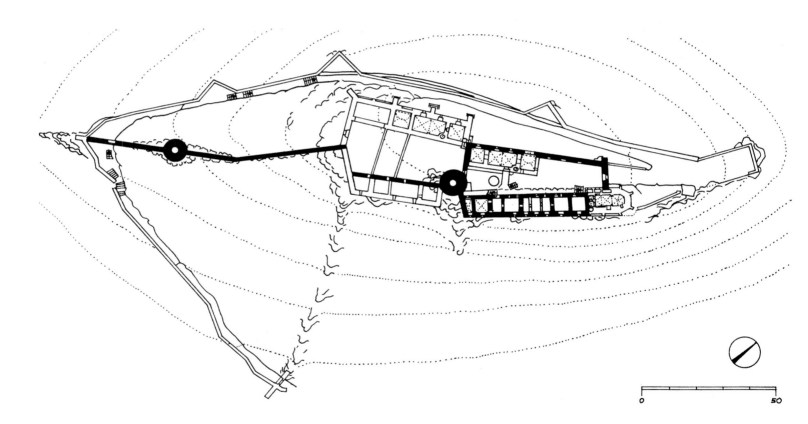

A rigorous study of sites, drawings and plans has proved that a uniform system of fortifications for royal cities was put into effect during the reign of Otakar II. Its elements can be described as follows. The main city wall was some 2 metres thick. The gateways usually took the form of towers built flush with the outer face of the wall. Mural towers were almost always circular at the angles of the wall and semicircular elsewhere. In front of the main wall there was an outer bailey of indeterminate size, enclosed by an outer wall rising from the ditch, in front of which stood a rampart. The depth and complexity of the fortifications greatly reduced an enemy's chances of bringing siege machines up to the main wall.

This defensive system was used for a number of

68

royal cities, the best preserved example being Čáslav. Most of the towers in the main wall are semicircular, standing at intervals of 28-40 metres. However, in a short stretch of wall on the south-west
side, facing the water which also formed part of the
defences, the towers were elliptical in plan. Following the royal order mentioned above, there were
gateways flanked with circular towers; but only the
tower protecting the former Brod Gate is now
standing.

The outer bailey of Čáslav was 6-14 metres wide.
Its outer wall, only 60-80 centimetres thick, rose
from a ditch 10-15 metres wide and protected by a
strong rampart; this still rises to a height of 5 metres
on the south-west side of the town.

Roman, Byzantine and possibly Islamic influences, brought to Europe by the Crusaders, were
probably at work in Bohemia. Since the medieval
fortifications of most European cities have not been
studied in depth, it is not possible to evaluate Otakar's achievement properly. However, our present
state of knowledge suggests that his royal cities were
far above the contemporary European standard because of their remarkable, distinctly un-medieval,
almost standardized uniformity of design, depth
and complexity.

Among the castles built for Otakar's son, Wenceslas II, is Konopiště (Benešov district), which has
a fully developed, regular rectangular layout. The
oblong eastern part constitutes the upper castle; a
large drum tower sits astride the middle of the east
wall, while a smaller round tower reinforces each of
the east corners. To the north and south the wall
joins up with residential wings.

The west side of the rectangular lower castle is
defended in the same fashion as the east side of the
upper castle. A circular tower stood at the northern
juncture of the two areas. Built into the sides of
some of the towers are slender cylindrical features
that formerly housed spiral staircases. The castle
was protected by an outer wall, a ditch and a rampart. According to recent scholarly findings the
castle was built at the turn of the 13th and 14th
centuries.

The large city of Znojmo in Southern Moravia was
built during the reign of Otakar II and Wenceslas II.
In places that were difficult of access, it was protected
by a single wall, but in other places the system of fortification was considerably more complex. The main
wall was up to 2 metres thick and some 6 metres high.
It was battlemented, and was defended by alternate
rectangular and circular mural towers at intervals of
50-80 metres; the towers were at least 4 metres higher
than the walls. At a distance of 4.5-10 metres there

was an outer wall above a ditch some 20 metres wide,
with a rampart beyond.

During the reign of Wenceslas II, the characteristic feature of urban fortifications was a tendency to
verticality. This was undoubtedly connected with
the arrival of the High Gothic style in Bohemia, and
manifested itself most impressively in the fortifications of the Old Town of Prague; unfortunately only
two tall towers, the monumental, originally triple-
towered St Gallen's Gate, and very small sections of
the wall have survived. The wall was 2 metres thick
and over 10 metres high; the lengths of the curtain
wall between towers averaged 60 metres. The outer
bailey was 15-20 metres wide and the ditch 25 metres wide and 8 metres deep.

Slovakia, the eastern region of modern Czechoslovakia, also has many castles and fortified cities.
The huge castle of Spiš was walled with stone as
early as 1221, and recent archaeological investigations have uncovered traces of a far older stone
castle on the site. The hall was built immediately
after the Tartar invasion of 1241, followed by the
conical watchtower of the upper castle in the third
quarter of the 13th century. The very existence of

82
Houska, Czechoslovakia.
Ground level plan of the
castle, which dates from
c. 1250-70.

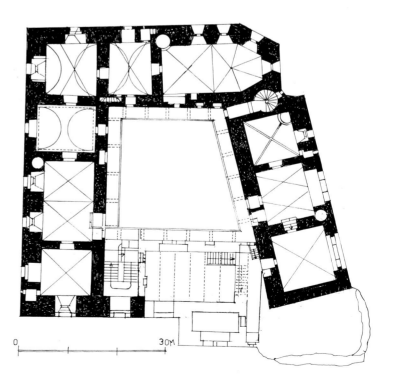

0   30M

69

the castle proved to be a stimulus to more intensive building in Slovakia.

By contrast with Bohemia and Moravia, flat-sided towers were more common in Slovakia than round ones. The large residential tower of the magnificent castle of Trenčín dates from the 1260s. According to recent archaeological findings, the masonry of the tower was partly of Romanesque origin.

The castle of Čachtice (Trenčín district) is a representative example of the more important late 13th century Slovak castles. In plan it is a trapezium with the lower corners cut off. In its south corner there is a tower, pentagonal in plan, with a sharply projecting beak (edge) facing outwards, towards a potential enemy. The courtyard is surrounded by buildings adjoining the wall.

There are fortifications of great interest on Hungarian territory, at Visegrád, which stands above the Danube on its northern bank as a bulwark against attacks from the west; at the time, the Bohemian state, which included Austria and other Alpine territories, seemed a formidable threat.

Visegrád was built from the mid-1250s. The lower castle was founded on a rocky eminence directly above the river, and its principal feature was a tall residential tower, hexagonal in plan, with protracted northern and southern angles. The tower is clad with carefully hewn blocks of stone. It was surrounded by a wall from which another wall sloped down to the river bank, guarded by a tower.

The fortifications of the lower castle met a wall reinforced with three towers, and this connected the lower castle with the triangular-plan royal upper castle rather higher up. In the middle of its east side stood a rectangular-plan tower with a sharply projecting eastern beak. The upper castle was enclosed by an outer bailey and a ditch.

The castle of Sümeg, to the north of the Lake Balaton, was in existence before the mid-13th century, and was monumentally reconstructed in later centuries. Its attractive ruins, on top of an unwooded hill, dominate the surrounding countryside for long distances.

The fortifications of Sopron, on Hungary's western border, developed in an unusual fashion. The main wall, 190 centimetres thick, had no towers. Its gateways projected into an outer bailey only 7.5 metres wide. The outer wall, 60 centimetres thick, was provided with semicircular bastions at approximately 30 metres intervals, partly built on to the remains of Roman defence towers. This means that when the medieval city was being founded in the 13th century, a new main wall was erected, and the outer wall was built on the trace of the decayed Roman wall.

The ruins of Bolków or Bolkoburg (Wrocław, Poland) are one of the most attractive of late 13th century Silesian castles. It has an oblong plan with a corrugated curtain wall and a strong watchtower in its south-west angle. A lower rectangular residential tower stood somewhere in its vicinity.

84
Konopiště, Czechoslovakia. Plan of the castle, built at the end of the 13th century. After Kašička.

◄ 83
Křivoklát, Czechoslovakia. View of the castle from the south-east, with the late 14th century outer wall in the foreground, and above it the early 13th century upper castle comprising the great tower and the royal hall.

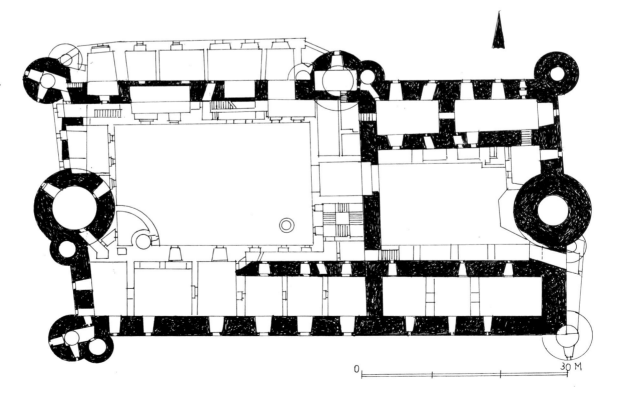

0   30 M

In 1230 the Order of the Teutonic Knights began a campaign to conquer the Chełmno region and Prussia; the Knights were technically crusaders, fighting to defeat and convert the pagan tribes on the Baltic, although the Order was in time to become increasingly politically motivated. About 1250 the first castle of Balga was founded on a hill above the sea. It has an irregularly hexagonal plan with a long north-eastern side, enclosed by a hexagonal wall with towers in the north-west and a ditch along the south-east and south sides. Only the foundations survive from this, the Order's oldest castle, which was built of brick.

In 1254 Otakar II took the cross and intervened to help the Teutonic Knights hold down Prussia. In 1257 he built the castle at Königsberg, named after its royal founder (König means 'king' in German); the city is now called Kaliningrad. The castle is believed to have had a rectangular plan with three

wings and a wall on the fourth side defining the inner courtyard, as at Houska in Bohemia.

The early castles of the Teutonic Knights seem to have been modelled on those of Otakar. Although the major phase of the Order's castle-building began early in the 14th century, some important works were executed closer to Otakar's time. These included the first phase of what became the principal seat of the head of the Order, the castle of Malbork or Marienburg (Gdańsk); in 1275-1300 its 'High Castle' (Hochschloss) and northern outer bailey were constructed. So was the castle of Lochstadt and the third seat of the Order, which was built near the town of Gniew or Mewe (Gdańsk), on the west bank of the Vistula. All of them had a four-wing rectangular plan.

Gniew was repeatedly reconstructed, but it is still possible to discern its original shape, with a slender tower in each of three corners; the fourth, north-

◀ 85
Čachtice, Czechoslovakia.
Early 16th century gateway to
the outer bailey, with the late
13th century upper castle in
the background.

circular corner towers in the walls and a strong tower serving as its gateway.

On the Danish island of Bornholm, the ruined castle of Hammerhus overlooks the sea. Built in the

86
Sümeg, Hungary. Panoramic view of the castle; in the foreground is a tetrahedral bastion, parts of which originated in the early 13th century.

east corner was occupied by a substantial tower until the late 19th century. The castle stands in the centre of an extensive outer bailey which is separated from the town by a ditch. Built of brick, it was begun in 1282.

Of the Order's many castles beyond its Prussian heartland, there is a particularly interesting example at Ventspils (formerly Windau), now in Latvia. Built towards the end of the 13th century on the coast of Kurland (Courland), it has a four-wing layout with an inner courtyard overlooked by a sturdy tower that projects slightly from the south-east corner. The castle entrance is near the large tower in the east wing. The castle was protected by an outer bailey.

On the opposite side of the Baltic, in southern Sweden, the construction of the royal castle of Kalmar began at the end of the 13th century. The castle had an irregularly rectangular plan with

mid-13th century, it had a rectangular courtyard surrounded with buildings, a massive residential tower and a large gateway tower.

Italian fortifications have long been the subject of intensive study, yet it seems unlikely that a final evaluation of their role has yet been made, whether in artistic or military terms. The golden age of Italian medieval fortifications began in the early 13th century during the reign of the Holy Roman Emperor Frederick II (1212-50). Frederick succeeded the Norman rulers of the region, transforming Southern Italy and Sicily into a power-base which he hoped to use in order to control his turbulent German realm. The castles of this period are distinctive, eclectic structures, excellently illustrated by a group of Frederick's castles with rectangular plans. These were probably inspired by small Arab fortresses in Sicily or elsewhere rather than classical or Byzantine models.

Frederick II was himself a remarkable personality, an innovator who was influenced by Eastern ideas while remaining in many respects a medieval man in the European mould. It was certainly rational of him to build up a compact, highly organized state in Italy rather than in his hereditary domains in Germany, where feudal decentralization had been taken to extremes.

Frederick's castles in Southern Italy and Sicily were only marginally related to the contemporary Hohenstaufen architecture of south-west Germany,

of the buildings, which are certainly outside the Italian artistic tradition.

Frederick's castle at Bari was built from 1233 onwards on the site of an earlier Norman castle. It originally stood on the coast, the line of which has since shifted. Bari is trapezoidal in plan, comprising a courtyard enclosed by four wings. A tower touches each of the south corners, and two smaller towers defend the north corners; one is hexagonal, the other quadrangular, and both are pointed. The Hohenstaufen atmosphere of the castle is accen-

although Lagopesole, discussed below, is to some extent an exception.

Italian castles were original in layout, monumental in mass and architecturally more advanced than their German equivalents. Frederick's castles were not built by German craftsmen, but mainly by local workers, but they were, however, partly influenced by Cistercian architecture. This Cistercian influence appears in the purity of the Gothic elements in some

tuated by the rusticated cladding of the walls. The interiors (arcaded corridor, double-span entrance hall and south-west part of the arcades) are also interesting. A ditch ran round three sides of the castle. The positioning of the towers in the corners harks back to the earlier Norman castle style.

The walls of Frederick's castle at Trani rise straight up from sea level. It has a classic, square, four-wing plan with four corner towers; the largest, on the south side, merely touch the angles of the walls. The south wing seems to have been the most important; it was protected against a land attack by an extremely thick wall, probably with a parapet which may have run along the east and west wings. The castle has not so far been subjected to intensive investigation. Historical documents give 1233 as the date of its construction; it was enlarged in 1249.

The most famous of all Frederick's castles is the inimitable Castel del Monte in Apulia, situated on the summit of a low hill in flat country. Its defensive functions were mainly served by the thickness of the walls (especially the tower walls), the height of the buildings and the hexagonal towers projecting out of the wall face. To some extent, defensive considerations were modified to fit the architectural concept of an octagonal layout with an inner courtyard and hexagonal towers at the angles. On the outside, the narrow loopholes in the stone cladding of the towers are very impressive. The towers are the same height as the adjacent curtain walls. The treatment of the ground and first floor interiors, the buttresses, the capitals and the massive ribbed vaults clearly shows the influence of Cistercian building. Surprisingly, in documents surviving from Frederick's lifetime Castel del Monte is mentioned just once, in 1240.

Castel del Monte is often compared with the late 12th century Alsatian castle of Egisheim, which has an octagonal tower with rusticated cladding. A similar plan, but without the angle towers, was used for the late 12th century castle of Büdingen in Hesse. And the castle at Boulogne sur Mer also has affinities with Castel del Monte, although its date (1231) makes any likelihood of influence very remote. However, its closest resemblance is to Bouillancourt en Sery in France (department of the Somme). Nevertheless, when all of this has been said, Castel del Monte is *sui generis* in the field of castle architecture, without significant predecessors or successors.

Lagopesole was founded by Frederick as late as 1242; it was not yet completed at the time of his death. The castle stands in a dominating position, visible from a great distance, on the top of a hill. It is rectangular, with four corner towers slightly projecting from the walls and standing at almost the same height. The peripheral walls are partly clad with rusticated stone blocks. The inner courtyard is entered through a gateway between a pair of massive pillars. Rusticated blocks also clad the entire surface of a substantial donjon in the other courtyard. The Imperial Hall is the most important of the buildings surrounding the principal courtyard.

◀ 87
Malbork, Poland; formerly Marienburg, built by the Teutonic Knights. View of the High Castle (Hochschloss) from the south-east. The wall in the foreground (pre-1340) surrounds the High Castle. The construction of the High Castle with the tower began around 1275 and ended with the consecration of the chapel in 1344.

88
Gniew, Poland; formerly Mewe, built by the Teutonic Knights from 1282 onwards.

89
Kalmar, Sweden. The castle, of the rectangular French type, dates from the end of the 13th century; the outer fortifications with roundels were constructed in the 16th century.

Very interesting is the style of architectural details of these castles, which are mostly Gothic.

Frederick's castle at Catania in Sicily originally overlooked the sea. In a letter of 1239 from the Emperor to its builder, Riccardo da Lentini, it is referred to as already under construction. The shape and layout of the castle are perfectly regular and symmetrical. It has a rectangular plan with four wings surrounding a square courtyard. Four almost completely round towers emerge from the corners, and the middle of each curtain wall is protected by a much slighter, three-quarter-circular tower. All the towers were taller than the walls.

As in other Frederican castles, the architectural details are mainly early Gothic. The style appears in the halls on the first floor, notably in the ribbed vaults, which are influenced by Cistercian architecture. German scholars maintain that Catania reflects French influence, particularly that of the castle at Angers; but a comparison between the two structures reveals the erroneous nature of such conclusions. In reality Catania represents the ultimate development of the Hohenstaufen castles, in which a delight in formal perfection came to take precedence over functional requirements. This phenomenon was without parallel in the medieval period; related designs, such as the splendid designs of French castles, are generally of a much later date.

This overriding of functional criteria culminates in the bizarre Syracusan castle of Maniace, on the island of Ortygia. The castle has a square plan with four circular towers in the corners of the curtain walls. The entire space within the walls was designed as an enormous hall, with a cross vault with massive ribs supported by half-columns along the walls and elsewhere by columns with early Gothic capitals. The castle is entered through an early Gothic gateway with a pointed arch. There is a hearth near the bottom of each corner staircase. The first floor was probably of similar design. The building was erected in the 1230s and '40s by builders influenced by early Gothic Cistercian architecture.

In Sicily Frederick II had another castle designed with arcades in the inner courtyard; it was built in the new town of Augusta, which he had founded.

However, Frederick's building activities were not confined to castles. Among his most celebrated achievements was the mostly destroyed palace of Lucera, of which all that remains is its square shell with a prominent external scarp; out of the scarp rises a half-barrel vault abutting the central tower-shaped structure. A similar tower was built by Frederick at Termoli, beside the Adriatic Sea, in about 1247.

Frederick also built castles outside Southern Italy, notably the Prato in Tuscany. This is an almost square-plan structure with corner towers no higher than the curtain walls. The main entrance is on the south-west side, with a tower to the left of it. On two of the other sides there is a rectangular mural tower in the middle. The battlements are crowned with swallow-tail merlons. The castle was still unfinished at the time of Frederick's death in 1250.

The Southern Italian castle of Oria underwent a complex development. Here Frederick did not construct an entirely new castle, as he did elsewhere, but built on an existing Norman fort; and the triangular plan of the castle is also exceptional. The low tower has been preserved from the Frederican period. Many alterations were subsequently made, notably by Charles of Anjou, in the French style of fortification. He had an extraordinarily massive wall built on the vulnerable town side of the castle in 1276-79, strengthening it in the centre and at the right-hand end with powerful round, high mural towers, a parapet walk on brackets and machicolations on top.

To the west of the town of Foggia in south-east Italy, some remarkable fortifications survive which date from the third quarter of the 13th century. There is a spur with steep slopes and a rather extensive flat summit on the western edge of the town of Lucera, and here the martial King of Naples, Charles of Anjou, built a castle adjoining Frederick's hall. Of somewhat irregular polygonal plan, it is protected by a single strong wall. Angle towers guard the west side, but there are much more elaborate defences on the vulnerable east side facing the town. In front of the wall a high, carefully constructed glacis (smooth stone defensive incline) rises up from the bottom of the ditch. In both east angles of the walls stand powerful round towers with loopholes; the north-east tower is called 'The Lioness'. The masonry of both towers consists of large stone blocks; the south-east tower is rusticated up to more than half its height.

The wall is reinforced with pointed rectangular towers at intervals of only 20 metres. Along the top of the wall runs a parapet walk protected by battlements on the outside (not preserved) and a continuous parapet wall on the inside. The top floor of the towers was above parapet level. The entrance to the town lay in a rectangular wall recess.

Charles of Anjou's castle dominates the Apulian countryside. Charles trusted only his own countrymen, putting the construction of the castle in the hands of Pierre d'Agincourt and the carpenter Jean of Toul. Consequently Lucera, built in 1269-75, provides evidence for the state of fortification as an art in late 13th century France. A surprising feature is the absence of any external reinforcement of the defences of the main wall; there is only the glacis and ditch on the east side. By contrast, the rectangular pointed towers are a highly progressive feature. In reality the fortifications at Lucera have the character of an urban system.

A remarkable example of a French castle far distant from the motherland is Castel Nuovo in Naples.

90
Trani, Italy. Aerial view of the town with the Emperor Frederick II's castle (begun in 1233) with a Renaissance bastion in the front.

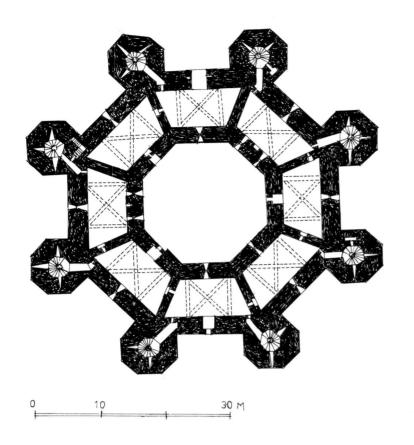

It stands in the harbour, overlooking the sea, and bears witness to the power of Charles of Anjou, who had it built in 1279-83 as his town residence by two French architects, Pierre de Caulis and Pierre d'Agincourt. The castle has an irregular pentagonal plan. On the short entrance side there are three massive towers influenced by French architecture. Two of them, almost completely circular, stand in the corners of the curtain wall; the south-west tower is adjacent to a U-shaped tower, both of them flanking the entrance gate. In the south-east and the northeast corners there are three-quarter-circular towers.

In the course of the 13th century Italian towns were also fortified. The main wall was reinforced with closely arranged rectangular towers. By con-

91
Castel del Monte, Italy. Plan of the 13th century castle. After Bruhns.

92
Castel del Monte, Italy. Frederick II's castle was built from about 1240.

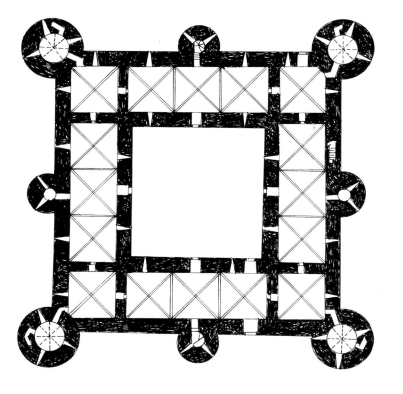

0   30 M

trast with fortifications in countries where a variety of wall towers were employed, Italian practice was largely uniform. Unfortunately, Italian town fortifications have not yet been studied in depth or reliably dated.

In 1220 the town of Cittadella, near Padua, was founded as a fortified centre to contain Treviso. It is therefore assumed that the walls still enclosing the irregular oval heart of the city were built shortly afterwards. The rectangular towers, mostly open at the rear, are one storey higher than the battlemented wall and project slightly from its face; 32 of the towers still survive. The stretches of curtain wall between the towers are very short. There was a ditch in front of the walls.

The small town of Monselice, in the Veneto, is dominated by a castle built by Frederick II. A wall with mural towers runs around the town. The small town of Monterrigioni, in Tuscany, has excellent fortifications. In plan, the walls comprise a rather

93
Catania, Sicily. Plan of the castle. After Bruhns.

94
Catania, Sicily. Aerial view of the castle within the city, known to have been under construction in 1239; it was protected by a ditch.

irregular trapezium with rounded corners. The tall towers outside the wall at intervals of 30 metres or more are open on the town side and have vaulted floors. The walls are protected by a ditch. The fortifications are believed to date from the third quarter of the 13th century.

In the early 1260s Frederick II's successor, Manfred, founded the town of Manfredonia on the Adriatic coast. On the land side it is rectangular in plan, the walls guarded by very closely spaced rectangular towers.

Very little is known for certain about the 13th century castle architecture of Spain, and even less about Portugal. Documentary evidence indicates that the castle of Bellcaire in Catalonia had a compact rectangular layout with circular corner towers and mural towers in the middle of two sides. It is therefore assumed to have been built in the 13th century. The castle was entered from the south. A

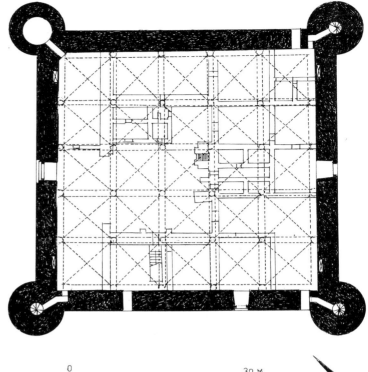

95
Maniace, Sicily. Frederick II's Syracusan castle, built in about 1240.

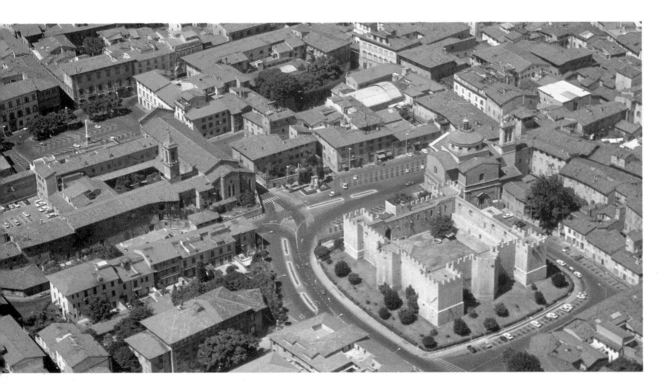

96
Prato, Italy. Aerial view of the Tuscan city with the castle, which was built before 1250.

pentagonal chapel projects from the face of the east wing. The west wing houses a hall.

The castle at Molina de Aragon, in New Castile, is of the same type, with six high mural towers. There is an outer bailey to the west and south.

Portuguese fortifications of the 13th century are represented by the castle of the Johannite Order

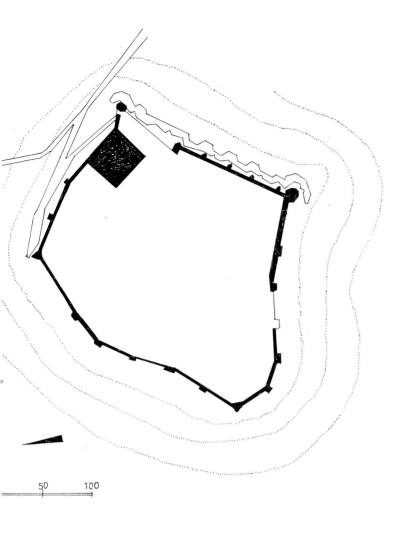

at Amieira, to the north of the town of Leiria, with its massive keep, high mural towers and battlemented walls.

The 13th century was of extraordinary importance for the development of medieval fortifications. Castles and fortified cities spread over vast areas of Europe, enriching the landscape with complex and dramatic silhouettes. Their architectural content became more intricate as the Gothic style took hold in a steadily widening area. Techniques and designs diversified and, as not only castles but also fortified cities became a common sight, the defence was for the time being in the ascendant over the attack.

97
Lucera, Italy. Plan of the castle. After Monumenti.

98
Lucera, Italy. Aerial view of the fortified area from the north. As well as Charles of Anjou's late 13th century castle, the ruins of Frederick II's hall are visible on the left (south-east corner); it was built from 1233.

99
Monterrigioni, Italy. City plan
showing the fortifications.
After Monumenti.

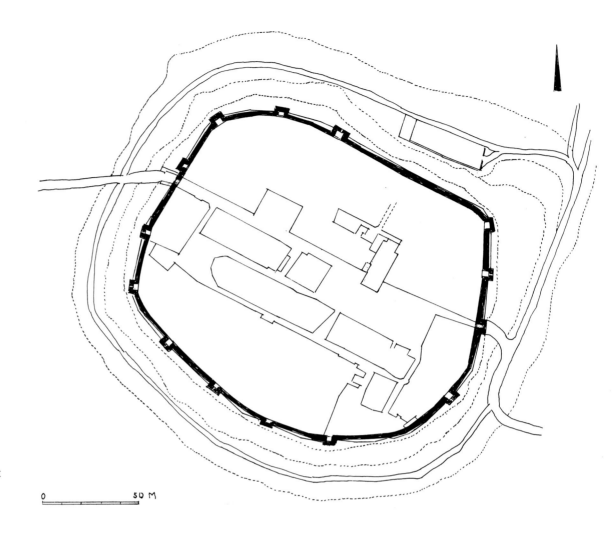

100
Monterrigioni, Italy. A distant
view of the city walls and
towers. Late 13th century.

0   50 M

101 ▶
Villandraut, France. Plan of
the castle. After Enlart.

The Fourteenth Century

Over much of Western and Central Europe, the 14th century was a period of consolidation and modification rather than innovation. The network of castles and cities was virtually completed, so there were relatively few entirely new examples. Spain was an exception to this rule, and in Italy too there were significant developments. Even the use of gunpowder and early artillery in the mid-14th century made little difference at first, since guns were not much used in siege warfare.

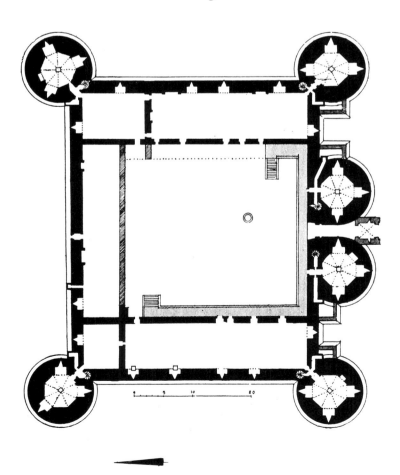

Generally speaking, then, the 14th century did not bring about any important changes in fortifications. However, castles tended to become ever more monumental, and architecturally and artistically splendid. This was most marked in France, where the various types of fortified structures differed conspicuously from those everywhere else in Europe.

In basic layout French castles remained emphatically centripetal, compact in both plan and mass. Outer wards and outworks were much less important in France than they were in Central Europe. Generally speaking, the only outside obstacle to the enemy advance was the ditch, for the outer wall was not made an integral part of the external defences.

The distinctive characteristics of French fortification can be seen in the romantic ruins of Pope Clement V's castle at Villandraut (Gironde), dating from the early 14th century. It is rectangular, the inner court being surrounded by three wings of buildings and the wall. Strong circular towers 20 metres high stand in the corners of the walls, and two similar towers guard the only gateway, on the south side. They were vaulted inside. The loops are cruciform. The castle is surrounded by a ditch 20 metres wide and 7 metres deep.

The nearby Château de Roquetaillade, near Mazères (Gironde), was built by the Pope's nephew and is similar in layout and construction. It dates from 1306 and was reconstructed by Viollet-le-Duc. Its sturdy circular towers are 28 metres high. In the centre of the castle stands a keep 35 metres high.

These splendidly regular buildings are of classical proportions, but it must be said that their defensive functions have retreated somewhat into the background. This group of castles also includes the ruins of Blanquefort (Gironde), whose remarkable keep

is closely surrounded by four U-shaped and two circular towers. The oblong interior has rounded corners. The oval peripheral wall was strengthened by unequal bastion towers in the 15th century.

The early 14th century castle at Lagarde (Ariège) has an oblong plan with four towers built into the corners. It is surrounded by an outer wall with U-shaped corner towers and semicircular mural towers; however, the defences are obviously of a later date.

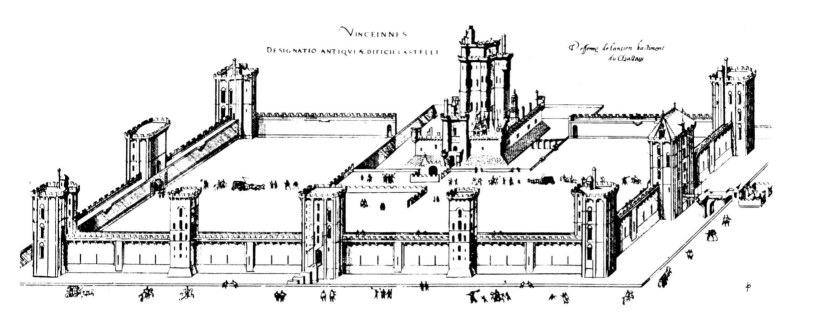

103
Vincennes in the 16th century. After Androuet de Cerceau.

◀102
Villandraut, France. Entrance façade of the papal castle. The wall and towers rise up from the ditch. Early 14th century.

104
Vincennes, France. View of the medieval great tower (keep), with the wall with a parapet walk and machicolations above the ditch in front of it. Late 14th century.

105
Villeneuve lès Avignon,
France. Gateway to the
stronghold of St André. 1366.

▶ 106
Saumur, France. View of the
castle, built before 1370, with
bastion fortifications from the
late 16th century in the
foreground.

The castle at Vitré (Ille et Vilaine) is generally dated to the 14th century. It is triangular in plan, with three corner towers in its peripheral wall, two U-shaped and one circular; the southern tower is very strong. A gateway guarded by two towers stands in the centre of the east side. The defence of the peripheral wall is strengthened by towers of semicircular and rectangular plan, two of which projected into the inner ward. On the south-west side there are small rectangular towers along the curtain walls. The castle is protected by a wide ditch.

One of the most monumental French royal castles is Charles V's at Vincennes, to the east of Paris. At its heart stands a large keep, now 62 metres high, with four round corner turrets. Above the parapet of its top floor there is an extension, and at its side stands a forebuilding that is only slightly lower. The keep is enclosed by a wall with bartizans in the cor-

ners and a typical French two-towered gateway. The entire building is mounted on an artificial base with scarps rising from the bottom of the ditch. The keep at Vincennes is a remarkable example of conservatism prolonging the existence of long obsolete architectural types. Construction began under King Philippe VI in 1336 and ended under Charles V thirty years later.

During this period a magnificent rectangular castle was added to the keep, which projects westwards. In the peripheral wall stand four massive corner towers, 42 metres high with articulated façades. The three central gateways in three sides of the peripheral wall were similar in design, but the towers on each side of the east gate were of equal height but less massy. The castle was surrounded by a ditch 22 metres wide and 14 metres deep.

An interesting example of a defensive system,

86

halfway between those of a castle and a fortified town, is the stronghold of St André, on a low hill above the southern French town of Villeneuve lès Avignon (Vaucluse). Completed in 1366, it has an irregular oval plan. Its sturdy peripheral wall is skilfully clad with hewn stone blocks, and has a battlemented parapet walk. The most imposing sight at St André is the monumental gateway with its two semicircular towers. The gateway, towers and connecting wall are crowned by machicolations on closely spaced corbels, and by battlements. Another battlemented section is situated in the west bend of the wall. The gateway was protected by outworks of which only small fragments of masonry survive.

Another remarkable stronghold is the Tour Solidor in St Servan sur Mer, opposite St Malo. It was built in 1369 and consists of three U-shaped towers within a trapezoidal-plan structure; the northern tower is more massive than the two southern ones. Battlements on corbels crowned the stronghold, the

defensive capabilities of which depended on its extremely thick walls and great height.

After the outbreak of the Hundred Years' War between England and France (1337), the French chivalry met with disaster at the battles of Crécy (1346) and Poitiers (1356). However, under Charles V (1364-80) French recovery was swift and complete. Among the ways in which this manifested itself was the construction of monumental residential castles of great aesthetic charm. A famous illuminated manuscript of the early 15th century, *Les Très Riches Heures du Duc de Berry*, gives a delightful picture of this development, which was necessarily short-lived, since the aesthetic achievement was in direct conflict with the defensive function of the castles. This has been shown by a reconstruction of the original appearance of the sumptuous castle of Mehun sur Yèvre (Cher), built from the early 1370s by Master Guy de Demartin for the very Duc de Berry who commissioned the *Très Riches*

ments. Conical roofs can be seen in the background.

The sides of the castle wall between the corner towers were complex and highly articulated; their present state is the result of a radical elimination and simplification of forms. The castle is entered through a gateway projecting from the south-west wing; its distinctive features are two bartizans on corbels and a small oriel with machicolations in the centre.

The illumination in the *Très Riches Heures* shows an outer bailey on the south-west side which has entirely disappeared. It was enclosed by the main and the outer walls, strengthened by small semicircular bastion towers; both walls are shown as battlemented. The outer bailey was entered through a gateway and closed by a drawbridge. The castle of Saumur was built from the end of the 1360s onwards.

In 1390 King Charles VI's brother, Louis d'Orléans, built the castle at Pierrefonds (Oise),

107
Avignon, France. One of the wall towers, seen from inside the city. 1355-77. After Viollet-le-Duc.

108
Avignon, France. The St Lazarus Gate, protected by a barbican (no longer extant), dating from 1368. After Viollet-le-Duc.

Heures. Only parts of two circular towers of unequal height actually survive, shorn of their intricate tracery, gables and other decorative features, which seem more appropriate to cathedral architecture than to a medieval fortress.

A better fate befell another castle shown in the *Très Riches Heures*, Saumur, which is sited on a terrace overlooking the River Loire. Saumur was radically reconstructed by Jean de Berry's brother, Louis d'Anjou. Here too the fortification function of the castle was almost suppressed. The nucleus of the castle probably consisted of four wings with four towers. In the *Très Riches Heures* polygonal towers, with façades articulated by pilasters, rise from the mass of the castle. At the top of each is a substantial parapet with machicolations supported by closely spaced stepped corbels and crowned with battle-

109
Alnwick Castle, England. View of the castle with the outer bailey in the foreground. After 1309 towers were added to the early 12th century shell keep. The peripheral wall was also reinforced by towers in the 14th century.

which was restored by Viollet-le-Duc in the last century. The castle has a regular rectangular plan with a slightly broken east side and a semicircular chapel tower projecting from the face of the wall. The corners are reinforced by circular towers, while semicircular towers punctuate the curtain walls on two sides. A large semicircular tower, known as Caesar's Tower, guards the gateway giving access to the castle from the outer bailey to the south-west. The towers are much higher than the walls. Above the parapet with machicolations there are high turrets typical of this élite group of French castles. Inside the castle, forming an independently defensible stronghold, Caesar's Tower is linked to a donjon with extensive residential quarters. The castle is surrounded by a wide ditch.

Louis d'Orléans also built the magnificent castle of La Ferté Milon (Aisne), which was left unfinished at his death in 1407.

First place among the urban fortifications of the 14th century belongs to Cahors (Lot). Along its partly preserved walls are rectangular mural towers open to the rear. The most remarkable feature of this town is the fortified stone bridge crossing the River Lot, the famous Pont Valentré, with three slender towers containing passageways; the towers at each end are machicolated. The foundation stone of the bridge was laid in 1308 and its construction was finished in about 1355, but the fortifications were only completed 30 years later.

The most complete system of urban fortifications in 14th century France was at Avignon (Vaucluse); it dates from 1355-77, towards the end of the 'Babylonish Captivity' when Avignon, not Rome, was the seat of the Papacy. The city wall, averaging 2 metres thick and 8 metres high, was defended by 35 much taller two-storey towers open at the rear. Along the curtain walls between the towers are 55

110
Warwick Castle, England.
North wall and gate. 14th
century.

turrets projecting slightly from the wall face. In the 15th century the tops of the walls and towers were strengthened with corbels, machicolations and battlements with cruciform loopholes. At the foot of the wall there was a moat 20 metres wide and only 4 metres deep. Access to the St Lazarus gate, in the north-east side, was controlled by a barbican of a square plan with round bastion towers in three corners. The open towers were an advanced feature, but as a whole the system, devoid of an outer bailey, was not an effective means of defence. It is clear, however, that the outer bailey was rarely incorporated into French city fortifications.

The magnificent fortifications of Dinan (Côtes du Nord) in northern Brittany, with twenty mostly U-shaped towers, originated in the 14th century. They were improved in the second half of the 15th century.

★

In 14th century England the pace of castle building slowed down. The unique Welsh castles built by Edward I had no successors except for the very interesting castle at Queensborough, discussed below. In the later 14th century French castle architecture exerted a significant influence.

During the 14th century the earlier Norman shell keep of Alnwick Castle in Northumberland was strengthened by the addition of seven slightly higher towers. Incorporated into the walls of the large bailey are higher towers with loopholes and battlements.

Dating from 1361-77, the destroyed castle at Queensborough in Kent had a consistently developed circular plan, visible in the castle itself with its U-shaped towers and in the outer bailey and the ditch. It anticipated the castle architecture of the 16th century.

Warwick Castle, above the River Avon, is a fa-

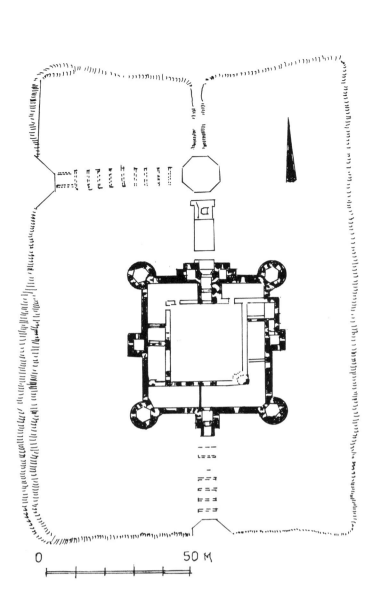

mous castle of Norman origin. However, its most remarkable features are the result of its 14th century reconstruction, notably the splendid north curtain wall with its magnificent gateway with slender towers and a pair of big polygonal end towers with machicolations on corbels. Also impressive is Caesar's Tower, a high, lobe-shaped structure with sophisticated machicolations and battlements.

The construction of Nunney Castle in Somersetshire began in 1373. The castle has the form of a high rectangular keep with four massive drum towers in the corners. Along the top edge of the remains, the corbels that once supported machicolations can be seen. The towers once culminated in conical roofs. The whole castle is French in character.

In 1385 King Richard II licensed one of his subjects to replace his manor house with a castle. This became Bodiam Castle in Sussex. Richard's intention was to strengthen the defences of the south coast, which appeared to be threatened by the French fleet. Nevertheless Bodiam was strongly influenced by French castle architecture. It is square in plan, with four walls around the inner courtyard, four round corner towers, and three square towers, each in the middle of a side. In the middle of the north side there is a massive gateway, its passage flanked by two towers projecting from the wall face. The castle is battlemented, and the gateway and mural towers are also provided with a parapet walk and machicolations supported by corbels. The towers and gateway are higher than the walls. The castle is surrounded by a very wide moat that greatly enhances its appearance.

The walls of Chester are the best preserved medieval city fortifications in England. They are of Roman origin, and may also have been added to by the Anglo-Saxons, but they were rebuilt in the 14th century, when they were extended to the River Dee. Several towers survive; they are semicircular or pentagonal in plan, and rise above the walls. Near the north-west bend of the wall, and projecting out of the wall face, stands the Water Tower; it was built in about 1325, so the wall itself must be earlier. On the north side there is a canal below the wall; on the west and east sides there was probably a moat, as the name of the gateway—Watergate—suggests.

Craigmillar Castle—the ruins of which stand on a ridge just outside the city of Edinburgh—consisted in the 14th century of only a massive rectangular tower with a building on the south side housing the staircase. In 1427 curtain walls were put up round the existing buildings on the west, north and east sides, creating a courtyard. Like the walls, the round

111
Bodiam Castle, England. Plan after Simpson.

112
Bodiam Castle, England. Sussex castle surrounded by a wide moat. Built from 1385.

corner towers rising above them are equipped with machicolations supported by stone corbels.

In the 14th century the ruins of Crichton Castle, standing above the River Tyne, in Midlothian, also consisted of a tall tower with an adjacent courtyard, in this case to the west of it.

★

Throughout the Middle Ages Switzerland was technically part of the Holy Roman Empire. However, from 1291, when the first confederation of cantons was formed, the Swiss became increasingly independent in reality. There was no unity among the cantons, and the nature of the terrain, broken by mountains with deep valleys, encouraged separate development and afforded little scope for the development of castle architecture.

The upper castle of Vufflens le Château (Vaud) consists of a sturdy residential tower surrounded by a wall with four lower towers. The lower castle is connected with the upper by the walls, and contains a rectangular hall with higher round corner turrets with conical roofs. Vufflens le Château was built between 1395 and 1420 by a vassal of the Duke of Savoy. It is Italian in character but, considering its date, very old-fashioned.

The walls of Murten (Fribourg) are the best preserved of Swiss city fortifications. The high wall is strengthened by open-backed towers; most are semicircular, although a few are rectangular. The entire system probably dates from the second third of the 14th century.

Outstanding fortifications with tall towers and gateways have been preserved at Fribourg. The towers are partly open at the rear. There is no outer bailey, the wall being protected only by a ditch. In

◀113
Vufflens le Château,
Switzerland. The main castle
is on the left, the lower castle
on the right, and the outer
fortification system in the
foreground. Built 1395-1420.

enich, to the south-east of Cologne. It is rectangular in plan, with an L-shaped outer bailey, and stands on an island. The oldest part of the castle is a five-storey residential tower in the north-west corner,

114
Murten, Switzerland. City walls, erected in about the mid-14th century.

1388 the wall was completed; the construction of outworks to the north-west began at the turn of the 14th and 15th centuries.

On the Plateau du Rham, to the east of the old part of Luxembourg, the remains of medieval fortifications have survived. They undoubtedly date from the early 14th century, when John, King of Bohemia, was also Duke of Luxembourg. The remains include a line of closely spaced semicircular towers, partly open in the rear, and a rectangular gateway in the north-east angle of the wall.

★

A typical moated castle belonging to the Elector of Cologne occupies the north-east corner of Lech-

the remaining corner being occupied by three towers. The construction of the castle began in 1306 and ended only in the mid-14th century.

A typical example of a Dutch moated castle is Muiderslot near Muiden. It has a compact rectangular plan, with corner towers of unequal height standing higher than the wall. In the middle of one side there is a massive gateway with a passageway leading to a drawbridge across the moat. Muiderslot is generally believed to be 14th century, and was built on the remains of a 13th century castle.

Some moated castles have a resemblance to Central European strongholds. Among them is Doorneburg, which was destroyed during the Second World War but has been meticulously restored.

Moated castles are also prevalent in the neighbouring parts of Germany. The most highly developed example of a rectangular-plan moated castle is Westerburg, near Halberstadt in the former Duchy

93

115
Fribourg, Switzerland. Sector
of the city wall around the
Auge quarter. Late 14th
century.

116 ▶
Muiderslot, Netherlands.
Aerial view of the castle,
which is protected by a wide
moat. 14th century.

of Saxony. In the 14th century it was added to an earlier structure now on its west side; the later building consists of three wings enclosing a courtyard in the south-east corner, in which there is a watch-tower.

The extraordinarily picturesque castle of Pfalz-grafenstein stands on a rocky island in the middle of the Rhine to the south of the town of Kaub; it was built before 1327, probably on the orders of Ludwig IV of Bavaria. Here, the presence of water has a special significance, since the function of the Pfalz-grafenstein was to levy a navigation tax on traffic up and down the Rhine. The oldest part is a pentagonal tower which was enclosed by a hexagonal wall only at a later date, perhaps in about 1340.

In Germany the 13th century tendency towards elongated plans petered out in the following cen-tury. This is visible in an interesting group of castles in the environs of Limburg an der Lahn. The oldest of them, Balduinstein, was founded in 1320 by Bal-duin of Luxembourg, Archbishop of Trèves (Trier) and uncle of John of Luxembourg. The main part of Balduinstein consists of a hall and a tower. Accord-ing to the *Limburg Chronicle* the castle was built 'in a novel way', which obviously refers to the fortifica-tions of the outer bailey. This lies beyond a wide ditch to the north; its east gateway is guarded by a tower, and two other towers strengthen the bailey on the north side. It is possible that the fortification of the outer bailey with projecting towers was in-fluenced by contemporary Bohemian practice.

In the southern part of the castle of Hohlenfels, built in 1355-63, the sturdy pentagonal tower is reminiscent of an earlier period. In its immediate

94

vicinity stands a residential tower occupying the east corner of the upper castle. The north corner of the plan is occupied by an octagonal tower. The upper castle is enclosed by a curtain wall; the outer bailey is irregular.

The ruined castle of Burgschwalbach (1368-71) is very similar. It has a compact but irregular hexagonal plan with some right-angled corners. At the south-east angle stands a round, partly seven-sided tower; a small outer bailey adjoins the south side. The culminating feature of the castle is a high, cir-cular, vaulted tower in the angle of the wall (5 metres thick), facing north-east. Directly opposite, in the south-west, is the hall. Both the walls and the high tower are battlemented.

One of the most striking castle ruins in Central Europe stands above the Franconian town of Stadt-prozelten, in the valley of the River Main. This magnificent castle has a complex building history. Its large square watchtower with rusticated stone blocks is Romanesque in origin. Then the early Gothic south-east hall was built from about the mid

117
Pfalzgrafenstein, Germany. A toll castle in the middle of the Rhine. The tower dates from before 1327, the surrounding wall from about 1340.

119 ▶
Stadtprozelten, Germany. View of the castle from the south-west, with the outer gateway and a postern in the foreground. On the right is the bastion tower of the outer defences (14th-15th century) with loopholes for crossbows and keyhole loops. On the left is a slender tower, in the background a large Romanesque tower (early 12th century).

118
Stadtprozelten, Germany. Plan of the castle ruins. After Dehio.

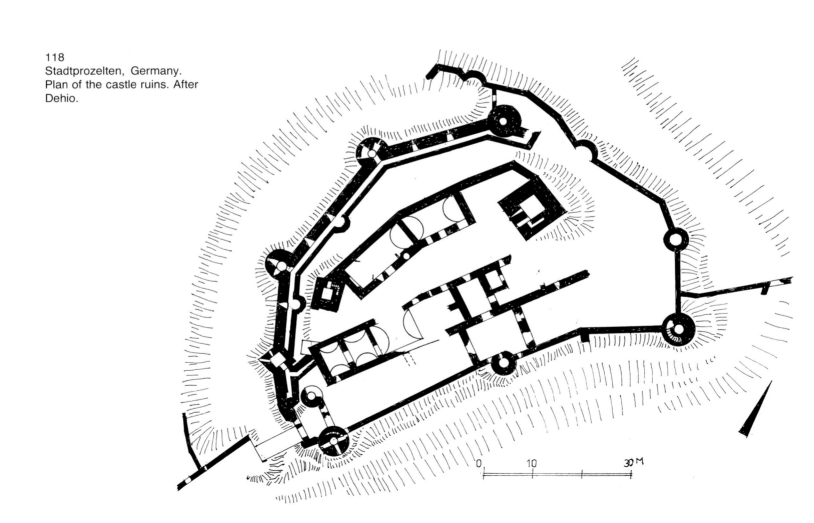

0   10   30 M

96

13th century. But as a visual ensemble the castle dates from the 14th century, when the smaller watchtower and the tall adjacent hall were erected. The outer wall of the hall joins up with the wall running round to the Romanesque old tower. The two towers with the hall in between them make a splendid spectacle. The remarkable outer defence system is obviously later (*c.* 1400). It consists of a wall with a number of bastion towers; most of them are circular, but two are semicircular and one is rectangular, placed aslant to present a sharp edge or

of arms of the Bohemian, Moravian and Silesian aristocracy in high relief.

Outstanding though these German castles are, they no longer display the unity so apparent in the German castles of the 12th, and especially the 13th century. Oblong plans were abandoned, and there was a tendency to employ compact and even concentric plans.

Politically, the period of Hohenstaufen dominance was replaced by an accelerated fragmentation of authority. In the 14th century the cities became

120
Lauf an der Pegnitz, Germany. View of the castle from the south, showing the projecting tower gateway, the big tower on the left, and the east hall wing on the right. 1356-60.

beak to the enemy. The outer fortifications were protected by a ditch.

The castle at Lauf an der Pegnitz, east of Nuremberg, was enlarged by the Emperor Charles IV in 1356-60. It comprises an irregular quadrangle, in the west corner of which stands an older tower clad with rusticated stone blocks. Projecting from the wall face, the rectangular south gateway gives access to the triangular courtyard enclosed by the wall and two wings. The first floor of the east wing houses Charles's Hall, a spot with a distinctive historical atmosphere; its walls are decorated with 114 coats

increasingly important, particularly the more or less autonomous imperial cities in the south-west and the cities in the north-east founded as outposts of German colonization. The situation was of course reflected in their fortifications.

The leading imperial city of Nuremberg (Nürnberg) is not far from Lauf. Only two small groups of remains survive from the fortifications of the early Gothic city. These once comprised two major systems, separated by the River Pegnitz, which were linked in 1320-25; three towers are still extant from this period.

121
Nuremberg, Germany.
Engraved view of the fortified
city with its castle in the
background; from Schedel's
Chronicle (1493)

122
Nuremberg, Germany. Part of
the city's main wall with
towers; the outer wall is in the
foreground. The main wall
was built between about 1340
and 1400, the outer wall in the
early 15th century.

After 1340 a new peripheral wall was constructed which has survived all the vicissitudes of the city's history. Work began in the Spittlertor area (the southwest bend of the plan), at first using rubble masonry. Soon, however, cladding with rusticated stone blocks was introduced. Surprisingly the wall, which is 7 to 8 metres high, is only 1 metre thick. It is clear that it was originally battlemented. It is strengthened by mural towers of unequal height, placed at intervals of 40 to 60 metres along the curtain wall; some of them partly project inwards from the city face of the wall. Altogether 83 towers have been preserved. The walls were provided with five main gateways, most of them guarded by circular towers. Secondary gateways existed in the form of passageways through tall rectangular towers.

The inner ring of walls was completed in about 1400. The next phase included digging a dry ditch averaging about 20 metres wide and 12 metres deep. This surrounded an outer bailey 15 metres wide, which was protected by a relatively low outer wall, strengthened by still lower towers at much longer intervals than those of the main wall. This fortification was completed in 1452. The appearance of the towers in both walls, particularly the inner wall, is enhanced by rusticated cladding.

However, Nuremberg's fortifications were far from advanced, and by the time they were com-pleted they were already obsolete. The city seems to have been protected by its great wealth, and by the resolution of its inhabitants, rather than by military technology.

The extremely picturesque Franconian city of Rothenburg ob der Tauber has fortifications that underwent a long and complicated development; even today, not all aspects of it have been elucidated.

The irregularly oval area in the western part of the present city was fortified as early as about 1200; two gateway towers have survived from this phase. During the 14th century the fortified area was enlarged to include the suburbs. Rather long stretches of wall separate the tall, slim mural towers, which are mostly recessed into the wall face, as are the gateway towers. The entire city was surrounded by an outer wall reinforced with narrow turrets on projecting supports. Pictorial sources suggest that the number of these turrets was far higher in the past than at present.

At about the end of the 14th century the Spittler suburb was fortified in a similar fashion. The construction of Rothenburg's system of fortifications is generally dated to the 14th century. As with Nuremberg, the towers of the outer wall seem to have been built at the same time as the wall itself.

By comparison with the sumptuous gateways of northern Germany, which were intended to be symbols of municipal pride, gateways in the south-west are less significant, even in the cities of some importance.

This tendency is exemplified by the former free imperial city of Dinkesbühl. Assessing its older fortifications is complicated by the fact that they were extended in 1372-1435. The present gateways consist of slender towers flanking a passage. The older gateways are sunk beyond the outer face of the main wall, while the gateways in the extended part of the wall project out of it. The Wörnitz Gate on the north-east side of the old city area, partly rusticated in its lower section, dates from the 13th-14th centuries. On the other hand, according to contemporary sources the Nördlingen Gate, though of similar design, originated in the early 15th century (before 1425).

In both its older and its newer parts the city wall is strengthened by variously shaped towers, mostly placed behind the wall. The curtain walls between the towers are surprisingly long. Clearly the narrow outer bailey was confined to the north side of the city, extending on both sides of the Rothenburg Gate. In the north-west and the south the main wall was protected by a double ditch and ramparts.

The city of Nördlingen, in Swabia, is a regular oval in plan and is enclosed in a continuous ring of walls; it makes an extraordinarily powerful impression. The original gateways are mostly sunk beyond the wall face. The wall is strengthened by towers at rather long intervals from one another. Part of the main wall was surrounded by an outer bailey. The whole city was protected by a ditch. The fortifications are dated to the 14th-15th centuries.

Weissenburg (Baden-Württemberg) was also once an imperial city. The construction of its walls began in the late 13th century, but in their full, extended form they date from the last quarter of the 14th century. The wall runs round the entire old city almost without interruption. It has a partly preserved parapet walk, towers between curtain walls merely 15 metres long, and twin-towered gateways. The wall was protected by a ditch.

In the German-colonized territories of the north-east, city fortifications are characterized by a basic overall similarity, varied by extremely diverse and individual gateway designs stemming from their symbolic role. As a result, scholarly studies have suffered, since writers have been tempted to neglect most of the fortifications and concentrate on the gateways.

In 1304 a licence was issued allowing the fortification of the city of Friedland (Neubrandenburg). Its stone wall was 6 metres high, with towers of various types on the more exposed south-east and east sides; the stretches of curtain wall were some 50 metres long. These parts of the wall were protected by a ditch and a rampart. At the same time the extraordinarily interesting Anklam Gate was constructed with a high passageway flanked by round towers. The gate was slightly narrower at the front

124
Friedland, Germany. The Anklam Gate from the city side. Early 14th century.

than at the back. The plan of the whole gateway has a curious, archaic shape, recalling pre-Romanesque churches. The stone masonry of the gate on top of its stone ground floor was erected before the middle of the 14th century. Its façade is decorated with panels and surmounted by gables with pinnacles.

At Wittstock (Potsdam) the fortifications (towers of various types and a partly double ditch) are of uncertain date.

125
Bernau, Germany. Engraved view of the city from the book by M. Merian (c. 1650).

battlements can be seen. The mural towers are closely spaced and only rarely semicircular. The only surviving gate, the Steintor, consists of a tower with a passageway and a defence gallery, connected with a circular tower. The exposed north side of the city was protected by a double ditch with ramparts. There was no outer wall.

The 'colonial' city of Templin (Neubrandenburg) was probably also fortified in the early 14th century. The stone wall has no parapet walk, is almost 7 metres high, and is strengthened by semicircular towers open on the city side and sited at intervals of about 30 metres. All of the towers were originally higher than the city walls. The outstanding features of Templin are its tower gateways, mostly built of

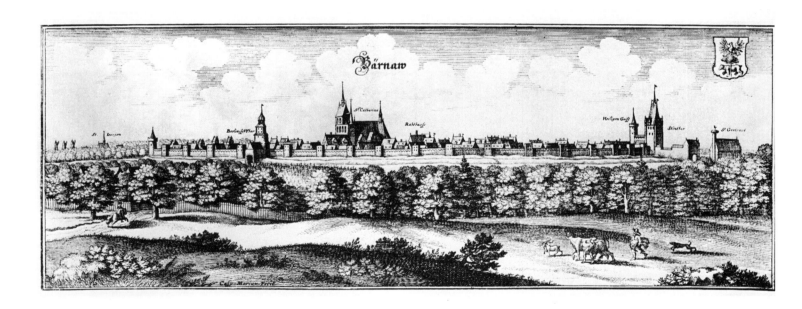

The fortifications of Tangermünde on the Elbe (Magdeburg) were built in about 1300. The walls are mostly of brick, the higher, semicircular and rectangular towers are partly closed at the rear, projecting out of the wall face, and occur at about 50 metre intervals. The corner towers are circular.

It is known that the fortifications of Bernau, in Brandenburg near Berlin, already existed in 1432, when they repelled a Hussite attack. They are commonly said to date from the 15th century, but a glance at Merian's engraving of about 1650 is enough to prove this wrong; and further confirmation is provided by the building material used on the walls (granite with additional brickwork at the top). In actual fact the walls of Bernau are of a character suggesting the early 14th century as the date of their construction. In Merian's engraving the filled-in

brick, which date from 1325. Two of them have a high and deep rebate to house the portcullis. The walls are decorated with blind arcades. The tops of the gates carry decorative gables on both the ouside and the city side.

The very important fortifications of Neubrandenburg undoubtedly date from the early 14th century. The rubble wall is 140 centimetres thick and attains a height of about 8 metres; the major part of it still survives. Originally there were 53 mural towers, open on the city side, higher than the wall and standing at intervals of about 50 metres. The wall was protected by a double ditch and ramparts. The mid-14th century Stargard Gate represents the culmination of the gateway style developed at Templin. The Treptow Gate at Neubrandenburg (c. 1400), with its richly articulated interior and exterior façades, is one of the finest gateways anywhere in northern Germany and the Baltic area.

Prenzlau (Neubrandenburg) has a partly preserved wall, made taller by additional brickwork, com-

ditch, on the outer side of which stands a circular tower connected with the south-east section of the outer wall.

126
Templin, Germany. Part of the city wall with towers. Beginning of the 14th century.

127
Templin, Germany. The Prenzlau Gate from the city side. About 1400.

plete with gateways and rectangular towers open on the city side (end of the 13th to the first half of the 14th century).

Less need be said about 14th century Austria, since there was a lull in castle-building after the intense constructive period in the 12th and 13th centuries. A revival began only in the 15th century, with the growing menace from the Turks.

On Austria's frontier with Bohemia, the picturesque city of Freistadt was situated on an important trade route. An early system of fortifications would have seemed necessary and likely, so it is surprising to find that even the latest research dates them to the late 14th century. The main wall is reinforced by semicircular towers, but the fragments that remain do not make it possible to determine the length of the intervening curtain walls. No gateways have been preserved in the main wall. The outer bailey is on average about 10 metres wide. The outer wall, enclosing the outer bailey, was strengthened with circular towers in the mid-15th century. Both of its tower gateways, the Bohemian Gate and the Linz Gate, were built in the 1480s and are situated in the trace of the outer wall. The town is surrounded by a

128
Neubrandenburg, Germany.
The Treptow gate from the
city side. About 1325.

In neighbouring Bohemia, the 14th century was a prolific period of castle-building in which existing structures were modernized and a number of new ones erected. The first phase witnessed the apogee of the oblong plan, which survived for some years after 1350. However, a preference for compact plans and shapes was making itself felt quite early in the 14th century. The culmination of the narrow, oblong plan is represented by the castle of Klapý or Hazmburk, on top of a hill in the vicinity of Litoměřice. The earliest part—the upper castle—has a compact oblong plan with pronounced rounded corners. On the highest point of the castle rock stands the White Tower. There was also a hall inside a high surrounding wall. Klapý was built in the early 14th century; the major additions thereafter were the work of Zbyněk Zajíc of Valdek, who acquired the castle in 1335. He had an outer bailey built around the upper castle, also with rounded corners, and added two more outer baileys, the smaller in the north-west and the larger in the south-east, which afforded access to the castle from the very big north-east outermost bailey. A ditch separated the upper castle from the south-east outer bailey.

At the lower, south-eastern end of the castle stands the circular Black Tower, surrounded by a wall. The extraordinarily impressive silhouette of the castle dominates the eastern basin of the River Ohře.

In eastern Bohemia the mighty castle of Lipnice (near Havlíčkův Brod) stands on the top of a hill above the small town of the same name. It is mentioned in historical documents for the first time in 1314, and represents a quite different architectural type from Klapý; in its compact silhouette and the mass of its towers the dramatic effects of earlier castles are eschewed. The south-east corner of the irregular, roughly rectangular plan is occupied by a partly ruined great tower, itself of asymmetric trapezoidal plan, 14.5×21 metres at its greatest extent and 35 metres high. This is in fact a real donjon, initially provided with a parapet walk with machicolations and battlements. The tower was roofed with a masonry barrel vault. The gateway giving access to the oblong courtyard is in a lower forebuilding. From its northern corner the main wall runs to meet the north-east corner of a second massive tower, this time square in plan, which is called Samson and also bears no resemblance to the slender watchtowers of the early Gothic period. The Samson Tower stands directly against a large hall building that seals off the castle in the north-west. The south-west side of the courtyard was closed by a chapel with a pentagonal presbytery, the nave of which forms the interior of another tower.

The castle of Kost stands on a rocky hill in the vicinity of Jičín. It has an irregular pentagonal plan with a massive residential tower in the south-east corner, flush with the main wall face. A smaller square tower stands in the north-west corner. The

104

great tower, with walls 3.2 metres thick and an irregular (17.6 × 14 metres) trapezoidal plan, is related to the main tower of Lipnice Castle.

The south side of the castle consists of a hall with a circular tower projecting from the south-west corner. It overlooked an irregular ward with a gateway. The outer bailey of the castle was entered by a further gateway protected by a slender tower near the north-west hall corner. Here, too, the compact plan and mass of the castle contrast strongly with older, mostly oblong plans.

The royal castle of Karlštejn, near Beroun, is quite unique. It was built for the Emperor Charles IV (and probably with his participation) by Vít Hedvábný. The foundation stone was laid in 1348 and its construction was completed in 1357, although work on the interior decoration went on for a few years more. Most of the castle's south side is occupied by the high imperial hall, which is closed by a semicircular tower to the east. (A similar hall closure was also used in Charles's castle of Radyně in western Bohemia.) On a slightly higher elevation to the north of the hall there is a roughly rectangular tower-shaped building; this is the collegiate church of the Virgin Mary, housing the Emperor's private chapel consecrated to St Catherine. Still further to the north, on top of the castle hill, stands an extremely massy rectangular tower, 25.8 × 16 metres in area and 37 metres high to the corbels; a

forebuilding to the south houses the staircase. The north wall of the tower is over 6 metres thick. On the second floor is the Chapel of the Holy Cross, the most magnificent and sublime interior in the castle.

The tower is enclosed by a separate set of walls with corner towers. Further north there is an irregular trapezoidal outer ward. The area west of the hall is closed by a wall with a gateway which separates it from the cramped, narrow lower castle to the west; and from this projects a fortified passage leading to the well tower. To the west of the upper castle there is an outer bailey sloping down to the first, northern gateway of the entire complex. The outer bailey on the south and east sides of the castle is only narrow.

In terms of fortifications, Karlštejn did not incorporate any new features. Its strength lay in the choice of its site and the massiveness of its masonry, and for these reasons it successfully withstood a siege by the Hussites. Karlštejn is not part of any historical trend, but its design was perfectly suited to military and imperial functions.

The typical oblong castle plan was revived as late as the 1350s for the royal castle of Kašperk (Klatovy district), in the Šumava Mountains. It was begun in 1356 and, exceptionally, the name of the builder is known: he was the same Vít Hedvábný who was responsible for Karlštejn.

At Kašperk the upper castle, with its extremely

129
Prenzlau, Germany. Part of the city wall with a tower and the Blindow Gate, seen from the city side. Late 13th and early 14th century.

narrow plan, is situated on the top of a hill; it consists of a long rectangular hall with a pair of towers close to its shorter sides, terminating in a gallery on corbels, battlements and a masonry hipped roof. The hall was protected by a narrow bailey enclosed by a battlemented wall. A ditch separates the upper castle from the oblong lower castle, which is defended by a tower open on the inside. The entire castle is surrounded by an outer bailey accessible from the south-east across the ditch. The gateway

130
Freistadt, Austria, The Linz Gate, in the outer wall of the city, 1480s.

was protected by a circular tower which no longer exists.

Radyně was a sister castle to Kašperk, very similar in layout and built almost simultaneously. It stands in a dominating position on a wooded hill in the region of Plzeň, western Bohemia.

The castle of the influential Rosenberg family, Dívčí Kámen (Český Krumlov district), was built from 1349 onwards on a spur above the River Vltava, and was provided with very complex outer fortifications. The small outer bailey is reached by a path between two walls which leads to the narrow lower castle area with a low round wall in the northern corner. The upper castle adjoins the lower castle to the south. It is almost rectangular in plan, the two wings and the walls enclosing an inner courtyard. The castle is protected by outer walls to the west and north.

The Rosenberg castle of Helfenburk (Strakonice district) in southern Bohemia was built from 1355 onwards. It too had superb fortifications, but although the hall was similar in design to that at Dívčí Kámen, its general layout was different. Dívčí Kámen and Helfenburk are both in ruins. Nevertheless the atmosphere of their courtyards already anticipates the Renaissance palace that was to supplant the fortified medieval castle.

The vast royal castle of Veveří, near Brno in Moravia, has important parts dating from the 13th century, but it was built and extended during the reign of the Emperor Charles IV. The builder of the phase dating from after 1350 was Charles's brother John Henry, Margrave of Moravia. A new hall, and a chapel on its east side, were built to the north of the early Gothic tower. However, John Henry's contribution was to lay out an extensive outer bailey that broadens outwards towards the west. Its west and south-west walls were straddled by four towers, one of which no longer exists. The outer bailey was reached through two successive gateways near its north wall.

At the very end of the 14th century the castle of Točník (Beroun district) was built by King Wenceslas IV of Bohemia (1378-1419); it is known to have been inhabited in 1402. Curiously enough, Točník is much more loosely laid out than the earlier 14th century castles we have just been discussing. It stands at the west end of an oblong hill with a deep ditch across it. Close to the ditch, in the south-eastern part of the plan, is an almost rectangular upper castle, including the large, three-storey royal hall, with its convex east side. It was extremely difficult to penetrate as far as the courtyard of the upper castle. A bridge (its stone piers still survive)

131
Klapý, Czechoslovakia. The White Tower amid the ruins of the upper castle. Early 14th century.

afforded access to the first gateway on the east side of the northern outer bailey. A second gateway led into the inner bailey, which consisted of two parts: the eastern area to the north of the upper castle, and the sloping, narrowing western area. Along the north-west side of the wall stands a long two-storey building, the residence of the burgrave. The south-east corner of the outer bailey is occupied by a tower adjoining the upper castle in the west.

City fortifications in Bohemia carried on along the lines laid down by Přemysl Otakar II. The principal change was the accentuated slenderness of towers, which were generally open on the city side.

The oldest example from the early 14th century is the royal city of Beroun, whose mural towers occur at brief intervals (18 to 38 metres at most) along the walls. Two gate towers, the Upper and the Lower Gate, have survived. In each, the arched passageway, still early Gothic in character, was sealed off by a portcullis. In front of the main wall there was an outer wall, a ditch and a rampart.

The walls of Tachov, a western Bohemian royal frontier city, date from the later 1320s. The main wall is provided with slender mural towers, open on the city side, at intervals averaging about 20 metres. Beyond the main wall lies an outer wall which has almost completely disappeared, as have the ditch and rampart.

In 1335 the fortifications of the royal city of Nymburk were under construction. Its main wall is reinforced with slender towers open on the city side, their close spacing (about 20 metres) being best seen in the section preserved along the south-east side of the city. Along the River Elbe a single wall was sufficient, but other parts of the city were protected by two moats—which still exist—with an outer wall between them.

The walls of Nymburk were built of brick; in combination with the moats they give the city an almost Dutch ambience.

The walls surrounding the royal city of Vysoké Mýto, in eastern Bohemia, have been almost entirely destroyed. However, three late 14th century city gateways survive; each consists of an arched passage, guarded by a tall tower on one side and a slender, low tower on the other.

Few medieval cities have preserved substantial parts of their fortification systems. Among the exceptions is Polička, founded by Otakar II in 1265, but fortified much later. The old city is still enclosed by a main wall 200 to 250 centimetres thick and 8 metres high. Semicircular mural towers, open on the

107

city side, stand at intervals of 35 to 60 metres; each has a stone barrel vault at first floor level. The towers were up to 13 metres high. A masonry recess has been preserved on the top storey of the tower, its presence indicating that there had formerly been a walkway with loopholes. Of the 19 towers, 18 still stand in various stages of preservation. The gates were torn down.

Beyond the main wall was an outer bailey 7-11 metres wide, enclosed by a towerless outer wall, 60-70 centimetres thick, of which only fragments have been preserved. It rose above a moat with a rampart in front of it. With the exception of the south side, where the city adjoined a broad sheet of water, Polička was protected by yet another, outer moat.

Documentary information concerning the fortifications of Polička are conspicuous by their absence. If it is valid to argue by analogy from the cities of Nymburk and Sušice, the entire system can be dated to the second quarter of the 14th century.

The New Town of Prague, founded by Charles IV in 1348, was a major feat of 14th century town planning. But only very short stretches of the main wall have been preserved from the fortifications, which were built in record time between 1348 and 1350. However, its appearance can be reconstructed from town views. The wall was battlemented and further strengthened by tall towers which projected into the outer bailey; surprisingly, the towers were closed on the city side. There were only four gateways, probably identical in design. The two storey central part with the entrance passage was protected on each side by a tower slightly projecting from the wall face. Still at the beginning of the 17th century

two of the gateways, the Swine Gate and the Vyšehrad Gate, were equipped with machicolations and small turrets. The outer fortification system was undoubtedly constructed on similar lines to those of other contemporary cities.

At Litoměřice in northern Bohemia, most of the fortifications survive; they constitute another monumental undertaking, and probably date from the 1370s. The main wall, more than 11 metres high, is battlemented. Rising above it, at short intervals, are the mural towers, open on the city side; they are concentrated in the most threatened, north-east sector of the fortifications. The outer bailey is enclosed by an outer wall above a ditch (no longer extant) bordered by a rampart.

The stone wall of the Silesian city of Paczków (Nysa, Poland) survives almost intact, along with its gates. Semicircular mural towers project from the wall face and stand open on the city side.

Despite its historical importance, Bohemian fortification architecture exerted no significant influence in neighbouring Slovakia, which then formed part of the large medieval Kingdom of Hungary. There, the ravages of the Tartars were made good and from 1308 the new Anjou dynasty paid particular attention to the defence of their Slovakian domains.

At the beginning of the 14th century the castle of Strečno (Žilina district) was built on a rocky eminence above the valley of the River Váh; it initially took the form of a massive tower with a small walled-in bailey. However, shell keeps without towers were also known in Slovakia.

Complex elongated plans were developed on a number of sites. The most important example is the

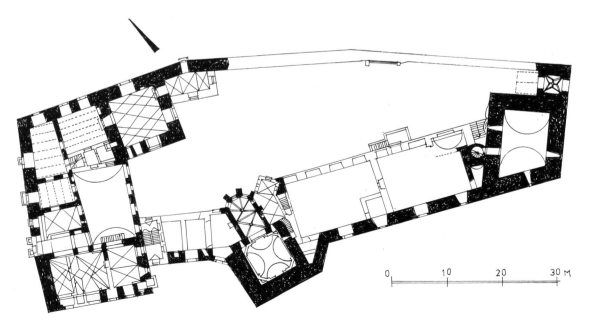

132
Lipnice, Czechoslovakia. Plan of the castle. First third of the 14th century.

133 ►
Kost, Czechoslovakia. View of the castle from the southeast. The late Gothic outer bailey is on the lower right, with the mid-14th century residential tower above it. On the left stands the circular tower (also mid-14th century) near the hall above the gateway leading to the outworks.

royal castle of Dobrá Voda (Trnava district), dating from the early 14th century. The upper castle is oblong in plan, the north-east side consisting of a narrow oblong hall with a tower on each side of it. In the south-east there is a narrow bailey with one projecting tower. Thus the castle of Dobrá Voda anticipated the interesting plan of the much later castles of Kašperk and Radyně.

The castle at Zvolen was built by the King of Hungary, Louis the Great (1342-82), probably from 1370. It consists of four wings around an oblong inner courtyard, with a tower in each west corner, flush with the face of the outer wall. On the ground floor of the west wing there was an arcaded corridor with rib vaulting. Unlike most Slovak castles, Zvolen Castle has retained its original ground floor layout. Originally it had no outer fortifications.

The city of Levoča (Spišská Nová Ves district) was one of the greatest commercial centres in medieval Hungary. Substantial parts of its complex fortifications survive, and have not yet been fully investigated. On the north and the west sides the city was protected by a steep slope above a stream, the Levoča, and its tributary. The east and south-east sides were more exposed to attack. The main stone wall was strengthened by shallow towers with barrel vaults above the ground floor. In front of the wall there was a narrow outer bailey protected by an outer wall and partly also by a ditch. This first phase of the city's fortifications can probably be dated to the second quarter of the 14th century.

The brick walls of Trnava are among the most remarkable examples of early urban fortification in Slovakia. Almost a regular oblong in plan, they are completely preserved along the west and east sides of the city, and were originally battlemented. The mural towers resemble those at Levoča; they are shallow, slightly projecting, oblong in plan and relatively closely grouped, leaving only short stretches of curtain wall. Towers of this kind were not used in Bohemian fortifications (except at Beroun), so comparative study and dating is difficult; and while the Czech art historian Menclová believes that the towers of Trnava were erected in the later 14th century, the official register of historic buildings and cities dates them some fifty years earlier. Possibly the towers of Levoča and Trnava are related in some way to the fortifications of Italian cities. The absence of an outer wall at Trnava is surprising; only

a ditch hindered an enemy from reaching the foot of the wall.

Castle architecture also flourished in the more restricted territory of present-day Hungary, where the terrain—mostly plains and lowlands—put certain limits on the variations that could be made on the plan and mass of castles.

The ruins of the baronial castle of Hollókó, to the north-east of Budapest, have a compact, irregularly polygonal plan. The residential tower is a substantial pentagonal, pointed structure.

At Csesznek, to the north of Veszprém, the upper castle consists of a narrow oblong courtyard, closed by two oblong towers. The lower castle, defended by towers, stands further to the west. Historians date the construction of the castle to the early 14th century, but it was probably completed somewhat later.

In the castle of Várgesstes, to the west of Buda-

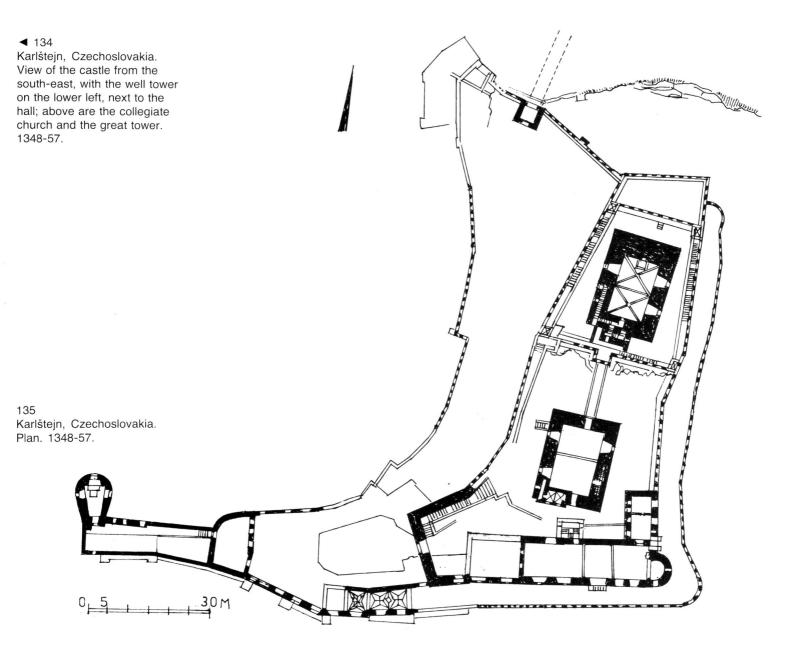

◄ 134
Karlštejn, Czechoslovakia. View of the castle from the south-east, with the well tower on the lower left, next to the hall; above are the collegiate church and the great tower. 1348-57.

135
Karlštejn, Czechoslovakia. Plan. 1348-57.

136
Kašperk, Czechoslovakia, begun in 1356. Plan, after Menclová.

0 ⊢⊢⊢⊢⊢⊢⊢ 50 M

pest, two inner towers seal off an oblong inner courtyard. The castle was probably built in the last quarter of the 14th century.

The secure authority and prestige of Louis the Great were manifested in the building of Diósgyör, near the city of Miskolc. The layout and construction of the castle represent a faithful application of the principles of Italian castle design, with certain modifications which largely sacrificed its value as a fortification to architectural considerations. The castle is oblong in plan, with an inner courtyard surrounded by typical single-span buildings. In each of the four corners stands a tower whose mass does not project beyond the castle; the towers were originally higher, but their upper storeys were subsequently demolished. The focal point of the defence was a continuous parapet walk with machicolations on closely spaced corbels, projecting around the entire periphery of the castle at the level of the roof eaves. Similar arrangements prevailed on the towers. The surviving architectural details, and the remains of the ribbed vaults of collapsed halls on the first floor evoke the royal magnificence of Diósgyör. Also lost now are its original outer fortifications.

Castles of the rectangular type were frequently built in late 14th century Hungary, especially during the reign of Charles IV's son, Sigismund (1387-1437). The purest representative of this type is the castle of the city of Tata, south of the Danube and west of Budapest. The castle had a square plan with four corner towers projecting only slightly from the outer face of the wall; now, only one corner tower and the adjoining wing survive. The gradual construction of the outer fortifications took place much later and belongs to a different phase of castle-building history.

The castle at Eisenstadt in Austria belongs to the same group. Dating from the last two decades of the 14th century, it is square in plan and originally had four corner towers projecting from the wall face.

Bran is a very impressive Transylvanian castle to the south of Brasov in Romania. It is built on a spur with steep slopes, accessible only from the west. It has a compact, irregular plan and a complicated silhouette. The castle was built on the orders of Louis the Great between 1377 and the 1380s. Its oldest part is the watchtower in the middle of the north side. The tower with a gateway on the south side is a striking feature thanks to its cladding of rusticated blocks. At the north-west end of the castle layout is a low circular tower. There is a massive wall with a tower on the vulnerable west side, which was also the location of the only outer fortification, a ditch.

In Poland (apart from Silesia, which formed a part of the Bohemian state), castle-building proceeded with great intensity in the 14th century. The new castles replaced existing soil and timber fortifications. From 1333 the principal builder was Casimir the Great (King Casimir III, 1333-70), who constructed a number of royal castles of stone and brick.

One of the oldest stone castles in Poland is also one of the most impressive. It is the ruins of the royal castle of Chęciny (Kielce), which stands on a rocky hill and is visible from a great distance in all directions. The castle is an oblong with curved sides. Its extraordinary appearance is enhanced by its two circular stone towers with brick superstructures. The west tower touches the inner face of the wall, whereas the east tower penetrates it. On the northern side of the east tower there was a gateway, on its southern side a narrow oblong chapel. The tower in the very extensive bailey to the west adds to the dramatic impact of its outline.

Chęciny was built by a Cracow bishop, John

112

Muskata, in about 1300, during the brief period when Poland was under Bohemian domination. It is the only Polish castle with an emphatically oblong layout. All other 14th century Polish castles had a concentric layout, sometimes without any outer bailey. Even Casimir the Great's castles were no exception. Bedzin (Katowice) had a massive circular tower and a hall surrounded by a double wall. This castle, dating from the mid-14th century, had an extensive outer bailey. Of the many other examples that might be cited, Lanckoróna (Cracow) was remarkable for its compact rectangular layout with a pair of towers.

An interesting feature of 14th century Polish castles is how varied their towers were. Apart from the usual circular and quadrangular shapes, there were also octagonal towers, for example at the royal castle of Boleslawiec (Łódź), at Kruszwica (Bydgoszcz) and at Rawa Mazowiecka (Łódź).

The main residence of the Grand Dukes of Lithuania was Trakai (Lithuania), on an island in Lake Galvé. The castle has a very regular rectangular plan; its rather small courtyard includes two ranges of buildings, differing in width and height, along its shorter sides; the courtyard is entered by a passageway in a tower. The castle was surrounded by a wall and separated from the rather large bailey by a ditch. There were three towers on the outer wall enclosing the bailey, two of them situated in the south-west corners and designed to be defended by firearms. The construction of Trakai is dated to the late 14th and the 15th century. Its layout is reminiscent of some late 14th century Bohemian castles.

★

The castles of the crusading Order of Teutonic Knights in the Chełmno region and in Prussia are interesting from both an architectural and a military point of view.

The castle of Golub-Dobrzyn (Bydgoszcz, Poland) was built of brick, complete with its outer bailey, in 1302-06. It has a typical rectangular design of almost square plan (39.5 × 42 metres). In the west corner the foundations of a square tower have been discovered. In the other corners, low turrets are mounted on top of the masonry. The castle was surrounded by a low wall.

The castle of Radzyń Chełmiński (Bydgoszcz) has been only partly preserved, but its initial state can be fairly reliably reconstructed. Built in the first third of the 14th century, it was one of the greatest fortresses of the Order at the height of its power.

The monastic nucleus of the castle forms a 52 × 52 metre square. Inside, in its north-west corner, there was a free-standing octagonal tower. The layout was regular, with buildings around a rather small inner courtyard: the four slender corner towers, which were much higher than the rest of the castle, had pyramidal roofs and battlements. There was a defence gallery below the eaves.

The castle was entered in the middle of the most important, south, wing, which housed the main hall

137
Radyně, Czechoslovakia. View of the upper castle from the north-west. About 1360.

and a chapel on the first floor. The gateway was at the back of a deep, high recess, and was closed with a portcullis on the outside. The inner courtyard was surrounded by vaulted corridors on the ground and first floor. All the castle's rooms were vaulted; the stellar vault of the chapel was among the oldest in the Baltic region. The entire castle was built of brick. The monotony of the vast, smooth façades was somewhat enlivened with black brickwork patterns.

The system of fortifications at Radzyń Chełmiński is also impressive. The castle stands on the west

the west end of the south wing a corridor led to a privy tower above a mill race. There was a trapezoidal bailey to the north, the so-called Mittelschloss (Middle Castle). After 1309 a radical reconstruction of the High Castle was carried out, in the course of which the chapter hall and the sumptuous chapel of the Virgin Mary, completed in 1344, were constructed in the north wing. With its presbytery, the chapel projects from the eastern façade of the castle. In the south the main tower adjoined the chapel. There was a stellar vault in the north wing of

138
Točník, Czechoslovakia. View of the hall from the southeast. About 1400.

bank of a lake. It was enclosed by a bailey with a wall and a ditch which separated it from the very large south bailey, which was in turn protected by a wall and a ditch. There was also a small bailey on the east side of the castle.

The castle of Malbork (formerly Marienburg; Gdańsk province) became the residence of the Grand Master of the Order in 1309. The original castle, built from 1280 above the east bank of the River Nogat, had only three wings with a wall on the east side; this was the Hochschloss (High Castle). At

the castle. The courtyard is surrounded by cross-vaulted ambulatories.

The Middle Castle, separated by a ditch from the High Castle, became the seat of the Grand Master. The most visually splendid part of the Middle Castle is the Grand Master Hall in a short wing projecting westwards towards the river; its west façade is extraordinarily impressive in design. The rooms of the hall and the west wing with a large refectory rank among the finest of all examples of medieval castle architecture. The south wing was built in 1380-98,

139
Nymburk, Czechoslovakia. Part of the main wall on the east side of the town. About 1330.

140
Polička, Czechoslovakia. Part of the main wall with towers on the north-west side of the town. Second quarter of the 14th century.

probably by Nikolaus Fellenstein. The Middle Castle was entered from the north through a newly laid-out oblong bailey, enclosed in 1335-41 with an outer wall and a ditch on two sides. The gateway was secured by a portcullis.

The fortifications of Malbork were not designed to be defended with firearms; nor were they designed to take account of the artillery that might be used by a besieging force. As a fortress, therefore, Malbork does not rank very high.

The castle of Brodnica (formerly Strassburg; Bydgoszcz) dates from the first half of the 14th century. All that now remains of it is an octagonal tower, 51 metres high and originally free-standing, near the north corner of the site.

Interestingly non-standard in design is the Order's castle above the Vistula at Swiecie (formerly Schwetz; Bydgoszcz). It was built of brick, probably in 1338-49. At the corners of its square plan

115

141
Zvolen, Czechoslovakia. View
of the castle from the south-
west, with the late 15th and
early 16th century outer
fortifications in the
foreground. The castle itself
was built from the 1370s
onwards.

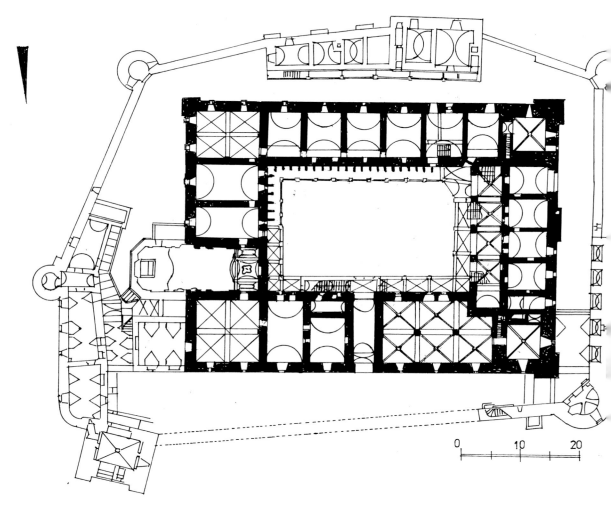

142
Zvolen, Czechoslovakia. Plan
of the castle. 1370 onwards.
After Menclová.

0   10   20

stood four circular towers, of which the north-east one, 34.5 metres high, is complete; it culminates in corbels supporting the machicolations and (restored) battlements. The castle was enclosed by a wall.

Other important castles of the Teutonic Knights included namely Kwidzyn (formerly Marienwerder; Gdańsk), from the second quarter of the 14th century, and the later 14th century Lidzbark Warmiński (formerly Heilsberg; Olsztyn).

The Pomeranian castle of Bytów (formerly Bütow; Koszalin) was built in 1398-1406 by Nikolaus Fellenstein, shortly before the power of the Teutonic Knights began to decline; it represents an effort on their part to cope with the new conditions created by the steadily increasing importance of artillery. Bytów is oblong in plan, with corner towers containing chambers for cannon; this was where the castle's fire-power was concentrated. The two south-east towers are octagonal, the west tower is circular and the north tower square. The main residential building stood against the inside of the north-west wall. The outer fortification system was built much later; before its construction the castle did not have great defensive strength.

Nidzica (formerly Neidenburg; Olsztyn), a city with a castle, was founded by the Teutonic Knights in 1381. Controlling the ford in the bend of the River Nida, it was a strong ling in the Order's defence system in this area. In plan the city was oblong, with the north-west corner slightly cut away where the river ran past it. The city wall was protected by closely spaced towers. There was an outer wall on the east side, and along parts of the north and south sides. A moat protected the east and south sides, the river serving the same function on the north and west sides. Entry to the city was through north and south gateways.

High up on the most vulnerable east side stood the castle. It was built of brick, was rectangular in plan, and had a massive tower in each east corner. In the centre of the curtain wall stood the gateway slightly projecting from the wall face. The main castle building was situated on the west side of the courtyard. Nidzica was completed early in the 15th century (its chapel was consecrated in 1404); shortly afterwards the power of the Teutonic Knights was broken.

Among other territories ruled by the Order were Kurland (Courland) and Livonia (Livland), ac-

143
Trnava, Czechoslovakia. Part of the wall on the east side of the town. Second quarter of the 14th century.

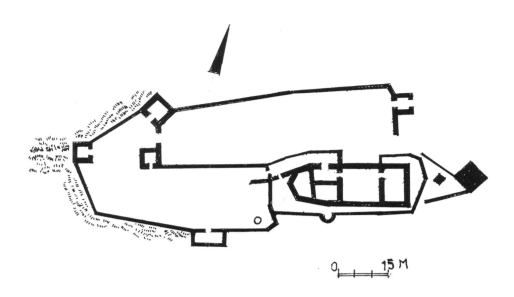

144
Czesznek, Hungary. Plan of the castle. After Gerö.

145
Czesznek, Hungary. View of the castle from the north-east, with the tower of the lower castle on the right. The view is dominated by the upper castle and its two towers. First half of the 14th century.

quired in the early 13th century, and Estonia, purchased from Denmark in 1346. Still further north along the Baltic coast, the Order's castle at Riga (Latvia) was begun in 1330 and completed very rapidly. Now extensively restored, it illustrates the remarkable uniformity of the Teutonic Knights' strongholds. It is square in plan, with buildings along all four sides. Slender towers project slightly from three corners; the fourth, north corner is occupied by a much bulkier square tower.

Kuressaare, on the south coast of the Baltic island of Saaremaa, was directly inspired by Teutonic Knights' castles, and in its restored form is one of the most impressive examples of Gothic architecture in the entire region. The castle of the Bishop of Ösel-Wieck, it stands in the city of Kingissepp (Estonia), also formerly known as Kuressaare or Arensburg. Its earlier development was complex; however, we

are interested in the final form of the castle, created between the 1340s and about 1380.

In plan the castle is almost square. Inside a thick peripheral wall stands a regular four-wing structure with a slender, slightly projecting tower in the northeast corner and a bulkier tower in the north corner. Two wings of the courtyard arcades are rib-vaulted.

The castle was protected by an outer wall and a ditch. In the 1430s another outer wall with numerous loops and embrasures (splayed openings) was built beyond it; and this was reinforced by three-quarter-circular bastion towers and partly protected by an outer ditch. In about the middle of the 15th century more high, semicircular and circular towers were added.

The castle of Narva (Estonia), mentioned for the first time in 1277, was established as the eastern-

118

146
Diósgyör, Hungary. Ruins of
the castle dating from the
reign of Louis the Great
(1342-82), with the 16th
century outer fortifications in
the foreground.

147
Tata, Hungary. Remains of
the castle. End of the 14th
century.

148
Chęciny, Poland. Plan of the
castle. After Guerquin.

149
Chęciny, Poland. View of the
castle ruins from the south,
with the upper castle (*c.* 1300)
on the right and the lower, late
15th century castle on the left.

most Danish stronghold in the Gulf of Finland; and after Estonia was purchased by the Teutonic Knights, its location immediately made it a vital outpost of the Order. Consequently, on the site of the original Danish stronghold a four wing castle, slightly trapezoidal in plan, was gradually erected around an inner courtyard. A massive tower stood in the north-west corner. On its west side the castle was protected by a vast fortified bailey, begun before the arrival of the Order. In the north the castle was linked with the city, which was also fortified.

The fortifications of Tallin are among the best

120

preserved and most impressive in the whole of Europe. The oldest distinguishing features are simple bay-like projections from the outer wall which date from the early 14th century; they were followed by slender rectangular towers. The major defensive points were the U-plan towers on the main wall, to the strengthening of which most later efforts were dedicated. These mainly consisted in increasing the number of towers (thus shortening the vulnerable curtain walls), the thickness of the walls and above all the height of the towers (from 20 to 24, and ultimately to 35 metres). In 1373 the number of towers was increased from 18 to 27, and 8 gates. 26 towers are still in existence. In front of the wall there was a ditch and a rampart. In 1510 and 1532 the fortifications were strengthened with a U-shaped gun roundel and a massive round gun tower.

The Danish castle of Gurre was built in the reign of King Valdemar IV (1340-75). It has an almost square plan with large, slightly projecting corner towers, one irregular, the remaining three of almost square plan.

The ruins of the castle in the small town of Vordingsborg date from the same period. The wall was reinforced with semicircular brick towers. The main tower was 27 metres high.

Valdemar IV probably also built the massive brick tower in Helsingborg on the east side of the Sund, now in Sweden. It has a diameter of 15 metres, is 30 metres high and has walls 4 metres thick.

Although Sweden is far from rich in medieval fortifications of any great significance, it does possess some of the most remarkable city defences in Europe. These are the walls of Visby, on the island of Gotland in the Baltic Sea. The extensive old part of the city is enclosed by stone walls with towers 15-20 metres high. They are open on the city side, have loopholes, and in a few instances the upper parts are three-sided. The towers stand at intervals of 40-100 metres along the wall; there are far fewer on the side facing the sea.

The walls were surmounted by battlements with embrasures. Between the towers there were projecting guard turrets (*échauguettes*) supported by corbels, but none now survive. However, 38 towers are still standing. The gateway, with an arcaded passage and a semicircular arch over the portcullis, forms an integral part of the fortifications. What is surprising is the absence of any outer fortifications.

The architectural influence of the Teutonic

150
Trakai, Lithuania. Castle on an island in Lake Galvé; late 14th and 15th century. View from the south with the 16th century bastion in the foreground.

151
Radzyń Chełmiński, Poland. Ruined castle of the Order of Teutonic Knights; view from the south-east, with the gateway in the centre. First third of the 14th century.

152
Malbork, Poland; formerly Marienburg. View from the south-west of the headquarters of the Teutonic Knights. The High Castle was completed in the first half of the 14th century. The privy tower is on the right, the Middle Castle with the Grand Master Hall (1380-98) on the left. The wall with the Bridge Gate, built after 1335, follows the line of the River Nogat.

153
Kwidzyn, Poland; formerly
Marienwerder. Corridor
leading to the privy tower.
Second quarter of the 14th
century.

Knights was felt even across the Gulf of Finland. The early 14th century castle of Hämeenlinna (Tavastehus) is directly modelled on the Order's castles in Livonia. It is rectangular in plan and had four towers, only two of which now survive.

★

Curiously enough, rather similar rectangular plans also prevailed in faraway Italy. Within the framework of the rectangular plan, Italian castle builders would go on to create a new fortification system which survived with adaptations until the end of the 19th century.

Although rectangular plans were the rule, one exception was the picturesque castle of Fenis in the Aosta valley, set against the background of the Alps. Its building history was rather complex, reaching back to the end of the 13th century (the tower at the gateway). A new phase of construction began about 1340 and ended in 1398. Against the pentagonal nucleus of the castle stand two towers with a walkway supported by corbels. The castle was enclosed by two walls and a ditch. The walls cul-

minate in battlements with swallow-tail merlons, a typical 14th century Italian touch that greatly enhanced the castle's picturesque appearance. There were also numerous keyhole loops. Building work on the castle was resumed in the 15th century.

In the small town of Ivrea, also in Piedmont, directly below the Alps, stands the Castello delle Quattro Torri, a roughly oblong castle whose tall corner towers are circular—a feature uncommon in Italian buildings. Work on the Castello began in 1358 and lasted almost to the end of the 14th century.

One of the most attractive city castles is the Castello Vecchio in Verona. It was built from 1354 onwards by Francesco Bevilaqua, at about the same time as the magnificent bridge across the River Adige, which it commanded. Sited directly on the river bank, the castle consists of two parts: the palace proper and a bailey on its north-east side, the two being separated by an area walled on both sides.

Above the bridge stands a tall, slender tower, through which there is a passageway with another tower in the background. The walls rise to battlements with swallow-tail merlons, to great visual effect. The upper castle is fortified by a simple wall with a tower in the south-west corner. The bailey, trapezoidal in plan, is protected by a wall with three higher towers on the city side. The fourth tower is situated in the north corner of the fortification. The castle was undoubtedly surrounded by a ditch. Like the castle, the bridge had swallow-tail battlements and was built of brick.

In Sirmione, at one end of the narrow peninsula near the southern shore of Lake Garda, stood the castle of the Scaligeri family. Although built as early as the 13th century, in general appearance it resembles the Castello Vecchio. At three corners of this rectangular castle stand towers of slightly greater elevation; from the fourth, south-east corner, a tall, slender tower rises up. On its east and south sides the castle is protected by an outer wall with higher towers. To the east of the castle there is a fortified harbour. The corner towers of the castle, the main gateway and the peripheral wall are battle-

154
Lidzbark Warmiński, Poland; formerly Heilsberg. Episcopal castle from the second half of the 14th century.

155
Bytów, Poland; formerly
Bütow. View of the castle of
Teutonic Knights from the
east. Built in 1398-1406.

156
Bytów, Poland; formerly
Bütow. Plan of the castle.
After Guerquin.

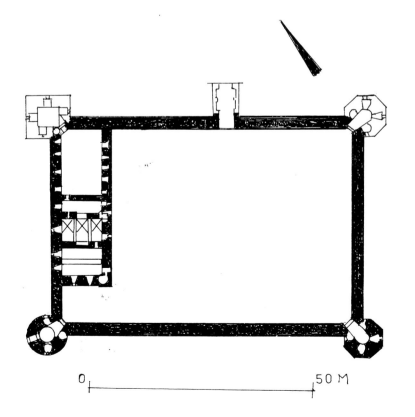

mented with swallow-tail merlons. The defences of
the main tower include a gallery on corbels. Sirmione was given its present appearance in the middle of the 14th century. With its attractive outline
and location on the shores of Lake Garda, it is an
extremely attractive sight.

Rocca Maggiore, the castle guarding Assisi in
Umbria from the north, is a somewhat uncon-
ventional example of Italian castle architecture. It
has a compact, not entirely regular plan, dominated
by a tower with a gallery on corbels which also runs
along the top of the wall and its mural towers. In
addition, an octagonal tower is incorporated into
the castle wall. The present appearance of Rocca
Maggiore dates from 1362-65.

The city castle of Narni in Umbria was built from
1366 onwards. The standard rectangular plan with
four corner towers is given a certain variety by the

125

157
Tallin, Estonia. Part of the city wall with towers, built from the middle of the 14th century onwards, with an early 16th century gun tower in the foreground.

158 ▶
Visby, Sweden. Part of the city wall with the gateway, seen from the outside. First half of 14th century.

fact that one of the towers exceeds the others in mass and height; they are only slightly higher than the walls of the building.

The city castle at Spoleto comprises a splendid double application of the rectangular plan. It consists of an oblong three-wing upper castle and a shorter, also oblong bailey meeting it in the west. The four corners are reinforced by towers of greater elevation. A further two towers stand at the junction of the two oblongs, the wider and higher northern tower having the character of a great tower or keep. The castle was built in the 1360s.

The construction of another Scaligeri castle, at Pondino in Northern Italy, began in 1379. It is square in plan, with four slightly projecting corner towers; probably they were all originally higher than the curtain walls. In the middle of the south side of the castle there is a gate tower equipped with Italianized machicolations.

Ferrara was well fortified during the Middle Ages. In its centre stands a Renaissance castle belonging to the Este family, the distinguished rulers of this large Northern Italian city-state. It is a four-wing rectangular structure with massive corner towers, enclosed even today by a wide moat. Its original design was modified by various later changes. Like the much lower peripheral wall, the towers are equipped with galleries with machicolations supported by plain, typically Italian corbels. The castle, built by Bartolini Ploti of Novara, was begun in 1385.

The city of Montagnana, in the Veneto, has remarkable fortifications, consisting of a battlemented wall protected by a ditch. The mural towers are pentagonal, mostly closely spaced, and open on the city side. Since rectangular towers were consistently used in medieval Italian fortifications, this wall is an interesting exception. In 1362 a castle was built directly against the wall; its high tower had a gallery on corbels with machicolations and battlements. The fortifications of Montagnana seem to have undergone a complex development; in their present form they undoubtedly date from the middle and later 14th century.

In the 1330s the Bohemian prince Charles—subsequently the Emperor Charles IV—founded the town of Monte Carlo, now in the province of Lucca. Its peripheral wall, with typical rectangular towers, has a notably irregular trace. The city is controlled by a small castle to the north-west; it is oblong in plan, with polygonal towers; around its top run closely spaced corbels supporting machicolations.

An outstanding example of 14th century urban fortification exists at Soave, to the east of Verona. In 1365 the Scaligeri family founded a small town there, with a rectangular plan with a slanting east side. This was added to the small Scaligeri castle that already stood on top of a nearby hill. The castle was untypical in plan. The battlemented wall with embrasures is reinforced by 24 towers, open on the town side, at intervals of 60-70 metres. Their upper storeys rise above the tops of the walls, the battlements being equipped with swallow-tail merlons.

We have described only a few of the very numerous 14th century Italian fortifications. This was not a period in which significant technical or architectural advances were made; but the next phase would witness a great leap forward.

★

There was also intensive building on the opposite side of the Adriatic. Only small parts of the fortifications survive at the charming city of Korčula, on the Dalmatian island of the same name. These date from two main phases of development. The older probably belongs to the late 13th or early 14th century. Its characteristic features are the slender towers that project from the face of the peripheral wall; only two survive, one on the western and the other on the southern side of the city. The southern tower has a secondary function as a gate.

Perhaps the most attractive medieval fortress to survive in the area is the city of Dubrovnik. Its fortifications were never subjected to serious assault, and

159
Fenis, Italy. Plan of the castle.
After Monumenti.

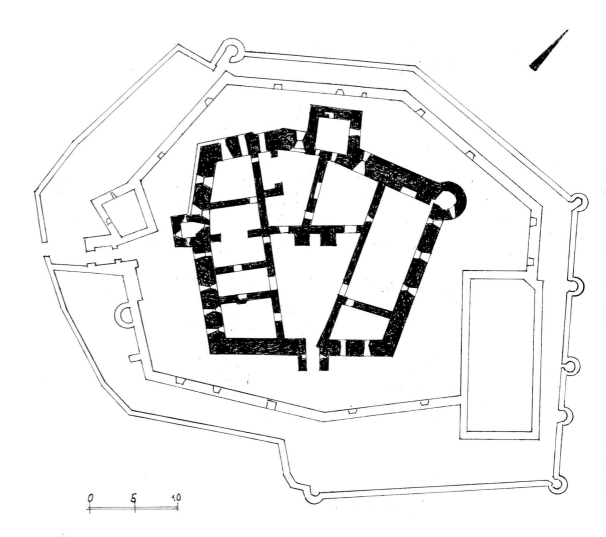

160
Fenis, Italy. The castle in its
Alpine setting; *c.* 1340-98 and
15th century.

0   5   10

have therefore undergone all sorts of small, gradual and local changes over the centuries. From these we shall try to isolate the building work of two periods, the 14th century and the late Gothic period (roughly speaking, after the fall of Constantinople in 1453).

The first really monumental fortifications at Dubrovnik date from the 14th century, when the original city wall was strengthened on the land and harbour sides with 15 typical rectangular towers, some of which still survive. They were higher than the wall, and their upper parts were open towards the city. Their original design was modified by later work on the fortifications. There was also an outer wall not far from the main wall, with a ditch in front of it. The final liberation of Dubrovnik from Venetian rule in 1358 was a major motive for intensive building of fortifications; at that time the city was already afforded further protection by an outwork known as Lovryenats in the south-east.

★

The lack of really comprehensive data makes it impossible to reach definite conclusions concerning 14th century castle architecture in the Iberian peninsula, which was both excellent and diverse.

161
Sirmione, Italy. The castle, standing above Lake Garda. The rectangular castle is surrounded by a wall with towers. About the mid-14th century.

162
Assisi, Italy. The castle of Rocca Maggiore, on top of a hill to the north of the city. Built 1362-65.

For this reason we shall present only a few examples, although the 14th century was undoubtedly the Golden Age of Spanish castles in particular. Some of them display a pronounced formal rigour which no longer had very much to do with the defensive role of the castle—a tendency that would reach its culmination in the following century.

Spanish castles are notable for their great variety, both of plan and appearance. Particularly remarkable are the elongated plans of the castles built on hilltops.

One of most original castle designs in Spain is that of Peñafiel (Valladolid), built on the top of a rocky hill devoid of trees or bushes. In a Western European context its oblong plan and narrow inner courtyard are rather surprising features.

Each end of the castle is strengthened by a U-shaped tower with a gallery and machicolations on corbels. Along the high, battlemented main wall, and extending slightly above it, there are slender semicircular turrets; these are interspersed, on no regular scheme, with large U-plan towers of similar design to the two end towers. All the towers, large and small, are closed on the inside.

Lying transversely across the layout is a donjon with machicolations on corbels. The line of machicolations is interrupted in the corners and in the centre of each side by small semicircular turrets supported by corbels at about two-thirds of the height of the towers. The entire castle is surrounded by a narrow bailey, which is protected by an outer wall and reinforced in its most vulnerable parts.

The fortifications of Peñafiel, begun very early in the 14th century, are reminiscent of urban defensive systems; only the mid-15th century donjon suggests a conventional castle building. The architectural expressiveness and unity of design achieved at Peñafiel are very surprising features.

Peñaranda de Duero in Old Castile has a similar layout with a great tower in the centre.

The castle of Almonacid, to the south-west of Toledo, was reconstructed in 1367-69. Here a massive tower stands in the centre of a polygonal shell. Above the battlemented walls rise four-sided towers, and beyond them lie a bailey and ditch.

The monumental ruins of Játiva, above the fortified town, probably also date from the 14th century. The castle is built on the narrow ridge of a high hill. Its central feature is a great tower, enclosed by two sets of walls with relatively closely spaced mural towers. The inner wall had a gateway guarded by two towers; in the outer wall there was a gate in a tower. The walls were battlemented. Játiva was among the best fortified castles in Valencia.

Castillo de Bellver, the royal castle at Palma, capital of the Balearic island of Majorca, is unique in Spanish or even European castle architecture. It is circular in plan, the main buildings being arranged around the periphery. The inner courtyard is surrounded by arcades with ribbed vaults, just as it was at Zvíkov in Bohemia. The wall is reinforced by towers which act as cantilevers. Beyond the ditch stands a machicolated circular tower which is connected with the castle by a stone bridge with a single pointed-arch span. The construction of the castle ended in 1344.

★

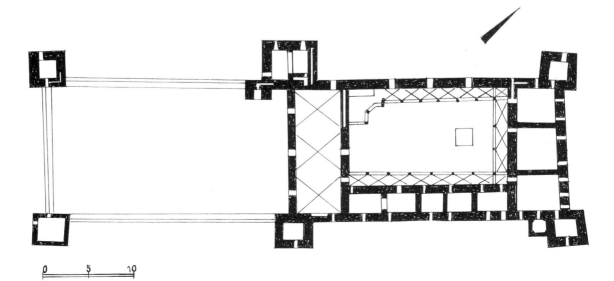

163
Spoleto, Italy. Plan of the castle and of the bailey on its south-west side. 1360s. After Monumenti.

◄164
Ferrara, Italy. Entrance façade of the city castle, built from 1385 onwards.

0   5   10

165

Montagnana, Italy. Plan of the
city, showing its walls. After
Monumenti.

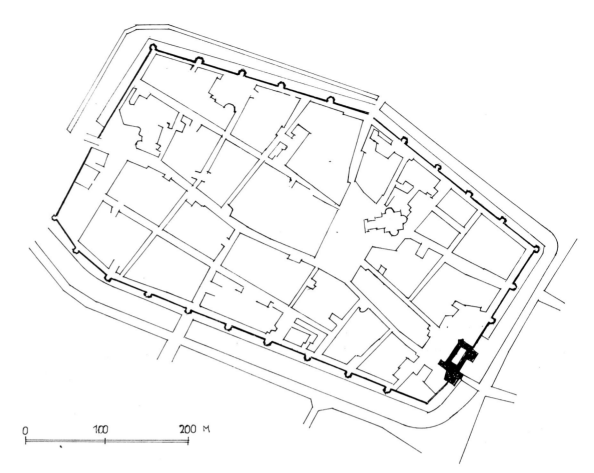

166

Montagnana, Italy. Aerial view
of the city. The walls date
from the middle years of the
14th century.

0   100   200 M

167
Játiva, Spain. Eighteenth century view of the castle ruins, which are probably 14th century.

168
Peñafiel, Spain. Castle plan. Early 14th century; the residential towers date from the middle of the 15th century. After Ebhardt.

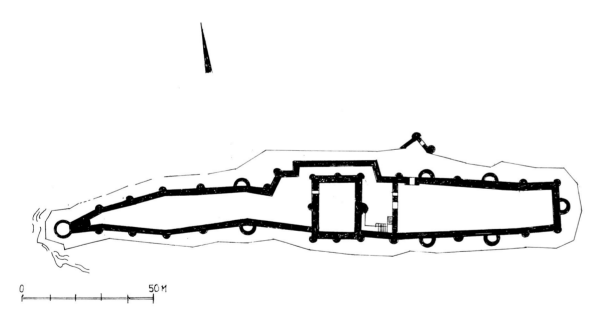

0   50 M

Thanks to economic and political conditions in the 14th century, castles and urban fortifications were erected all over Europe. Not only quantity but also quality characterized the period, notably in France, Germany, Bohemia, Hungary, the Baltic and Spain; aesthetic considerations became more important — almost inappropriately so in France. Technically, on the other hand, there were almost no signs of the great changes that were soon to occur, transforming war and siegecraft; and in this sense the 14th century represents the apogee of the medieval art of fortification.

The Fifteenth Century

The age-old art of fortification, with its roots in the world of classical antiquity, began to decline in the 15th century and eventually fell into complete oblivion. This was due almost exclusively to the development of siegecraft technique, and in particular to the development of artillery. Guns appeared in the early 14th century; they had come into general use within a few decades, and towards the end of the century the destructive effect of bombardments on fortifications was already being felt. However, it was not until the mid-15th century that artillery became the decisive factor in a siege —so decisive that the besieged were compelled to adopt new measures in order to put up a significant resistance.

The first phase of this development in Central Europe took place during the Hussite wars (1420-34), in which the Bohemians fought to secure their 'heretical' religious arrangements against a crusade proclaimed by the Pope and the Holy Roman Emperor. From this struggle emerged the principle of active defence and the tactic of trying to distance the vital centres of a fortress from the impact of the besieging artillery—the beginnings of the bastion system described hereafter. Meanwhile a weakened and divided France passed through the critical phase of the Hundred Years' War, finally emerging triumphant in 1453. In the same year, after a siege in which artillery played a major role, the great city of Constantinople fell to the Turks. This event reverberated throughout Europe, and fear of the Turkish peril —and Turkish artillery—stimulated strenuous endeavours to construct new and more effective fortifications.

The successes of French arms made this seem all the more urgent. During the reign of Louis XI (1461-83) France consolidated in the wake of the Hundred Years' War, and the employment of artillery made considerable progress. This culminated under the next king, the martial Charles VIII (1483-98). During Charles's campaign in Italy, the effect of French guns shooting metal balls was a cruel surprise to the defenders of Italian fortresses, which were compelled to surrender one after another.

The experience of these wars proved that stone or brick walls with towers no longer represented a reliable means of defence. It became clear that systems of fortification must undergo radical change. It is therefore not to be wondered at that the revolution in fortification construction began on Italian soil. Another factor was the vulnerability of the Italian peninsula to attacks from the sea. At the same time, the Republic of Venice actually controlled through her fleet most of Dalmatia and Corfu, Crete, Cyprus, and other Greek islands.

It is certainly no accident that in the late 1450s —that is, almost immediately after the fall of Constantinople—Mariano di Jacopo il Taccola designed a bastion-protected fort for Pope Calixtus III. However, the transition from the traditional fortification system to the bastion system was a long and complex one, full of interesting experiments and novel designs.

★

During the early 15th century, the development of French castles was characterized by a tendency to accentuate their compactness of plan and appearance. The focus remained the more or less rectangular castle with deep foundations and very thick walls rising to a considerable height.

A classic example of this kind of splendid medieval castle is Tarascon (Bouches du Rhône) in the South of France, which stands on the summit of a rock on the east bank of the River Rhône. The white walls of the castle were built up to a height of 48 metres and were provided with battlements and machicolations on corbels. The layout of the castle was derived from the traditional French rectangular plan. Facing upstream, the strongest side of the castle is defended by two mural towers, one circular and one rectangular, with a smaller, nearly square mural tower between them. On the opposite side, the castle is protected by a widely projecting corner with a roughly semicircular tower. The buildings enclose a narrow courtyard.

On the north side there is an elongated bailey; of its fortifications, all that survives is a wall on the land side with three higher towers, culminating in machicolations and battlements similar to those of the castle proper. Tarascon was built between 1400 and 1449.

In the period 1431-35 the castle of Domeyrat (Haute Loire) was reconstructed. It has a roughly oblong plan with circular corner towers. It is surrounded by quite a large bailey with an outer wall and U-plan towers.

Lassay (Mayenne) was built very rapidly in the course of 1457-58. The castle is polygonal in plan; its closely spaced U-plan mural towers, rising above the wall, terminate in corbels intended to support brattices. The twin-towered north gateway was protected by an oblong barbican.

To make effective defensive use of the horizontal trajectory of cannon balls, fortifications had to be made substantially lower. At the same time, the need for a greater concentration of artillery fire led to the building of larger bastion towers, and this gave rise to artillery roundels, the principal products of the 15th century revolution in fortification.

In Europe, these originated in France. At Coucy le Château (Aisne), dating from the late 1230s, the circular corner towers of the upper castle are some 22 metres in diameter, hardly penetrate the masonry of the outside wall, and can probably be regarded as pure roundels. Also circular in plan was the 'Major Barbican' of the upper city (Cité) of Carcassonne; it dated from the reign of St Louis, projecting in front of the fortifications to the northwest of the city castle until it was torn down in 1816. The demolished U-shaped barbican of the Laon Gate, in the city of Coucy, dates from the 13th century; it was 90 metres in diameter, and was also one of the predecessors of the roundel. During the course of the 14th century the use of large circular mural towers, only minimally attached to the corners of curtain walls, developed fully. An example is

the castle belonging to Pope Clement V in Villandraut (Gironde).

The development of artillery, particularly under Louis XI (1461-83), brought about a reduction in the height of towers, mostly to a point level with the tops of the walls. Simultaneously the walls were greatly thickened. The principal circular tower of the castle of Ham (Somme) was built in the reign of Louis XI but was destroyed during the First World War. Its walls were as much as 10 metres thick. As the Gothic period came to an end and the Renaissance began, these circular towers came to be generally called bastion towers or bastions.

Guérande (Loire Inférieure) in southern Brittany is an attractive example of a small town fully enclosed by walls with four gateways. The most sumptuous is the St Michel Gate, with two semicircular towers flanking the recessed entrance area. The gateways, like the lower wall, are provided with machicolations on corbels. The wall is battlemented, and was certainly protected by a ditch. The construction of the granite walls of Guérande began some time around the middle of the 14th century; they were radically reconstructed before the mid-15th century.

The fortifications of the city of Beaune (Côte d'Or) in Burgundy offer interesting examples of 15th and early 16th century defences. Long stretches of curtain wall are punctuated with high bastion towers, mostly of a pronounced oblong plan, with rounded ends or semicircular bastions; it is clear that they were originally open on the city side. In the south bend of the wall a trapezoidal castle with two small semicircular bastions projected from the wall periphery. The fortification system also included a moat.

In the course of the 15th century the settlement below the famous monastery of Mont St Michel (Manche), on an island near the Channel coast, was fortified. Prominent among the low, U-shaped or segmentally projecting bastion towers is a more massy, tetrahedral (four-sided) east bastion with a sharply projecting point, designed for artillery and dating from the reign of Charles VIII. It is one of the oldest surviving examples of this innovatory type of fortification.

Not far from the Mediterranean, on what is now French soil, stands the unique fort of Salses (Pyrénées Orientales), built at the end of the 15th century for Ferdinand of Aragon by the engineer Ramirez. The walls of the rectangular castle are 6 metres thick, and there are four U-shaped corner roundels. The west side is strengthened with a mural tower. Large, U-shaped ravelins (roughly triangular defensive works sited in the ditch) protect the east and south sides, the latter with a gateway. The ravelin giving access to the gateway is reinforced by another bastion tower. The entire fortress is surrounded by a deep ditch.

Salses is among the most important fortifications constructed in the period around 1500.

★

Building and rebuilding increased the number and quality of Swiss castles in the 15th century. The picturesque early medieval moated castle of Hallwil (Aargau), standing on two islands, was partly rebuilt in 1419.

Aigle (Vaud) is a castle in a dramatic setting, with the Alps in the background. Its definitive form dates from the reconstruction carried out after 1475, when the peripheral wall with circular bastion towers was erected, surrounding the castle with a low pyramidal trace and several free-standing buildings.

Bellinzona became part of Switzerland only after the battle of Giornico in 1478. The complex fortifications guarding the valley of the Ticino were mainly built by the dukes of Milan after 1422 and between 1450 and 1466. The Castello Grande, mentioned in historical documents as early as 1242, stood on a hill close to the river; it had two towers of different sizes and an outer bailey. Further to the east stands the better preserved Castello Montebello, which is roughly triangular in plan. Its peripheral wall, with continuous machicolations and typical swallow-tail battlements, is strengthened with round and square corner towers. The castle is reached through a gateway with a drawbridge. Both are fortified by a low wall with rectangular open towers of equal height. Between the Castello Grande and the river there was a massive wall, known as the Murata, with a wide parapet walk and small bastion towers. A third fortress, Castello Santa Barbara, situated higher up, does not actually belong to the same defensive ensemble. It dates from the period after 1479 and has a square plan with an inner courtyard and towers of different sizes projecting from two corners of the wall face.

The fortifications of the town of Lucerne must also be mentioned; they were mainly built in the 15th and early 16th century.

★

The military significance of English castles waned in the 15th century, but they became extremely important as symbols of status and power. An example is the brick-built tower of Tattershall Castle in Lincolnshire, which dates from the 1430s; neither its general appearance nor its sumptuous period interiors have much in common with the stern, massive keeps of earlier times.

In Scotland the ruins of Ravenscraig Castle in Fife are of particular interest. The castle was built on a rocky headland directly above the Firth of Forth. Its defences were strengthened by a pair of bulky, partly rounded towers of different sizes, in effect serving

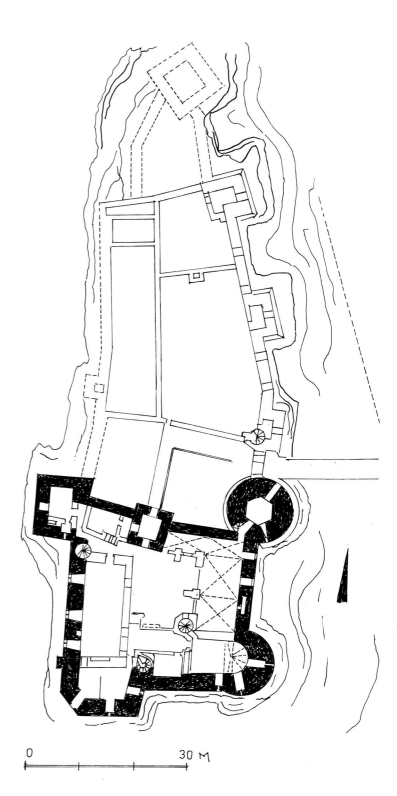

0   30 M

as roundels, and by outer walls of extraordinary thickness. Built by King James II in 1460, Ravenscraig was therefore already designed to resist artillery attack.

Affleck Castle (Kirrienmuir) is quite different. Although also built in the 15th century, it is a powerful rectangular keep with machicolations on corbels and a small staircase forebuilding.

Change began to make itself felt in the Low Countries too. After 1470, at the Dutch castle of Wedde a peripheral wall was built round the existing tower-shaped nucleus; it formed a square with three slightly convex sides and four corner bastion towers.

★

In the Holy Roman Empire the main 15th century developments were the rebuilding of the residential parts of castles, sometimes to great artistic effect, and the improvement of castle fortifications. Urban defensive systems were also improved. Our knowledge of the subject is less complete than it might be, since scholars have paid relatively little attention to the period and the existing materials are widely dispersed.

The partly ruined castle of Alzenau, near Aschaffenburg, was erected at the very beginning of the 15th century. It is oblong in plan, with a bailey to the south-west. The heart of the castle, with its rectangular hall, is protected in the north-east by a wall 5 metres thick and rising to height of 15 metres. The

◄ 169
Tarascon, France. Plan of the castle. After Salch.

170
Tarascon, France. View of the castle from the south-east, with the bailey in the background, right. First half of the 15th century.

upper castle is surrounded by a low and narrow outer bailey defended by a north-east U-plan bastion tower. The massive wall on its vulnerable side was intended to protect the castle from artillery fire.

We have already mentioned the castle of Landeck in the Palatinate in an earlier medieval context. In 1416 its defences were strengthened by the construction of an outer wall with bastion towers, all but one (which was rectangular) U-shaped in plan; the wall enclosed an outer bailey. To the north there was an outworks with a gateway and a U-shaped bastion tower, protected by a ditch. The main line of defence was thus transferred from the wall of the Romanesque castle to the wall round the outer bailey.

The castle of Haut Koenigsbourg, or Hochkönigsburg, in Alsace (now Bas-Rhin), was remodelled into a powerful fortress in the later 15th century. Exceptionally large U-plan roundels for gun emplacements were built in both west corners of the outer bailey; the southernmost roundel was particularly massive. It was possibly during this phase that the east side was strengthened by the construction of a rectangularly bent wall with an almost circular bastion tower in each corner. The entire castle is surrounded by an outside wall with small, open, semicircular bastion towers.

The castle of Eltz, in the valley of the Mosel, dates from the 15th-16th centuries. It is remarkable for its picturesque appearance, enhanced by its lovely landscape setting.

One of the most splendid castle ruins in Germany stands east of Wertheim, in a once strategically significant position near the confluence of the Tauber with the Main. A medieval fortress of complex design, it was repeatedly strengthened. During the earlier phase of its development, the defences included the wall around the upper castle in the west and north-east, on which there were several circular mural towers reinforced by semicircular open bastion towers.

To the south and south-east the castle is flanked by a wide ravine. The new 15th century fortifications, with U-plan bastion towers designed for artillery engagements, were erected to the south of the ravine.

The east side of the famous Heidelberg Castle (Palatinate) was strengthened with three circular roundels of unequal mass, two of them intended as gun emplacements.

The border castle of Burghausen (Upper Bavaria) stands on a narrow ridge above the west side of the town; at the foot of its west slope is a lake, the Wöhrsee, formerly an arm of the River Salzach. In

172 ▶
Aigle, Switzerland. The outer fortification system was constructed after 1475.

171
Hallwil, Switzerland. A moated castle, partly rebuilt from 1419.

138

1480-88 Burghausen was transformed into a powerful fortress by an impressive feat of reconstruction undoubtedly inspired by the threat from the Turks, whose armies had penetrated deep into East-Central Europe. The castle is 1,100 metres long and is divided by neck ditches into six sections. The entire fortress is protected by walls with towers, partly already intended to serve as gun emplacements. All this was probably done by Benedict Ried, later famous for his work on Prague Castle.

The castle of Breuberg, in the town of Neustadt in Odenwald (Hesse), is well preserved. The outer fortification system dates from 1480-1515, and features a wall with a sloping face rising directly from a deep ditch, and four artillery roundels of unequal size (one of them semicircular in plan).

The monumental 14th-15th century fortifications of south-west German cities were described in the last chapter. Here we need only add that the Hospital Gate (Spitaltor) in the town of Rothenburg ob der Tauber is secured by a late 15th century barbican which in plan resembles a figure of 8 open at the top. Its gallery is equipped with a large number of closely spaced oillets (openings for missiles etc.).

Querfurt (Halle) was one of the outstanding Romanesque castles, and the improvements made to its defences during the later 15th century were also remarkable. In 1461-79 the outer wall was reinforced by three U-shaped roundels differing slightly in plan from one another; their walls contain loopholes for arquebuses to fire through. Heavy barrel vaults support the gun emplacement platforms. At the same time a very thick wall was built along the west side of the north-west section of the castle; it

was completed in 1479. It is provided with casemates (covered chambers for gun emplacements) and artillery loopholes as well as loopholes for firearms.

Built in 1484-1503 for the archbishops of Magdeburg, the castle in the north-west corner of Halle an der Saale is entirely different in character. It is an irregular rhomboid in plan. The outside walls have loopholes, and the artillery roundels at the corners are only shallowly integrated into them. The two east roundels are far more massive than their western counterparts.

The castle at Meissen (Dresden) was a fine medieval fortress. Its eastern part, Albrechtsburg, was built by Arnold von Westphalen between 1471 and (probably) 1485; it is known for its splendid exterior design and interior layout, which are of European importance. However, this phase is not of major importance in the history of fortification.

The town of Aschersleben (Halle) was refortified in the 15th century with a stone wall, a bailey and a ditch. A stream forms its south-west boundary. Along the walls are closely spaced towers, mostly rectangular, with battlements and machicolations on stone corbels. Even the masonry roofs of the towers have been partly preserved, as has the tall tower of John's Gate. The fortifications date from about 1442. In the 16th century a circular artillery roundel was built in the south-east corner.

The barbican shielding the Marian Gate at Naumburg (Halle) dates from 1455-56 and in plan resembles an irregularly compressed arch. It is one of the earliest Central European examples of this type of fortification.

Work on the fortifications of German 'colonial' cities remained quite intense. At Brandenburg (Potsdam), a city of some historic significance, the fortifications were completed in the 15th century. They included four gateways that still survive; each consists of a tower (two circular and one octagonal in plan) with a passageway beside it. Their layout resembles those of some 13th-14th century gateways in Bohemia and Moravia.

At Jüterbog (Potsdam) the 14th century stone fortifications were rebuilt in brick after 1480. Only five mural towers have been preserved. The main wall was surrounded by a bailey. Three gateways are of architectural interest, one in the main wall and two in the trace of the outer wall. The Zinnauer Tor consists of the pointed arch of the gateway, guarded by a tall circular tower on the right and a lower rectangular tower on the left.

Great importance was attached to the appearance of city gateways during the late Gothic period. The two early 15th century outer gateways of Neubrandenburg, the Stargard Gate and the Treptow Gate, for example, have brick façades of high aesthetic quality. Their defensive function has been forgotten, but they are supremely effective as symbols of the city. A number of other examples might be mentioned, perhaps the most important being the Neustadt Gate (Neustädter Tor) in Tangermünde, which dates from about 1450.

Artistic expression and effective fortification tend to be incompatible requirements. Nevertheless, in the colonial cities of north-east Germany, a highly decorative approach developed as early as the 14th century. The gateways of these cities represent a curious, isolated phenomenon in the history of European fortifications.

★

The ruins of the Lower Austrian castle of Aggstein stand near the Danube in the attractive Wachau region. Most of the castle was newly built after 1429 on the narrow, elongated site of an older building. There is a gateway at a point about one third of the way along the wall from the south-east, above a ditch that no longer exists. The wall is 6 metres thick.

Not far from the Austrian border with Bohemia

◀ 173
Bellinzona, Switzerland. Two castles guarding the Ticino valley. On the left is the Castello Grande with its two towers, in existence since at least the 13th century; the Castello Montebello stands much higher on the right. The final appearance of the castles dates from the 15th century.

174
Lucerne, Switzerland. Part of city fortifications. 15th-early 16th centuries.

The Alpine region constituted a borderland that was most frequently threatened from the east, in the late Middle Ages by the Turkish peril which haunted the whole of Europe. From the 15th century this peril led to a revival of building activity, the outcome of which was a number of strong castles, sometimes of quite exceptional size. The process culminated in the 16th century.

Widely diverse types of castles occur in the large area from Hungary to Switzerland, and from the Bohemian border to Venice and Milan. As well as distance and political divisions, the varied configuration of the ground was an important factor. In Tirol especially there were a great many castles whose layout was determined by geographical, political and similar considerations.

stands the monumental lowland castle of Heidenreichstein, protected by two moats. Its bailey is entered from the north, along the west side of the castle proper; in the middle of this there is a sturdy residential tower, accessible at a height of 14 metres from a circular staircase turret. In plan the castle is an irregular quadrangle, defined by very high walls with circular corner towers of different mass and height. The north-east view is particularly impressive. The oldest parts, including the residential tower, belong to the 14th century, but most of the construction work was done in the 15th.

One of the most impressive medieval fortresses is the castle of Hohensalzburg dominating the city of Salzburg. This former castle of the archbishops of Salzburg is the result of several centuries' development which began in the early feudal period. An advantageous terrain made possible the gradual development of the fortifications. The castle was enclosed by a wall protected by a large bailey that was particularly extensive on the east and south sides. The reconstruction of the oldest parts was effected between 1465 and 1519. The wall around the bailey is reinforced by towers of the most varied plans (rectangular, U-shaped, polygonal). Two irregularly shaped roundels, known as the upper and lower bastion towers, were built on the southern perimeter. In the 16th century the defensive capability of the castle was strengthened by the construction of an outermost eastern bailey with bastion towers. At the same time three gateways almost square in plan were built along the route into the castle from the north, and the north-eastern triangular-plan bastion tower was erected.

The famous castle of Hochosterwitz, standing on a solitary rocky hill, is one of the most remarkable sights in Carinthia. The castle proper was converted into a Renaissance mansion. Nonetheless the entire, virtually unique fortification system, designed as an outpost against the Turks, is redolent of the Middle Ages and hardly affected by occasional Italianate modifications such as quadrangular bastions. To the south-east the castle hill slopes very steeply away. At its foot stands a gateway giving access to a very large area with a steep slope on the northern side of the castle. Along the foot of this slope there are six more gateways. To the north-east there is a small projecting bailey defended by a tower. On the western side of the castle the big eighth gateway, the Landschaftstor, leads to another bailey, protected by a pair of towers below the ninth gateway, the Reisertor. From here the road climbs along the north-west side of the castle to the twelfth gateway, the Brückentor, giving access into the north bailey. The fourteenth gateway leads into the innermost bailey around the castle itself.

This brief description is far from exhausting the picturesque complexity of the castle plan. It can be assumed that the general system of fortification is late medieval in origin but redesigned during the Renaissance period between 1570 and 1586.

By contrast, the toll castle of Finstermünz, on the Engadin border of Tirol, is small, and attractive in a very different fashion. In the middle of a bridge across the River Inn stands a tower with a passageway through it; it corresponds with a tall, five-storey tower building on the right-hand bank of the river, adjoining a wall with a parapet walk dating from the reign of the Emperor Maximilian I (1493-1519). On top of a rock further north there is another tower known as Siegmundseck, after a Duke of Austria. The toll castle was built in the 1450s and extended under Maximilian I.

★

Bohemia was the most important country in Europe for the early development of fortification systems based on the use of, and resistance to, artillery. The armies of the Hussites—followers of the religious reformer Jan Hus, who engaged in an epic struggle to maintain Bohemian independence—were the first to use artillery in an organized fashion and on a large scale. It was in Bohemia that a new type of gun, the howitzer, originated; and the Hussites also devoted much attention to fortification problems. The fundamental change in the character of urban fortification began during the Hussite wars—namely the transfer of the principal line of defence from the main wall to an outer wall, closer to the enemy.

The process can be seen at work in the fortifications of the royal city of Čáslav, which figured prominently during the Hussite wars. The outer wall of the 13th century fortifications was strengthened on the north-east and south-east sides of the city with semicircular, rectangular and tetrahedral bastion towers, the latter with a sharp point facing outwards from which the defenders could enfilade an enemy mounting an assault on the walls. It is generally supposed that the tetrahedral bastion towers were built on the orders of the Hussite leader, Jan Žižka of Trocnov, while he was staying at Čáslav in 1422-23. They are the oldest wall bastion towers in Bohemia and Moravia, and the first examples of a fortification structure of bastion type.

Of even greater significance are the fortifications of Tábor, a city founded in 1420 as a direct result of the growth of the Hussite movement. Its main wall, about 6 metres high, was reinforced by many much higher, semicircular towers at irregular intervals (from 25 to 70 metres). However, from the very beginning the main line of defence was the outer wall, standing 10 to 15 metres in front of the main wall. As well as a roofed wooden gallery, it possessed several tall, elongated bastion towers with semicircular, triangular and, in one instance, bihedral ends; here we again encounter the sharp point of the bastion tower, hitherto found only in the fortifications of Čáslav. The walls were partly protected by a ditch and a rampart. The gate on the south-west side is still in existence. The eastern Prague Gate was protected by a polygonal barbican with extremely thick outside walls.

The main wall of Tábor can be considered a tradi-

175
Eltz, Germany. Built at the
end of the 15th to early 16th
century.

tional fortification work, but the bastion towers of
the outer wall demonstrate the innovatory skill of
the Hussites. Given the role played by Tábor in the
Hussite wars, the city's fortifications must have been
constructed in the very first years of its existence,
soon after 1420. The barbican was in place by 1451
at the latest.

A slab bearing the date 1434 tells us when the
outer fortifications of Velké Meziříčí, a castle in
southern Moravia, were completed. These consist of
a wall above a ditch with masonry revetment. The
wall is 4 metres thick and is reinforced by three
bastion towers of unusual design.

The Hussite system of fortification was widely
copied in the cities of Bohemia and Moravia, especially by the reign of George of Poděbrady (1458-71).
Both the Tábor bastion towers and the barbican
were frequently copied. The three-quarter-oval
barbican of the Žatec Gate in Kadaň is dated to
1458. The barbican of the Prague Gate at Slaný (no
longer in existence) was similar to that of Tábor,
dating from 1472. The west side of the leading
Hussite town of Žatec was reinforced in the same
year by three elongated bastion towers in the outer
wall with gun emplacements. Two had trihedral
ends; the other was semicircular. The towers were
equipped with keyhole loops for arquebuses and
large rectangular loops for guns. The curtain walls
were 100 metres long.

The almost intact outer fortifications of the royal
city of Kouřim must also be described. The outer
wall rises directly above the surrounding ditch, and

176
Halle an der Saale, Germany.
Plan of the castle. 1484-1503.
After Wäscher.

was reinforced by numerous bastion towers with mainly semicircular (but occasionally rectangular) ends. Several of the semicircular bastion towers have an elongated form comparable with those of Tábor. The curtain walls between the bastions are 40-60 metres long; the outer face of the ditch is protected by a substantial rampart. On the western side of the city in particular, the atmophere is still distinctly late medieval.

It is a significant tribute to the influence of Hussite techniques that 'Tábor' should have been the name chosen for the barbican (no longer extant) of the Vienna Gate at Znojmo, a strongly fortified city in southern Moravia. Three massive semicircular towers stood at its corners, and it was machicolated and enclosed by a wall of its own. The barbican was constructed in 1462.

Of uncertain date are the fortifications of the north side of Bechyně, a town to the south-west of Tábor. The main wall is reinforced at short intervals by open tetrahedral bastion towers with their points projecting outwards towards potential attackers. In front of the main wall there was a bailey and a ditch with a rampart. In type the north wall of Bechyně would seem to belong to the reign of George of Poděbrady (1458-71) at the latest; but a later dating

—to the last quarter of the 15th century—is also sometimes proposed. In any event it can be considered as the oldest known system of fortifications based on the bastion principle. Some scholars even state categorically that the bastioned fortification was invented by the Hussites.

An example of a newly fortified small town from the late Gothic period is Vimperk in south-west Bohemia. The charter of incorporation that licensed the construction of fortifications was issued in 1479. These consist of a single wall 140 centimetres thick, with embrasures, reinforced by tall, vaulted circular towers at irregular intervals. The towers are connected with the wall by vaulted bridges about 2 metres long. The defences on the northern side were supplemented by a separate ward comprising a thick-walled circular tower and a small, roughly oval yard enclosed by a wall and protected by a ditch.

Similar outworks, usually situated on top of a hill and dominating the approaches to castles and towns, were built to keep enemy artillery at a distance, out of range of vital spots within the main walls. Perhaps the most remarkable is the big south bastion tower at Český Šternberk, a castle in central Bohemia. It has a rounded end projecting into the field, and is said to have been built in about 1470.

It is characteristic of the late medieval period that powerful barons rather than kings should have taken the initiative in constructing fortifications. Second only to the Pernštejns was the western Bohemian family of Rýzmberk. It was they who built the monumental moated castle of Švihov, to the north of Klatovy in western Bohemia. Fortified between 1490 and about 1510, Švihov is undoubtedly one of the most remarkable moated castles in Europe. Ingenious engineering made it possible to flood large areas to the east, south-east and south of the castle, which stands in the rectangular bend of a mill race. The construction of the inner castle, with its compact plan, began in 1490. Its corners were reinforced by substantial U-plan bastion towers;

177
Tangermünde, Germany. The Neustadt Gate (outer face). About 1450.

178
Heidenreichstein, Austria. View of the castle from the north-east, with the massive residential tower in the foreground. 14th-15th centuries.

The first floor houses a vaulted casemate with niches containing loopholes.

Another type of fortification was the shield wall, an especially thick wall built to protect a castle on its most vulnerable side. At the end of the Gothic period shield walls attained unbelievable dimensions. One outstanding example was built in the late 15th century by the powerful, aristocratic Pernštejn family. The shield wall in their Moravian castle of Helfštejn (Přerov district) was 7-9 metres thick, 90 metres long and 12 metres high. It has two slightly projecting, rounded artillery bastion towers. Beyond the narrow courtyard lies a neck ditch separating it from a gateway dated 1480. This gives on to a large bailey enclosed by an outer wall with open, U-plan bastion towers equipped with keyhole loops. William of Pernštejn had the shield wall built some time after 1480.

179
Hohensalzburg, Austria.
Unusual view of the castle
from the north-east, with the
16th century triangular bastion
adjoining the medieval wall on
the right and the armoury
(partly Gothic) on the left.

180 ▶
Hochosterwitz, Austria. View
of the castle from the east
showing the complex
approach system with
numerous gateways. The late
Gothic castle was rebuilt and
extended in 1570-86.

they were higher than the wall, to which they had obviously been added later, after a change in the construction plan. Only the pentagonal eastern end of the chapel and the rectangular gateway tower project into the moat that surrounds the entire structure. The fortifications of the castle proper were extremely advanced, and a comparison between Švihov and most contemporary moated castles in western Europe reveals just how sophisticated it was.

The inner castle was entirely surrounded by the bailey. Its construction began in the west, evidently under a conservative-minded builder who reinforced the wall with two tall rectangular towers, one almost semicircular bastion tower and one circular tower near the south-west corner. The bailey was entered from the north through a rectangular tower. Because the western part of the bailey fortifications were built in a partly obsolete style, the Master of the King's Works, Benedict Ried, was called to Švihov in 1505. He is generally credited with the design of most of the now vanished outer fortifications, which are known from some remarkable documents and from archaeological investiga-

146

tion. The polygonal trace of the outer wall was strengthened at the angles by large artillery bastion towers, U-shaped in plan, open on the inside, and the same height as the wall. A small bastion tower stood roughly midway along the north curtain wall. The entire bailey was surrounded by a moat connected with the mill race.

Near Pardubice, his new residence in eastern

between two walls with loopholes. This road terminates at a second gateway leading to a minor bailey. Across a ditch stands a third gateway in a tower, giving access to a large lower ward with a well. On its north-east side there was a large three-quarter-circular roundel. Its outer wall was supported by a large embankment. It was equipped with gunposts, and culminated in a parapet walk with

Bohemia, William of Pernštejn built the castle of Kunětická Hora at about the same time as Švihov. The castle stands on top of a solitary hill, visible from a great distance. The strength of Kunětická Hora, due to its natural position, was considerably enhanced by a typical medieval device, namely the accumulation of obstacles along the main route into the castle. The earlier inner castle and western bailey were enclosed by a wall, interrupted in the east by a large U-shaped roundel.

The castle is entered from the north. The first gateway leads to a typical Pernštejn road enclosed

embrasures and loopholes. From the third gateway the road proceeds to a gateway in the wall along a bailey with a semicircular north bastion tower. A fifth gateway gave access to the sixth gateway, which at last led to the castle proper.

In the area in front of the north-east roundel there was a low wall running right down to a point below the south-east corner of the upper castle; another massive roundel stood there. A third roundel, in the south-west corner of the castle plan, was destroyed by quarrying.

The castle of Kunětická Hora is a Bohemian

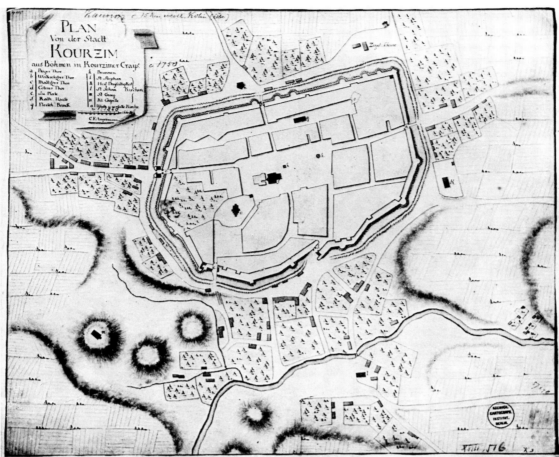

counterpart of the Hochosterwitz castle in Carinthia. However, it differs from the latter by introducing huge roundels largely made of earth, a development which represented a complete abandonment of the medieval fortification system, and one logically motivated by the relative weakness of masonry in the face of artillery fire. Effective defence of the castle naturally required a very large garrison. The castle was built to serve as refuge for the entire local population in the event of a Turkish raid, which seemed a real threat in the late 15th century.

In the 1480s the Master of the King's Works, Benedict Rieth, or Ried, began the construction of new fortifications at Prague Castle. The southern outer wall was strengthened with three artillery bastion towers. The approach to the east gateway was protected by a barbican (later dismantled). The defensive capability of the northern outer wall was increased by adding a parapet walk supported by a line of pillars. In front of a bend in the wall to the north-east, Ried built a circular bastion tower called Daliborka, which was linked to the outer bailey; the tower was finished in 1496. Further west, the closed, semicircular White Tower was added to the outer wall. Much later, in the mid-16th century, Mihulka,

181
Kouřim, Czechoslovakia. City plan; coloured drawing from about 1750. State Library, Berlin.

182
Bechyně, Czechoslovakia. Plan of the fortifications on the north side of the city, with a continous line of bastion towers. Second half of the 15th century.

the sturdy circular tower on the north side of the castle, was built.

The city of Budissin, or Bautzen, in Upper Lusatia, formed part of the Bohemian state until the Thirty Years' War of 1618-48. Its fortifications, dating from the 13th century, were greatly strengthened in the late Middle Ages. The entire fortification system is clearly shown in a 17th century engraving. The main line of defence was transferred from the principal to the outer wall, around which ran a ditch and a rampart. Circular bastion towers were built on the outer rampart slope; they were connected to the outer wall by necks walled on both sides. The gateways in the principal wall were de-signed after the Bohemian model, guarded by a tall tower on one side. In the outer bailey and the ditch, a roughly oblong gateway precinct linked up with the U-shaped barbican. In front of the rampart, bastion towers and barbicans stood yet another low wall. The fortifications of Budissin functioned in impressive fashion as a single, uniform defensive system.

The defended area included two churches and a castle with a bailey to the west. The south-west fortifications around St Michael's Church, right on the bank of the River Spree, included the Old Water Tower (Alte Wasserkunst). Substantial parts of the city fortifications have been preserved.

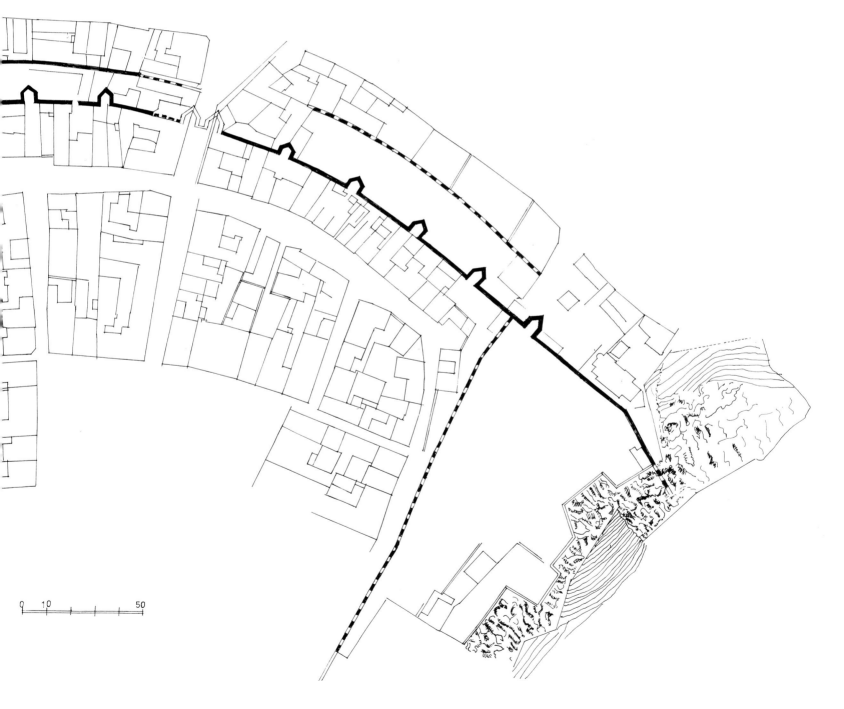

0 10   50

183
Helfštejn, Czechoslovakia.
Gateway with wall and bastion
tower. 1480.

184
Kunětická Hora,
Czechoslovakia. Plan of the
fortifications, built from 1491
onwards.

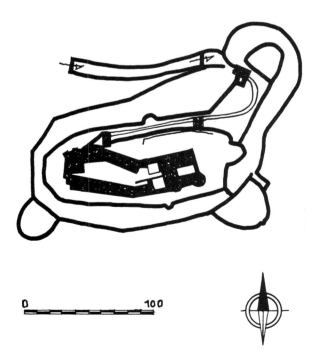

The Bohemian state also included Zhořelec or Görlitz. In front of the Reichenbach Gate a circular barbican, begun in 1490, still survives. It is 19 metres in diameter, and the thickness of its walls ranged from 1.7 to 4.5 metres. Its parapet walk was supported by corbels.

To sum up, the turbulent history of 15th century Bohemia led to important new developments in the art of fortification. One of the most significant was the shift to active defence, undertaken further forward and nearer the enemy. The building of rectangular bastion towers and the introduction of earth works in the late 15th century were also advanced procedures.

★

Different conditions prevailed in Slovakia, which was relatively untouched by the Hussite wars. Here a very important role was played by Sigismund, Holy Roman Emperor and King of Hungary, who was the Hussites' principal adversary.

The castle of Beckov (Trenčín district) occupies a very effective position on the very edge of a rocky

150

eminence above the River Váh, close to Slovakia's border with Moravia. Of medieval origin, it was practically rebuilt at the very beginning of the 15th century, although retaining its early Gothic tower. It is irregular in plan. To the east and south is a bailey enclosed by a wall continuously curved in outline. Further south lies a narrow hexagonal outermost bailey, reached through a tall gateway.

The early 15th century was also a period of intensive construction at the nearby royal castle of Trenčín, which King Sigismund took great pains to strengthen. Architecturally the castle was much improved, notably by the construction of the east hall and the chapel; but of far greater significance was the transformation of the castle into a very powerful fortress. A semi-oval bailey was built on the south side of the castle. Another large bailey was added in the north-east, extending to the banks of the River Váh. Both of its corners were reinforced with bastion towers; only the circular south-west tower, known as the Dungeon, survives. New gateways, and the building of city walls below the north-west side of the castle, further improved its defences.

The principal royal castle in Slovakia during the reign of Sigismund was at Bratislava (Pressburg). It was built in 1423-37 as both a palace and a

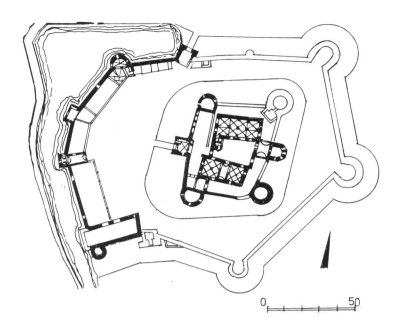

185
Švihov, Czechoslovakia. Plan of the moated castle. After Menclová.

186
Švihov, Czechoslovakia. View of the moated castle from the west. The moat and outer bailey fortifications are in the foreground, the gateway tower in the background. Construction of the castle began in 1490.

151

187
Bratislava (formerly
Pressburg), Czechoslovakia.
The castle was built in 1423-
37. In the foreground the wall
drops to a late Gothic gateway
in the east.

188 ▶
Spiš, Czechoslovakia. View
from the west, showing the
upper castle with its late 13th
century circular tower, the
upper bailey a little lower to
the left, and the large lower
bailey, built from 1442
onwards, to the right.

huge fortress. The nucleus of the castle was based on the 14th century rectangular layout. It stands in a dominating position at the westernmost end of the castle area. The west side of the trapezoidal royal hall also functions as a shield wall 7.5 metres thick and three storeys high. The north wall is 6 metres thick. In the south-west corner of the hall stands a rectangular tower with rusticated cladding, which is also used on the other corners of the building. There is a Gothic hall in the south wing. All that remains of the fortifications of the vast bailey are parts of the wall including two slightly elongated bastion towers with circular ends in the north and an imposing late Gothic gateway in the south-east corner.

Spiš Castle (Spišská Nová Ves district), spreading out over a large hill commanding the surrounding countryside, ranks among the most splendid of European ruins. Its compact, irregularly shaped nucleus, comprising buildings dating from the 13th and subsequent centuries, was protected from the 14th century onwards by a gradually expanding south-west bailey. However, the enormous expanse of the castle results from the creation of an outermost bailey from 1442 onwards, during a period when Spiš was garrisoned by Czech forces. It extends some 200 metres downhill from the upper bailey. Its south-east side is relatively straight; the north-west side is emphatically concave; the west side, determined by the rocky terrain, is extremely

irregular. The wall is reinforced with three towers, the middle one functioning as a gatehouse. With the departure of the Czechs in the mid-15th century, the outermost bailey ceased to function as such.

The fortifications of the Slovak city of Levoča (Spišská Nová Ves district) were strengthened in an interesting fashion during this period. Near the main wall, elongated bastions were constructed along the outer wall; they were variously rectangular, U-shaped and tetragonal in plan. The rectangular tower is the oldest; the most recent is the bastion tower with a trihedral pointed end.

The proximity of these bastion towers to the main wall was retrogressive, violating the principle that the line of defence should be moved as far as possible from the main wall, up to the outer wall. In Levoča this was probably impossible because the fortification forefield was too narrow. It seems very likely that the U-shaped and tetrahedral bastion towers originated under the influence of Hussite fortifications, and their construction should be back-dated to the years before the mid-15th century.

★

During this period the kingdom of Hungary extended as far as the Adriatic Sea, incorporating

152

parts of Dalmatia. This exposed it to Italian influences, apparent, for example, in the south barbican of Buda Castle, dating from about 1430; it took the form of an oval bastion tower with gun loopholes in its 5 metre thick wall, and was known, significantly, as the Torre d'Italia. At that time Hungary was directly in front of the Turkish line of march into Europe, and there were repeated wars between the two. For this reason the Hungarians' relative lack of well-prepared fortified positions (with the exception of Transylvania) is all the more curious. A particularly surprising omission is the lack of defences in depth, arranged to exploit the advantages of flanking fire; and this is true of both castles and cities.

The ruined castle of Varpalota, to the north-east of the town of Veszprém, was mainly 15th century in origin. It had a trapezoidal layout with thick outside walls, one side being segmentally convex. The corners were fortified with four towers.

In eastern Hungary, not far from the Romanian border, stand the ruins of the castle of Gyula. Oblong in plan, with a projecting tower, it was surrounded by outer fortifications of which only a corner roundel for cannon has survived.

The entrances to a number of castles were protected by low circular barbicans, representing the fortress's only projecting gun emplacement (examples: Nagyvázsony, Siklós).

A distinctive feature of Hungarian castle architecture is the survival of substantial residential towers almost down to the end of the Middle Ages. The most remarkable example is the great tower of the castle of Sárospatak, dating from the end of the 15th century; the interiors were radically redesigned during the Renaissance. The bartizans, initially situated in the four corners above the main cornice, distantly recall the design of Norman keeps. The number of closely spaced loopholes in the upper storeys emphasizes the tower's primary function as

a defensive retreat, obviously built in response to the Turkish threat. The outer fortifications were completely altered in the course of a major Renaissance reconstruction.

Southern Transylvania is a surprisingly exciting region for the student of castle architecture. Here, on the very frontiers of the Western Christian world, we encounter a quite distinctive cultural atmosphere and building tradition. The possibility of a Turkish invasion was realized even in the late 14th century, and led to the elaboration of a specifically Transylvanian and very efficient type of defence system based in fortified churches. These are known to have existed in Europe during the Romanesque period, but nowhere else were they as effective, successful and influential as in Transylvania; for some time, indeed, they were the region's chief means of defence.

The large church at Cristian, or Grossau, is enclosed by a wall, above which rise several projecting towers. In the south corner of the wall there is a separate octagonal bastion tower.

The fortified church at Biertan, or Birthälm, standing above the village, makes the same sort of impression as a strong castle. Along the main wall were tall towers projecting inwards. In front of the main wall were two more outer walls. Some vital points were interconnected by covered corridors.

The church at Vorumloc, or Wurmloch, was rebuilt as a fortified structure at the beginning of the 16th century. In the course of this reconstruction the portal of the west tower was filled in. The most impressive feature of the church is the modified presbytery; its buttresses, linked by means of high arcades, supported the defence gallery. In the background of the individual arcades, narrow loopholes can be observed. The church was enclosed by a wall with a pair of tower gateways and mural towers. The east gateway was built in 1501, which may be considered the date when the entire fortress was constructed. Inside the wall are closely spaced cells intended to hold supplies in the event of a siege.

The fortified church that makes the most vivid impact on the imagination is probably the one at Prejmer or Tartlau, which has an almost circular inner peripheral wall. The walls were as much as 5 metres thick and 12 metres high, equipped with loopholes, embrasures and machicolation, and reinforced by mural towers. The defences were further strengthened with a moat and a small outpost. The entrance, via a vaulted passageway, was sealed off by a portcullis. But most remarkable of all are the two-storey annexes inside the wall, containing store rooms and temporary dwellings to be used in times of danger and sieges; there were no less than 275 of these at Prejmer. The church's fortifications originated in the 15th century and were improved in the 16th.

The church fort at Harman (formerly Honigberg) is comparable with Prejmer in layout. Features that survive are the strong oval main wall with six towers projecting from its outer face.

At Cîlnic (formerly Kelling), in 1430 the villagers obtained possession of a small feudal castle with a residential tower, which they converted into a strong peasant fort with a triple wall.

The following two examples of 15th century Polish castles testify to the survival of the compact plan. Czersk, to the south of Warsaw, was built at the end of the 14th century, and a number of its older features are immediately obvious. The castle is brick-built and polygonal in plan. Its south-east corner is occupied by a circular tower; a second circular tower stands at the northern end of the western section of the wall, only slightly integrated into it. The castle's impressive silhouette is enhanced by a tall tower above the gateway near the north-east corner. Originally, however, both circular towers were the same height as the wall, as at Ciechanów (below). the tower above the gateway was erected later, in the mid-16th century. The hall stood on the north side of an extensive courtyard. No traces of other fortifications have survived.

The brick-built castle of Ciechanów, to the north of Warsaw, dates from about 1429. It has an extremely simple plan. The north-south oriented rectangle has a circular bastion tower in each of the south corners; they were originally the same height as the walls, but were later reconstructed. Between them was the south entrance to the castle. The hall stood along the north side of an extensive inner courtyard. Neither documents nor visual materials indicate the existence of outer fortifications, whose place was evidently taken by the river and the surrounding marshy territory.

The barbican of Cracow's Florian Gate is a splendid piece of architecture, dating from 1498-99, during the period when the city was the capital of Poland. The barbican is roughly circular in plan, and is equipped with loopholes for arquebuses and guns on three storeys. The wall rises to a top floor supported by corbels; its roof is decorated with small turrets. The barbican was built of brick, only the mouldings being of stone.

★

154

The Teutonic Knights never fully recovered after their devastating defeat at the battle of Grunwald (1410), but they took measures to slow down their decline. After the siege of Malbork in 1410, a bailey with gun bastion towers was constructed on the east and north sides. Further improvements followed in 1447-48, immediately before the Teutonic Knights went into an unmistakable decline. It was then that the Plauen-Bollwerk was built; this was a bastion tower filled with soil, with a platform for a gun emplacement on top—a quite remarkable structure to have been erected before the middle of the 15th century.

A fundamental change took place in the appearance and functional organization of the Order's castles during the later period of its existence. Perhaps the clearest example of this is furnished by the

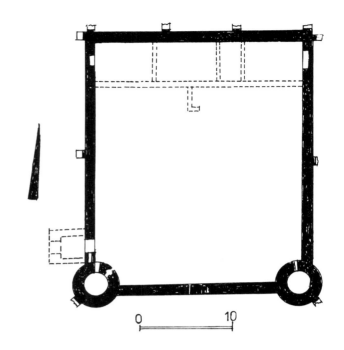

189
Ciechanów, Poland. Plan of the castle. Before 1430. After Guerquin.

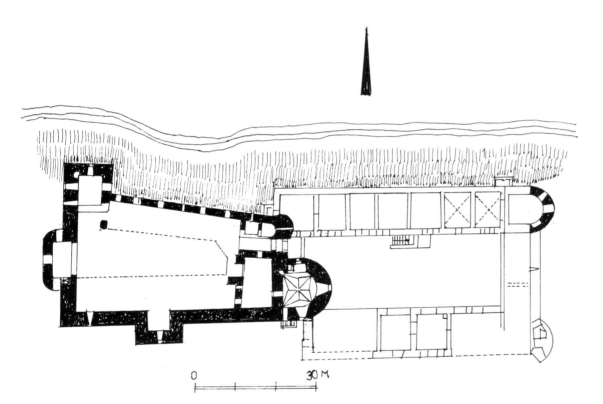

190
Bauska, Latvia. Plan of the castle founded in 1443 by the Teutonic Knights. After Tuulse.

ruins of Bauska, a border castle in southern Courland (now part of Latvia). Founded in 1443, the castle stands above the south bank of a river. An irregular, elongated trapezium in plan, it has massive peripheral walls on the south and west sides. Bauska was entered from the east, through a gateway guarded by a pair of U-plan bastion towers of unequal dimensions. The south tower has the character of a large gun roundel, but was used at the same time as a residential area. The north bastion tower, projecting slightly from the outer castle wall,

is much smaller. On the south side, a rectangular tower open on the inside projects from the face of the wall. A similar structure housing a chapel stands out above the river in the north-west corner of the castle. Also interesting is a shallow building with rounded corners projecting from the west side. The ruins of the east wing structures—the most important part of the courtyard—still survive, unlike the other (north and south) wings. The outer fortifications of the castle are conspicuous by their absence; they may have disappeared, or they may

155

never have been built because the garrison was not large enough to man them. The entire castle was designed for intensive defence by arquebus and cannon fire.

The Order's castle at Riga (Latvia) was badly damaged by a burgher revolt; after their defeat, the townspeople were forced to rebuilt it. Begun at the end of the 15th century, the work lasted until 1515. The devastated interiors were provided with late Gothic vaulting. From the point of view of fortification the most significant change was the construction of two powerful circular gun towers near the south and north corners of the castle plan, replacing a 14th century tower.

Examples of 15th century Scandinavian castles are relatively rare. In 1499 the small castle of Glimmingehus was built in southern Sweden, at that time under Danish rule. It has the character of a fortified house surrounded by a moat and equipped with battlemented walls. A Rheinish master-builder,

Adam von Düren, took part in the construction. Similar buildings, of no great military significance, are found in Norway, which was also at that time part of Denmark.

The castle of Bohus, not far from Göteborg, has an irregular rectangular plan with three corner roundels. It was built in the middle years of the 15th century.

The best example of a late Gothic Norwegian castle is furnished by the ruins of Steinvikholm, to the north of Trondheim. It is irregularly trapezoidal in plan, with irregular-plan gun roundels in two corners. The walls of the roundels are 5 metres thick; all the other walls are 4 metres thick.

The castle of Olofsborg, known to have been under construction in 1477, is a monumental example of Finnish fortification architecture. It is rectangular in plan, with conical towers which were subsequently heightened.

★

In Italy, although the Renaissance was well under way by 1400, the art of fortification remained faithful to the medieval formula for a good deal longer. However, this formula was modified substantially as rectangular corner towers were replaced by circular towers, which shortly afterwards became artillery roundels. In the last quarter of the 15th century the first examples of pointed bastions appeared. By then, urban fortifications of the traditional type were in decline.

At Mantua the Castello di Corte, also known as

higher than the curtain walls between them and projecting to a greater or lesser extent from the faces of the walls. At the top, all the way round, there are machicolations on corbels and a roofed parapet walk. The castle is strengthened by a bailey whose wall towers are small-scale versions of the main castle towers.

Torrechiara, in the province of Emilia, dates from 1448-60 and is a rectangular castle with four towers and machicolations on corbels very similar in design to Vignola. It is surrounded by a wall with a project-

◄ 191
Mantua, Italy. The Castello di Corte was completed in 1406.

192
Ravenna, Italy. The citadel, Rocca Brancaleone, built in 1457.

the Castello di San Giorgio, was completed by Bartolino Ploti in 1406. It is a classic castle of rectangular layout with four towers projecting from the corners. The towers and the curtains between them were equipped with typical Italian machicolations on simple, high corbels. The castle was surrounded by a moat.

The castle at Vignola, near Modena, was built towards the middle of the 15th century but nevertheless illustrates the standard older Italian style of castle architecture. The corners of its rectangular layout consist of rectangular towers of various sizes,

ing rectangular gateway in the north-east corner, similar in appearance to the towers. The entire castle is protected by a ditch.

Celano, in the Abruzzi Apennines to the east of Rome, is of the standard type, with rectangular corner towers the same height as the walls. The towers are topped by more slender extensions. This two-storey castle differs from others in possessing a two-storey arcade around the oblong inner courtyard. Some architectural details led one authority, Bodo Eberhardt, to include Celano among the castles of Frederick II, who did indeed capture and restore

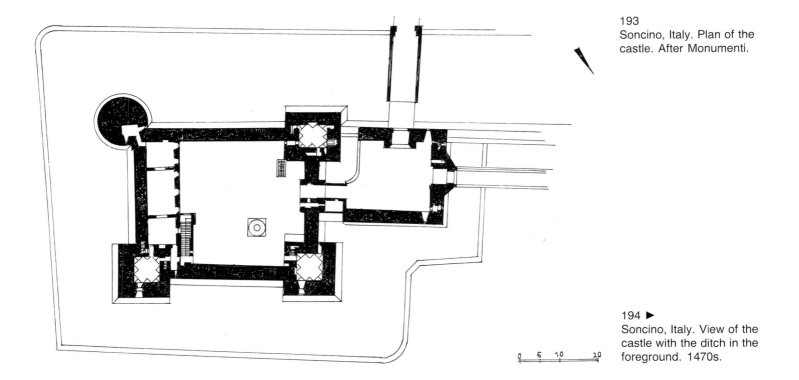

193
Soncino, Italy. Plan of the castle. After Monumenti.

194 ▶
Soncino, Italy. View of the castle with the ditch in the foreground. 1470s.

the town. However, the prevailing architectural appearance of the castle brings this early and undoubledly tempting attribution into question, and the first half of the 15th century is a more generally accepted dating. The castle is surrounded by a wall that bends several times; it is protected by small rectangular and U-plan bastion towers.

The huge Castello Sforzesco in Milan was built from 1450. It has an almost square plan with 200 metre sides. Two rectangular towers rise up from the north-west corner, while two circular towers touch the south-east corners. The inner and outer gateway buildings are highly decorative. The interior area is asymmetrically divided into the castle proper (in the north-west) and a bailey. The outer fortifications have disappeared.

At Castel Gavone, in Finalborgo in Liguria, the tall end tower was built after the middle of the 15th century; it presents the enemy with an edge, and is fully finished with diamond boss dressing. The tower is topped with a gallery on corbels.

In 1457 a citadel called Rocca Brancaleone was inserted into the north-east bend of the walls of Ravenna, at that time a Venetian possession. It consisted of a square with four circular corner towers, a south bailey and a roundel in the south-west corner.

Rocca Pia, a castle at Tivoli, a town near Rome, was built in 1460 by Pope Pius II. It is an impressive structure. In the corners of the walls stand circular towers with machicolations and battlements. One of the towers, much higher and more massive than the rest, is like a donjon and gives Rocca Pia the air of a medieval castle. A parapet walk on high corbels runs along the curtain, which is slightly lower than the towers.

The picturesque castle of Soncino, in Lombardy, dates from the 1470s. It has a circular south tower, the remaining towers being rectangular. Its standard Italian castle appearance is enlivened by the consistent use of swallow-tail merlons on the battlements, which also crown the bridge and the entrance gateway into the castle.

The rectangular castle in the Central Italian town of Volterra has circular roundels, the same height as the curtain walls, in its corners. There is a taller, free-standing circular tower in the centre of the courtyard.

A number of similar castles were built, for example, at Forlì to the north-west of Rimini, and at Imola near Bologna. They have a square plan with circular roundels in the corners. The central tower is situated in the centre of the plan at Imola and on its north-west side at Forlì.

The contemporaneous castle of Senigallia, on the Adriatic coast north of Ancona, has U-shaped roundels with extremely massive walls. It was built after 1474. The castle at nearby Pesaro, also on the coast, was built in 1474-1505 to a design by architect Luciano Laurano. It is surrounded by a ditch. The front walls of these castles are battered (slant downwards).

The fort of Sassocorvaro, to the north-west of Urbino, has an interesting ground plan. It was built

from 1474 onwards. In 1483 a famous Italian military engineer, Baccio Pontelli, designed a fort at Ostia, the former Roman port on the left bank of the River Tiber. Its central section is trapezoidal in plan. In the corners of the trapezium are two three-quarter-circular artillery roundels with massive walls. The entire shorter side of the central part opens into a massive, tetragonal, sharply pointed bastion slightly projecting to the left. The tall, massive circular tower in the centre of the bastion is a throwback to past principles of design, and the curtain walls and the roundels are still equipped with parapet walks on corbels and battlements. However, the fort was also provided with a very advanced feature in the form of underground listening galleries.

In spite of some backward-looking features, the fort at Ostia, completed in 1486, was the oldest Renaissance fortification work that directly anticipated 16th century developments.

In 1488 the foundation stone was laid of Sarzana, a fort to the east of Spezia. It was designed by two famous architects, the brothers Antonio and Giuliano da Sangallo. Sarzana was in most respects traditional in layout. In plan it is a rectangle, divided into two parts. Circular roundels stand against the walls (and at the same height) in the corners and in the centre of each long side. A substantial circular tower stands in the centre of the courtyard of the north-west section of the fort. In the south-west there was a bailey, later destroyed.

During his famous Italian campaign of 1494, Charles VIII of France showed an interest in the fort of Sarzana. Nevertheless Sarzanello, a stronghold built in 1493-94 on a hill above the town, is far more rewarding and also more progressive from a technical point of view. It has a somewhat irregular rhomboid plan consisting of two bastions of different dimensions. Both are triangular; the corners of the east bastion are extended by U-shaped projections, whereas the west has one corner slightly chamfered. A ditch surrounds and separates the bastions. A covered way was added at a later date.

Sarzanello anticipates the remarkable Italian fortresses of the 16th century. The fortified city of Civita Castellana was provided with bastions for its defence in 1494-97.

★

There were very interesting developments in the art of fortification across the Adriatic, in Dalmatia. The fall of Constantinople to the Turks in 1453 shook the entire Christian world, and had immediate repercussions on directly threatened places such as Dubrovnik. The walls of the city were gradually strengthened until they were 4-4.5 metres thick and 22 metres high. To defend the highest (north-west) bend of the wall, which was most exposed to a land attack, the Florentine architect Michelozzo Michelozzi designed a monumental U-plan tower with a parapet gallery on corbels and battlements; the tower, called Minceta, was built in 1461. It was protected by a mantle wall with three storeys of casemates. In the outer wall, low, open, semicircular bastion towers with an emphatically slanting outer face were built to protect the towers of the main wall. The fortifications of Lovryenats were also substantially improved during this period. In the 16th century Dubrovnik's defences were greatly strengthened once again.

Attractively sited on an artificial island, the Dalmatian town of Trogir was protected by a battlemented stone wall with higher rectangular towers. Parts of this 14th century system of fortifications are still in existence. From 1420 onwards, under Venetian rule and with the Turkish threat an ever-present reality, its defences were greatly strengthened.

In the north-west corner of the city, on its land side, stands a single low, substantial, circular tower with a parapet walk and machicolations on closely spaced corbels. On the opposite, south-west side, facing the sea, stands the stronghold of Camerlengo, a castle whose high walls are machicolated and battlemented. Towers rise up from the four corners. The tall polygonal tower in the south-west corner of the castle is extremely massy. The north-west tower has a rectangular plan; the plans of the other two are polygonal. The Venetian fortifications of Trogir probably date from the period following the mid-15th century.

The importance and exposed position of another Venetian possession, Korčula, prompted the grad-

195
Senigallia, Italy. View of the castle. After 1474.

196 ▶
Sassocorvaro, Italy. Plan of the fort built from 1474 onwards. After Volpe.

ual strengthening of its walls with massive towers and bastions. Three towers are still in existence, clad with dressed stone blocks and terminating in a parapet walk, machicolations on corbels, and battlements. The circular tower in the south-west corner of the walls dates from 1444; the other two were gun towers with a U-shaped plan, open on the city side, and were built in the 1480s. Moreover two low, distinctly cone-shaped stone roundels were built at the ends of the south wall and projecting beyond it. The west roundel, circular in plan, has survived down to the present day. The roundels are generally dated to about 1500, but the possibility that they are actually somewhat later cannot be entirely discounted.

A remarkable synthesis of European and Byzantine techniques can be seen in the superb citadel of Smederevo, a Serbian city near the confluence of the River Jezava and the Danube. It was built from 1428 onwards with the express consent of the Turks to defend the Serbs' Danubian border against the Hungarians. This situation was a curious one at a time when fear of the Turks was stimulating new

fortifications and new techniques throughout southeast and even in parts of Central Europe. And so although Smederevo actually falls just outside the 'European' framework of our study, it is included here because of its special interest.

The 'Major' Citadel is roughly triangular in plan, with the 'Minor' Citadel in its north corner. The relatively low wall with parapet walk and battlements is reinforced by battlemented towers; most are rectangular and at least partly open on the inside, but a few are semicircular and closed. On the most vulnerable south side there were mural towers at intervals of a mere 38 metres; the longest stretches of curtain wall were, naturally, on the Danube side.

✸

Spain and Portugal have distinctive characters because of their histories as outposts of Christendom. This was true of the arts, and also of architecture —particularly secular architecture, most effectively represented by castles. It is in these that the originality and independence of Iberian architects can best be observed. However, it is important to realize that the Spanish state was created only in the last years of the 15th century. In 1469 Isabella of Castile married Ferdinand of Aragon, and the link between the two states proved permanent. Then in 1492 the last Moorish stronghold, the Kingdom of Granada, fell, and Spain emerged with more or less her present boundaries. In the same year Columbus reached the New World, and within a few decades Spain and Portugal had become the first modern colonial powers. Portugal's ambitions were centred exclusively on her colonies and maritime trade, but Spain also became a European great power. However, this development belongs to the next, 16th century chapter.

Aragon's cultural development was linked with that of the South of France and the Mediterranean. It developed side by side with the very different culture of Castile, situated between south-west France and the Islamic world of the Moors, which was the more distinctively Spanish; its most striking feature was the significance attributed to form in all areas of human expression. All of these influences also appeared in the construction and design of castles. A notable characteristic was the way in which the structures were of necessity adapted to the terrain, a respect in which Iberian castles differed somewhat from those of France and Italy. In late medieval Spanish castles, this characteristic gradually became less pronounced, to the benefit of a

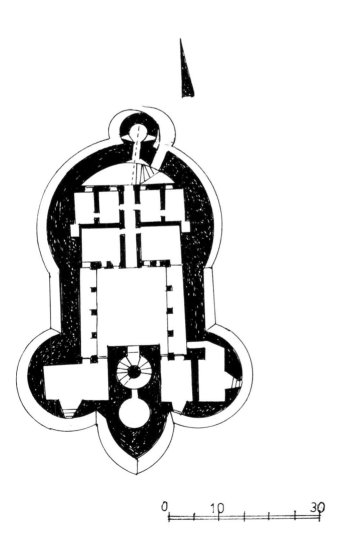

0   10   30

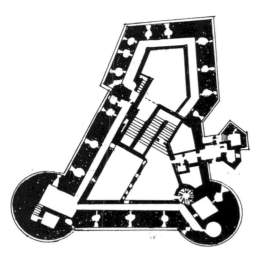

197
Ostia, Italy. Plan of the fort.
After Monumenti.

198
Ostia, Italy. Aerial view of the
fort with the circular tower in
the centre of the bastion on
the right. The design of the
fort was prepared before
1483.

more formal design of both plan and elevation, which finally became the universal norm and culminated in the famous castle of Coca.

Another characteristic of Spanish castle-building was a certain conservatism, visible in the survival of massive residential towers as vital elements right down to the end of the Middle Ages. In this respect Spanish castles differed considerably from those of other Mediterranean countries.

The rectangular castle layout was also employed until the end of the Middle Ages. Outer fortifications were extremely important, along with arrangements to allow the effective use of flanking fire. However, a comprehensive assessment of Iberian castles can only be made after they have been described in summary analytical fashion. Unfortunately the dating of some castles remains problematic.

The 15th century may be called the golden age of Spanish castles, since they were built at a time when Spain was becoming steadily more powerful, and they served symbolic as well as military functions.

The construction of the magnificent castle of Manzanares el Real (New Castile) is dated to about 1435. It was square in plan, with three circular towers and a large rectangular residential tower.

In 1440 a Master Fernano de Cerreno is mentioned in connection with the renovation of Castillo de la Motta in Medina del Campo (Valladolid). This brick-built castle consists of a trapezoidal area with a massive residential tower in the north corner of the inner wall. On the top storey, small bartizans are grouped on each side of the corners, supported by corbels. At the top of the tower there were machicolations and battlements on corbels. The inner wall is reinforced by slightly higher rectangular towers and two small semicircular turrets on corbels. The castle is surrounded by a bailey, around which runs an outer wall with semicircular mural towers. Two such towers guard the southern gateway. Along the curtains of the inner and outer walls are small semicircular turrets supported by corbels. The walls are battlemented, with a loophole in the centre of each

that it must have been newly built during the latter part of the reign of King John II (1406-54).

Formal refinement is also the keynote of the late Gothic castle of Fuensaldaña, in the province of Valladolid. The centre of its layout is occupied by a rectangular donjon. At its corners stand slender circular towers which rise from the ground to a height slightly above that of the main mass; each terminates with a parapet walk and corbels, battlements and a pair of small pyramids. In appearance this recalls the swallow-tail battlements of Italian castles. At the centre of the donjon's north side is a small turret supported by a corbel about two thirds of the way up the wall. In the middle of each of its shorter sides the donjon is met by the low wall of a bailey to the south of the castle. The wall has circular corner towers standing at the same height and furnished with decorative battlements. In the middle of the short side the motif of the projecting miniature turret, used on the donjon, is repeated. Fuensaldaña was built in about the middle of the 15th century.

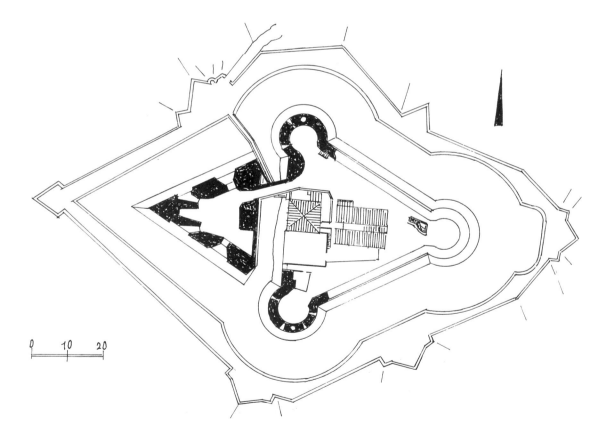

199
Sarzanello, Italy. Plan of a stronghold built in 1493-94. After Monumenti.

merlon. The outer wall has also a lower walkway with keyhole loops. The castle is surrounded by a ditch excavated from the rock. The main part of the castle has been dated to the 13th century, but in its entirety it gives such an impression of perfect unity

Palazuelos (Guadalajara) is a reduced version of Fuensaldaña. At its heart is a bulky square-plan donjon with typical round bartizans in the corners. Its north-east side adjoins a square walled ward with a U-plan tower at each east corner. The castle is

200
Dubrovnik, Yugoslavia. View
of the harbour with
fortifications. The corner
bastion dates from 1647-57.

201
Dubrovnik, Yugoslavia.
Fortifications on the north side
of the city, with the Mincheta
tower (1461) in the
background and the main
wall, reinforced after the fall of
Constantinople, on the left
(1453-55).

164

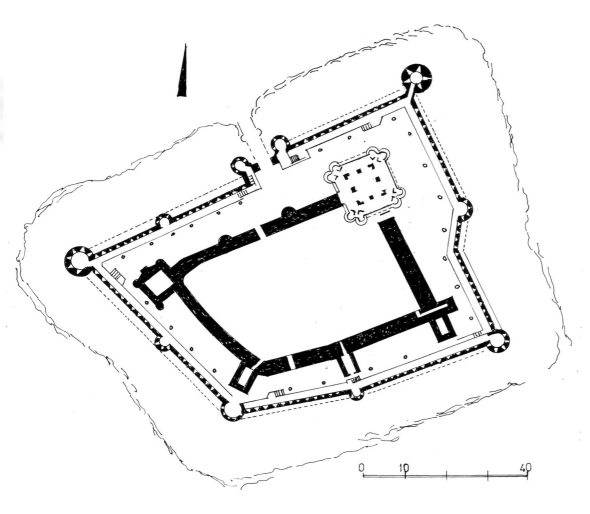

202
Castillo de la Mota, Spain.
Schematic plan of the castle.
After Ebhardt.

0   10   40

203
Castillo de la Mota, Spain.
View of the castle with the
outer wall and the gateway in
the foreground. First half of
the 15th century.

surrounded by a bailey whose outer wall has pronounced rounded corners. The gateway, guarded by a circular tower on either side, stands on the south side.

Guadamur, to the south-west of Toledo, was built between 1444 and 1462. It has a rectangular plan with three solid three-quarter-circular corner tow-

tury. In the corners of its square plan stand three circular towers only slightly higher than the wall. The fourth corner is occupied by a taller, larger, circular residential tower. The castle is protected by a bailey; its outer wall, the lower part battered down to the ditch, is reinforced by one semicircular and three U-plan corner bastion towers. The gateway is

ers. A fourth tower stands near the west corner. In the centres of the curtain wall there are bastion towers with two projecting faces coming to a point. The castle is protected by an outer wall with low U-plan bastion towers in the corners and pointed, projecting bastion towers in the centres of the curtain walls. The entire castle is surrounded by a ditch.

The magnificent ruins of the castle of Pioz (Guadalajara) can probably be dated to the mid-15th cen-

guarded by a tower on each side; both are almost circular in plan.

Jadraque (Guadalajara) stands on the top of a bare hill that dominates its environs. The plan, although derived from the rectangular model, was adapted to the terrain and is notably elongated. The battlemented wall is reinforced by taller, mostly U-shaped towers open on the inside. In the north-east are some remains of masonry, perhaps from a

◄ 204
Coca, Spain. The most
splendid of all Spain's
medieval castles, built before
1473 by the Archbishop of
Seville.

205
Rhodes. Engraved view of the
principal city of the Greek
island in 1493, from Schedel's
Chronicle.

wall. On the south-east side stands the lower castle, with a gateway framed by a rectangular and a U-shaped tower. The castle was protected by a bailey, the trace of whose walls follows the curvature of the towers, which thereby function (except on the north-east side) as low roundels. The main castle probably dates from the 15th century.

The most splendid of all Spain's medieval fortresses is Coca, near Segovia, which is breathtaking even in its ruinous state. It was built by the Archbishop of Seville, Alonso de Fonseca (d. 1473). The layout of Coca is a perfect formal composition, already quite alien to the Middle Ages. Its almost square nucleus is reinforced by polygonal corner towers of the same height as the curtain walls between them. In the fourth corner stands a taller, massive, slightly oblong tower. The curtains of the main wall are divided by semicircular turrets. The castle is surrounded by a wide bailey, around which runs a lower wall, divided in similar fashion to the main wall: there are slightly higher polygonal towers in the corners, while the curtains are divided in the middle by robust towers, and at the sides by slighter bartizans on corbels. The gateway is guarded by a pair of semicircular towers.

The design of the castle and that of the outer bailey are identical. The mass of their corner towers is largely concealed in their upper regions by the closely spaced groups of solid pentagonal bartizans on corbels. The main tower has more robust round turrets on its corners and, between the corners on each side, a pair of smaller bartizans.

The outer wall is equipped with keyhole and gun loopholes. Both the main and the outer walls have a parapet walk, high battlements and small pyramids. There are loops below the closely spaced merlons, which are decorated with fluting.

Only fragments survive from the stepped masonry of what was an outermost wall along the line of the ditch, with roundels and bastion towers. The castle was built of brick, and the masonry was not plastered.

Coca gives the impression of being an unreal, fairy-tale castle, never really intended to endure a siege. Formally speaking, the castle combines the functional features of a medieval castle with the requirements of architectural effectiveness; but the individual defensive elements were subordinated to such an extent that their original function was overlaid and they were probably incapable of fulfilling it.

The standard type of Castilian castle was also found in the south of Spain. The ruins of Villena

(Murcia) have a compact layout with a bulky rectangular residential tower in the south-west corner; at its top are corner bartizans and, between them on each side, central turrets on corbels. All the other corners of the castle are reinforced by small circular towers. There is also a lower outer wall, strengthened by small bastion towers of semicircular or U-shaped plan.

One of the oldest Spanish castles built to cope with artillery is Grajal de Campos (Palencia). It is square in plan, with U-shaped roundels in all four corners; they are of the same height as the inner walls, the lower parts of which form large scarps. Each roundel has a parapet walk on corbels with battlements and embrasures. The towers are equipped with oblong loopholes for firearms. The curtain walls too are battlemented. Their gun loopholes, horizontal and oblong, are somewhat lower than their equivalents on the towers. The upper part of the curtain walls is punctuated by small, typically Spanish, semicircular turrets projecting on corbels from the wall face; there are also battlements with embrasures.

Of Portuguese castles, Alvito is particularly worthy of mention. It has a square plan and circular corner towers, a design that is employed repeatedly in Spain and Italy.

In the Iberian peninsula the 15th century was a period of exceptional importance. Many new castles were built, and many more were reconstructed. A distinctively Spanish style of castle architecture emerged, emphasizing maximum regularity of plan and exhibiting an increasing tendency towards the articulation of individual architectural elements. Only the basic square plan, more or less modified according to the circumstances, was taken over from earlier times. However, the aesthetic character of Spanish castles is entirely indigenous, showing no traces of foreign influence but redolent of the national culture.

Between 1291 and 1522 the island of Rhodes was the headquarters of the Knights of St John after their expulsion from the Holy Land. It therefore became an enclave of Western Christian culture in an area otherwise dominated by the Byzantine Greek and Turkish cultures. The late Gothic fortifications of the city of Rhodes date from 1476-1505, although additional improvements were made until the final siege. They rank among the finest examples of late medieval military architecture, and constitute a unique application of the techniques of the late Italian school.

The main wall was built in front of an earlier city wall. It was strengthened with rectangular towers, supplemented in the next building phase with strong U-plan towers. The northernmost gateway on the vulnerable west side, the Porte d'Amboise, is flanked by a pair of rounded towers and is typically French; most of the other gateways are tower gatehouses. Along the west and south sides of the city the wall was reinforced at its angles by powerful bastions. Two of them, close to St George's Gate and the Coschino Gate, are tetrahedral, with a sharp point; the other two are pentagonal. Apart from the stretch running along the line of the harbour, Rhodes's wall was protected by a gigantic ditch excavated from the rock, 30-45 metres wide and 16-20 metres deep. On the side facing the anticipated line of attack there was an earth rampart, 14 metres wide, on which stood an outer wall with battlements and loopholes.

In 1530 the Order was expelled from Rhodes and transferred its headquarters to Malta, which was to become the scene of another epic siege.

★

To sum up, the 15th century was a period of radical change almost from its beginning, thanks to the increasing importance of artillery in siege warfare. These changes appeared first in Bohemia. The principal line of defence was shifted from the main wall to the outer wall, now reinforced by bastion towers. Some bastion towers began to be designed with tetrahedral plans, with a point thrusting out towards the attackers; at Bechyně, all of them took this form, a fact that supports the theory that the bastion system was a Bohemian invention. Barbicans came into general use, and gun roundels appeared. The Ottoman Turkish thrust deep into Europe caused alarm throughout Christendom and stimulated intensive building and rebuilding of fortifications in Hungary, Germany, and other Central and East European territories.

In the later 15th century, Italy was in the forefront of new developments, while the castle architecture of the Iberian peninsula assumed an extraordinary and quite distinctive character of its own.

The Sixteenth Century

The 16th century was one of the most turbulent periods in European history. The unity of the Western Church was shattered. Knowledge was vastly expanded as a result of the voyages to America and India at the end of the 15th century, which also brought great wealth to Europe. The spread of the Renaissance disseminated new styles, a new culture and new ideas. Under the Emperor Charles V (1516-56) the Habsburg dynasty dominated the Continent, and it gradually became apparent that their true power-base was Spain, which under Charles's successor, Philip II (1556-98), came close to establishing a European hegemony.

Although divided, Italy too played a major role. Spain and Italy were both deeply involved in the struggle against the Turks in the Mediterranean, its milestones being the siege of Malta (1565) and the naval battle of Lepanto (1571), which halted the Turks' apparently irresistible advance in the region. This Mediterranean community was also manifested in the construction of fortifications. It was in Italy, too, that the techniques were devised which strengthened the defences of Central Europe against the Turkish advance. Moreover, whereas Spanish engineers were mainly employed in the Spanish Empire, their Italian counterparts were active almost everywhere in Europe. In France, however, Italian fortification techniques were not widely adopted, despite the fact that the French kings Charles VIII (1483-98), Louis XII (1498-1515) and François I (1515-47) all undertook campaigns in the Italian peninsula.

Italian fortification techniques were so influential throughout the 16th century that there is a case for describing Italy first of all in this chapter. However, in the long run this change of order would be confusing, so here we confine ourselves to a few general remarks that will clarify developments in other

206
Schematic representation of the fortification systems of the Old Italian and Neo-Italian schools of fortification. After Stankiewicz.

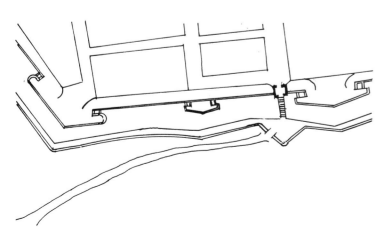

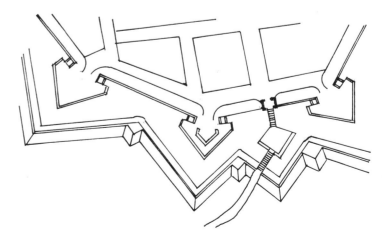

169

countries, which we shall then describe before we embark on a detailed treatment of Italy itself.

The main principle of the Old Italian fortification school was the use of very shallow bastions, their faces meeting at an obtuse angle. The short flanks were recessed, forming 'retired flanks' behind lobe-like features called orillons. Behind them were artillery casemates to enfilade the ditch. Along the outer edge of the ditch ran a covered way protected by an earth rampart 7-8 feet high.

The Neo-Italian fortification system greatly improved the defences both in depth and by heightening individual elements. The faces of bastions now met at an acute angle. Above them there were cavaliers founded on top of the bastions. The much shorter curtain walls were protected by tri- or tetrahedral ravelins built in the ditch. The course of the covered way was interrupted by places of arms.

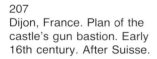

In 16th century France, castles began to give way to Renaissance mansions and palaces, although they continued to be described as châteaux. It is extremely difficult to distinguish between the two, since the plans of French Renaissance châteaux, with their powerful roundels, derived directly from late medieval castles. Arguably the genuine military function of such châteaux did not survive the reign of Louis XII (1498-1515); for example, in the magnificent early Renaissance Loire château of Azay le Rideau (Indre et Loire), built from 1518 onwards, the fortification elements are entirely non-functional in character.

The castle at Dijon (Côte d'Or), the former capital of Burgundy, no longer exists. It was reinforced in the early 16th century by a massive circular roundel with vaulted casemates and artillery loop-

207
Dijon, France. Plan of the castle's gun bastion. Early 16th century. After Suisse.

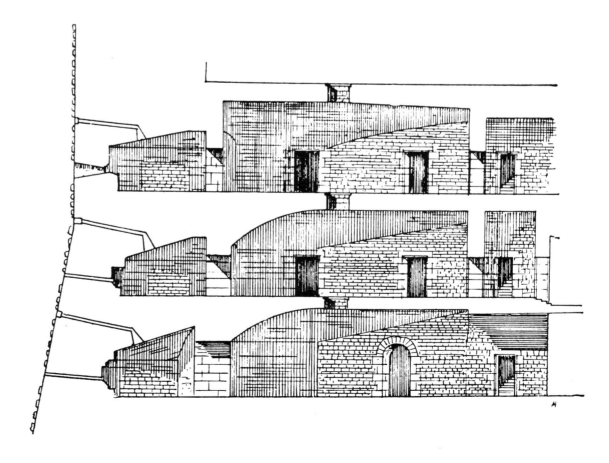

208
Dijon, France. Section of the castle bastion. After Suisse.

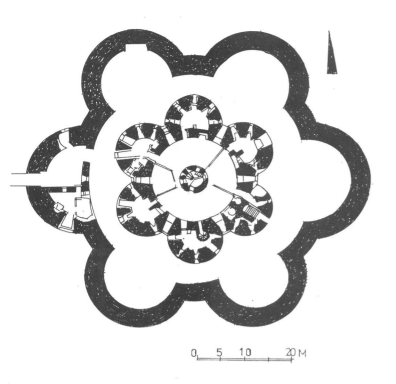

0 5 10   20 M

209
Deal Castle, England. Plan of
the castle. After O'Neil.

210
Deal Castle, England. Coastal
fort built by Henry VIII, with
the ditch controlled by the
bastions in the foreground,
and the central tower in the
background. About 1540.

211
Berwick-upon-Tweed,
England. Plan of the fortified
city. Construction of the
fortifications began in 1558.
After MacIvor.

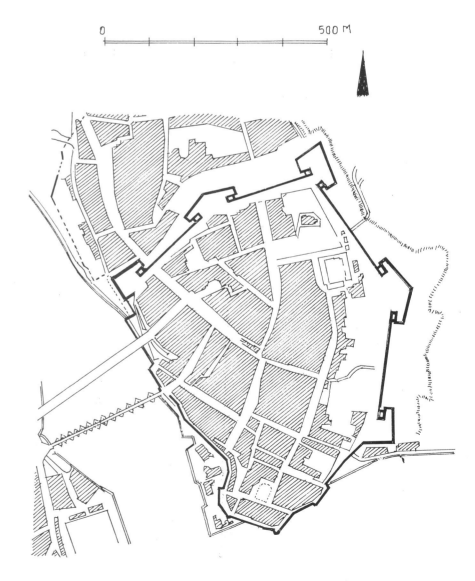

0   500 M

holes. At about the same time the fortifications of
the town of Langres (Haute Marne), originally
Roman, were improved after having been modified
in the previous century. The structures dating from
the early 16th century included the semicircular St
John's Tower on the north side of the castle. In 1517
its south-west corner was reinforced by a gun
roundel, circular in plan, with a rear annex known as
the Navarra Tower. The low, battered outer walls,
clad with rough-dressed stone blocks, are equipped
with gun loops on two superimposed levels. The
walls are up to 6 metres thick.

In 1524 the legendary Château d'If (famous for,
among other things, its role in Alexandre Dumas's
novel *The Count of Monte Cristo*) was built by order
of François I on an island outside Marseille for the
protection of the city.

Interesting French examples of Neo-Italian fortifications included a little town in the south-west of
France which has dwindled to a village. The stone
fortifications of Brouage (Charente Inférieure)
were built during the reign of Charles IX (1560-74).
The curtain walls were short (the west curtain was a
good deal longer than the rest), being interrupted by
four corner and three midspan tetrahedral bastions.
The west and the south-west curtains were further
protected by ravelins. The fort was the work of
d'Argencourt.

212
Schaffhausen, Switzerland. The Munot, a roundel defending the city, with walls meeting it on both sides. Built in 1564-85.

214 ▶
Willemstad, Netherlands. Aerial view of the fort founded in 1583.

213
Antwerp, Belgium. Plan of the citadel, built in 1567 but no longer extant. After Romaňák.

Between 1558 and 1574 the castle at the frontier city of Sedan (Ardennes) was substantially fortified by the addition of four corner bastions; the wall thickness was increased to 7 metres.

The construction of fortifications in France intensified after the end of the religious wars under Henri IV (1589-1610), who was preparing to challenge Habsburg supremacy in Europe. The foremost French engineer of the day, Errard de Bar le Duc, fortified Sedan and other cities, and also rebuilt the defences of Laon, a fine example of a medieval fortified city.

Despite all this activity, however, it is clear that no distinctive French system of fortifications was devised during the 16th century.

From this point of view, developments in England were much more interesting. A new situation was created by the schism with the Church of Rome under Henry VIII (1509-47), which alienated the Habsburg Emperor Charles V and left England dangerously isolated. Henry reacted promptly to the danger by ordering the construction of a chain of

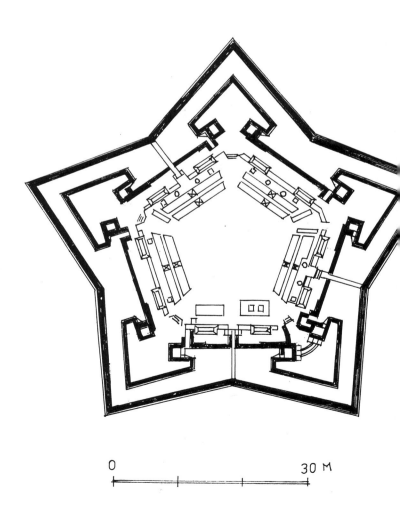

0   30 M

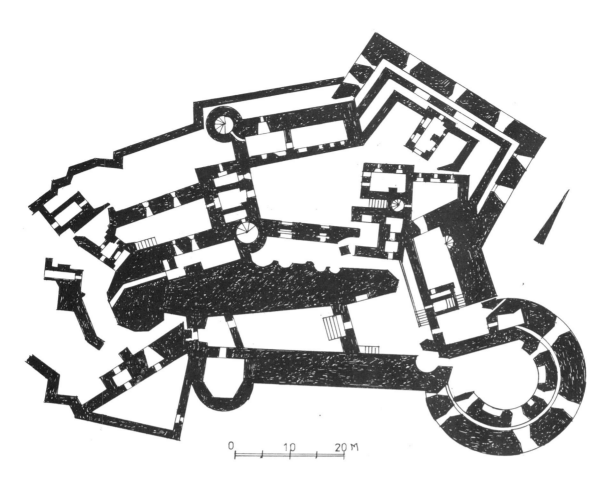

215
Nannstein, Germany. Plan of the castle. The extremely thick wall is of medieval origin; the roundel was built about 1550, the north-east bastion in 1590. After Dehio-Gall.

0   10   20 M

216
Rheinfels, Germany. Ruins of a medieval castle converted into a fort from 1568 onwards.

174

forts along the south coast; and these constitute an independent, specifically English style of fortification.

On the east coast of Kent, Henry built the forts of Deal, Walmer and Sandown (since destroyed). The plans of both surviving forts are entirely regular. The layout of Walmer Castle is the simpler of the two. In the centre there is a massive roundel, circular in plan, which opens on to four U-plan gun bastions which are surrounded by a ditch.

The most remarkable of the Henrican forts is Deal, which has survived almost intact over more than four centuries. The layout comprises a symmetrical, concentric, six-lobed plan. The centre consists of a bulky circular roundel surrounded by six U-shaped, only slightly lower gun bastions which engross almost the entire periphery, leaving only a few metres of wall between them. A sort of dry ditch serves as a communication corridor to the outer defences, which consist of six low U-plan bastion towers. Their vertical walls rise up from the bottom of a wide ditch; the trace of its counterscarp follows the periphery of the fort. This stronghold with 145 loopholes for firearms, so beautifully regular in plan, was undoubtedly influenced by contemporary depictions of forts in the 'ideal cities' it was fashionable to design. Deal Castle was built in about 1540.

Further west along the coast, Henry built Camber Castle in Sussex; Calshot Castle and Hurst Castle on the Solent in Hampshire; Portland Castle on the Isle

217
Weissenburg, Germany. The outer fortifications of the Elling Gate (Ellinger Tor) of 1520, with the 14th century inner gateway in the background.

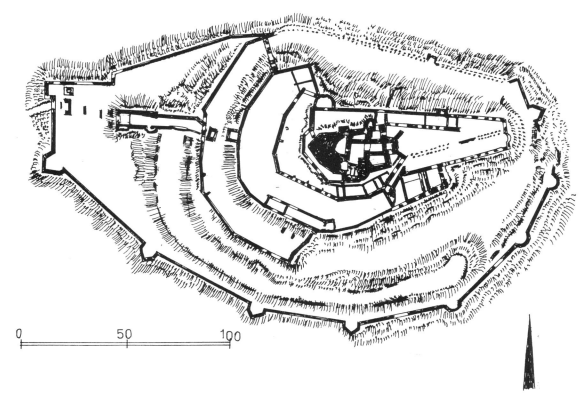

218
Landsee, Austria. Schematic plan of the castle ruins. The outer fortifications date from the 16th and 17th centuries. After Dehio.

175

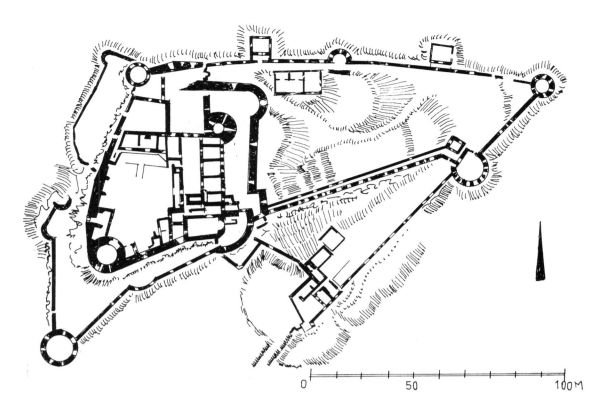

219
Hohenwerfen, Austria. Plan of the castle as reconstructed in 1530-85. After Dehio.

221 ▶
Heinfels, Austria. Castle ruins. The outer wall with roundels dates from the 16th century, the main part with the residential tower from the 13th-14th centuries.

220
Kufstein, Austria. Castle converted into a fort in 1518-22.

of Portland, Dorset; and St Mawes and Pendennis in Cornwall.

The fort of St Mawes has a three-lobed plan with a central tower, while Pendennis has a solitary tower encircled by a wall; it was surrounded by bastions somewhat later, during the reign of Queen Elizabeth (1558-1603).

Henry VIII's forts were designed as part of a uniform overall strategy for defending the south coast. The indigenous architectural design of the individual buildings is a notable achievement, since they are also perfectly suited to their respective functions. Unlike medieval castles, the Henrican forts are exclusively military in character, without residential or symbolic functions; in other words they are not in the strict sense castles, but forts. At the same time their appearance is very impressive from a purely architectural point of view. Their designers included Sir Richard Lee, Edward Ryngley and a Bohemian, Stephan von Haschenperk.

The only Renaissance fortified city in Great Britain is Berwick-upon-Tweed, on the border between England and Scotland. It was built by Sir Richard Lee with advice from an Italian designer, Giovanni Portinari. Construction began in 1558 and, with an interruption, was completed at the end of the 1560s. These fortifications were of the Old Italian type. They did not enclose the entire city as defined by its medieval walls, but excluded roughly its northern third. They consisted of five bastions

linked by curtain walls, longer in the east than in the north-west. The bastions were equipped with orillons with casemates, varying in layout. The south-west and the south-east bastions are simple; both central bastions are characterized by extraordinarily long faces meeting at an obtuse angle, and short flanks. The north bastion (the Brass Bastion) has a pronounced asymmetrical form with unequal faces and an acute angle at the apex. The battered walls are clad with rough-dressed stone blocks and rise up from a wide ditch.

Carisbrooke Castle, near Newport on the Isle of Wight, originated in the 12th century as a Norman keep standing on a low elevation; but its chief significance lies in its 16th century fortifications. It is slightly oblong in plan, and is enclosed by a bat-tlemented wall with reinforced corners. In two corners tetrahedral bastion towers were erected to the same height as the wall. The castle was separated by a ditch from the outer fortification system with low tetrahedral bastions whose faces met at a near right angle. This fortification system protected a much larger area than that bounded by the walls of the upper castle. It was built in 1597-1600 by Federigo Gianibelli, after a design by Peers.

★

The most interesting 16th century Swiss fortification is the Munot, which stands on a headland over the Rhine. It was built in 1564-85 in the immediate vicinity of Schaffhausen and consists of a substantial

222
Feldkirch, Austria. The fort of Schattenburg. The residential tower with a hall dates from the 13th century, the outer fortifications from the 16th.

circular roundel connected to the city wall. A ramp leads from the casemates on ground floor level to the upper artillery terrace.

★

In Flanders the most interesting early 16th century fortifications were erected at the great port of Antwerp, then at the height of its prosperity. The older fortifications of the city had disappeared by this time, but they were replaced in 1540 by defences in the Old Italian manner, built by a German named Franz. A more progressive design, however, was that of the citadel erected in 1567 on the south side of the city. It was the work of the foremost Italian fortification engineer, Francesco Paciotto from Urbino. It too no longer exists, but it is known to have had a regular pentagonal plan with bastions; these were equipped with orillons, and had short flanks and long faces meeting at an only slightly obtuse angle. The shape of the bastions represented a considerable improvement on those of the Old Italian school. The interior of the citadel was laid out on the schematic plan of an ideal city, with the buildings arranged symmetrically and parallel with the curtain walls. The citadel was surrounded by a star trace ditch.

Flanders was part of the far-flung Habsburg empire under Charles V, after which it passed to Philip II of Spain. From 1565 resistance to Spanish rule gathered strength, and after a long struggle the Dutch won their independence. (The southernmost part of Flanders, roughly corresponding to modern Belgium, remained a Habsburg possession.)

These events inevitably prompted the rebellious Dutch to build new forts to protect their territory from Spanish counter-attacks. In 1583 the principal Dutch leader, William the Silent, founded the fort of Willemstad in the Rhine delta, on the south bank of the Waal. Its fortification system has been preserved intact, and it makes an impressive appearance in the flat landscape, rising immediately above the water level of a great river.

Willemstad was directly influenced by the Old Italian school, with various improvements in details. It comprises a seven-pointed star with tetrahedral bastions in the corners; the outer sides meet mostly at acute angles and have no orillons. Access from the east was controlled by a single ravelin, built on the outside of a wide moat protecting the fort along its whole periphery and interrupted by dykes only on the river side. A narrow canal passes through the north curtain wall, giving access to a small river port. A covered way follows the course of the moat, beginning at the dykes; the base of the covered way is protected by a narrow outer moat. The city has a perfectly regular orthogonal plan with a square at its centre. The fortifications had no masonry revetment, which speeded up the construction work and reduced its cost. The oldest use of earth fortifications—which were to be of major importance in the future—is generally supposed to have been a Dutch innovation, introduced at Breda in 1533; but, as we shall see in due course, the earthworks at Pardubice in eastern Bohemia are of much earlier date.

★

In Germany and the rest of Central Europe, late medieval fortification techniques prevailed for most of the early 16th century.

Neuscharfeneck is a castle in the Palatinate, not far from the northern boundary of Alsace; it dates from the early 13th century but was rebuilt mainly in the second half of the 15th century. It is remarkable for its gigantic, purely medieval east shield wall, standing above a ditch; the wall is 58 metres long and 12 metres thick and was designed for artillery warfare. It probably dates from the period after 1530.

The north-west shield wall of the very old Palatine castle of Madenburg, not far from Landau, was probably also built in the early 16th century. The wall is 5 metres thick and runs to a sharp bihedral point in the middle, which is equipped as a gun emplacement.

The fortifications of another castle in the Palatinate, Ebernburg near Alsenz, were also improved in the 16th century. The massive wall around the castle proper is strengthened on the south-east side by two light U-plan gun roundels.

Finally there is the powerful castle of Nannstein, not far from Kaiserslautern, which has an exceptionally thick wall on the south-east side of the lower castle. In its east corner stands a huge circular gun roundel. In 1590 a large rectangular bastion with closely spaced loops was built on the north side of the castle.

All these castles in the Palatinate are now in ruins.

Hardenburg, near the town of Bad Dürkheim in the Palatinate, is a mighty castle whose fortifications were designed to cope with artillery warfare by generally medieval means. Its east bailey is protected by a shield wall with a circular tower at each end. The extent of the castle above it is determined by three roundels dating from the early 16th century. The huge north-east roundel, called the Stout Tower (Dicker Turm), is clad with partly rough-dressed stone blocks. The south-west roundel is also of gigantic dimensions. And, dating from about 1550, the remarkable West Bastion comprises a magnificent multistorey gun tower standing high above the ditch.

In 1527 the outer fortifications of the city of Nuremberg were strengthened in two places by circular bastion towers. From 1568 onwards the castle of Rheinfels was converted into an up-to-date fortress.

The citadel of Jülich, in the Rhineland, is an exceptional work, built in 1547 to the designs of the Italian architect Alessandro Pasqualini. It has a regular plan with four bastions with orillons. The citadel also acquired ravelins, with a fully developed covered way including places of arms, erected in front of the curtain walls; but it is questionable

223
Radkersburg, Austria. Part of the wall with bastions. The city's fortifications were erected from 1545 onwards.

whether they were already there in the second half of the 16th century.

The outer fortifications of Heldrungen (Halle) were constructed between 1512 and 1517. They consisted of a rampart with earth corner bastions, protected by a wide moat. This was only slightly later than the use of earth ramparts at Pardubice in Bohemia.

The outworks of the Elling Gate (Ellinger Tor), at Weissenburg in Bavaria, date from 1520. They are among the most attractive examples of fortification architecture in Germany.

★

The Turkish threat to Christendom culminated in the first siege of Vienna in 1529, after the shattering defeat and death of Louis II (1516-26), King of Bohemia and Hungary, at the battle of Mohacs in 1526.

As a result, the Austrian dominions of the Habsburgs, together with Slovakia, parts of Hungary, Croatia and Dalmatia, suddenly became the embattled front line of Christian Europe. The consequences quickly became apparent in a surge of castle-building, which at first took a purely medieval form.

The eastern marshes of the Austrian Habsburg dominions became known as the Burgenland— literally the land of castles, a name singularly appropriate to their history in the 16th and 17th centuries.

The most powerful castle in the Burgenland, dominating the surrounding countryside from the top of a hill, was Landsee, which was Romanesque in origin. The main castle area, narrowing sharply towards the east, is surrounded on the west and south sides by a narrow bailey of irregular oval plan. There was also another, outermost bailey.

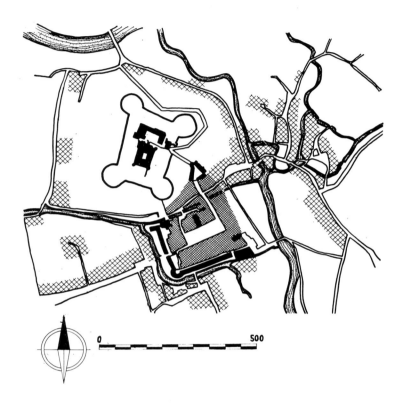

224
Pardubice, Czechoslovakia. Schematic plan of the city, the castle and fortifications, from a survey of 1839.

226 ▶
Pernštejn, Czechoslovakia. The main castle with adjoining tower. Reconstructed in the late 15th and early 16th centuries.

225
Pardubice, Czechoslovakia. Earth roundel with an outer wall. The fortifications were completed in 1511.

181

In the 16th and 17th centuries the castle fortifications were strengthened on the west side by an extremely complex system of ditches and ramparts. The outer wall rises from the bottom of the inner ditch, which runs along the entire south side of the castle and also turns to the north. In the west it is separated by a massive rampart from the wide, irregularly trapezoidal outer ditch. Along its outer face there is another wall, strengthened with tetrahedral pointed bastions, which originally surrounded the entire castle hill. The first gateway into the castle stands in the western part of this wall, and three more gateways had to be negotiated before it was possible to enter the western, outermost bailey.

Standing on level terrain, the castle of Roggendorf, at Pöggstall in Lower Austria, underwent a complex development. The more or less rectangular main castle was enclosed by a bailey which was in turn enclosed by an outermost bailey. Beyond these there was a ditch and a rampart with rounded corners. The most interesting fortification feature is a substantial three-storey south gun roundel, almost circular in plan (50 metres in diameter), outside the south ditch. It in fact functioned as a barbican protecting the south gateway; originally it had two entrances and was surrounded by a ditch. Beyond the rampart there is an outworks near the south-east end of the castle, terminating in a U-plan bastion tower. The principal period of improvement in the fortifications was the 16th century.

The castle of Hohenwerfen in Salzburg is documented as being in existence as early as 1077. It stands in a magnificent Alpine landscape, controlling the gorge of the River Salzach. Despite its Romanesque and Gothic past, the general appearance of the castle was determined by a major reconstruction that took place between 1530 and 1585. On its east side, an oblong bailey was added with a circular bastion tower at its furthest point. The north wall was reinforced by three bastion towers, two rectangular and one semicircular. Along the south side of the bailey a long roofed stairway runs up from the second or inner gateway to the upper castle. This gateway, guarded by a strong U-shaped gun roundel to the south-east, connects the bailey with an outworks below its south wall. On the south-west side of the outworks stands the first or outer gateway, controlled by a segmental bastion tower in the south-east corner of the upper castle. In the south-west corner of the west bailey there is a circular tower. The circular tower at the north end of this bailey, and the tower in the north-east corner of the hall, also date from the 16th century.

The general character of the fortifications at Hohenwerfen castle is still late medieval. This is all the more interesting because the castle stood near one of the main routes along which Italian culture was carried into northern Europe.

The defences of Heinfels in South Tirol were strengthened by the addition of a large eastern bailey of somewhat irregular trapezoidal shape, and a narrow bailey around three sides of the castle. The three corners and the long sides of the castle layout are reinforced by small semicircular bastion towers and four U-shaped bastion towers and roundels, probably dating from the early 16th century.

After being captured by the Emperor Maximilian I in 1504, the castle of Kufstein on the Tirol-Bavarian border was converted into a powerful fort. Between 1518 and 1522, on the site of the Gothic castle, Michael Zeller built a massive gun tower with walls 5-7 metres thick, known as the Imperial Tower. At the same time the two massive roundels in the northern and southern corners of the castle were reconstructed, along with the small circular tower in the west angle of the wall. Along the south side there is a bailey that was repeatedly reconstructed.

The nearby castle above the town of Rattenberg, in the valley of the River Inn, was also rebuilt for Maximilian I by Michael Zeller. Between 1503 and 1521 it was converted into a strong late Gothic fortress. The castle consists of two parts on different levels, the entirety being an irregular oval in plan. It was strengthened by three strong circular gun roundels. A circular tower stands in front of the gateway on the north-west side of the castle. The inner south wall of the older northern part of the castle and the walls of the upper castle are supplemented with small, mostly U-plan bastion towers. The fortifications of the town were also reconstructed, probably at the same time.

The forts of Rattenberg and Kufstein represent the last attempts to apply medieval fortification techniques to the new situation created by the rapid development of artillery.

The Gothic castle of Schattenburg, above the town of Feldkirch, in the Vorarlberg, was also converted into a fort during the 16th century. On the north-east side of the oblong, compact main castle area there is a trapezoidal outworks with a small bastion tower. From there the access road climbs between two walls to the upper castle, guarded by a pair of U-shaped roundels in the bends of the outer wall.

The Turkish threat prompted the fortification of endangered cities. One such is Radkersburg in Styria, which was fortified by the Italian engineer

Domenico Allio over several decades from 1545. The surviving features include parts of the walls, the ditch, and tetrahedral, mostly asymmetrical bastions whose outer faces meet at right angles or, less frequently, obtuse angles.

Except at Radkersburg, engineers in this region continued to place their faith in the medieval method of protecting strongholds against artillery by increasing the thickness of stone walls, particularly of gun towers. A significant shift of the defences towards the enemy was really only achieved at Landsee in the Burgenland. It is curious that the principal line of defence in both of Maximilian's Bavarian castles, Kufstein and Rattenberg, should have been concentrated in the castle proper.

★

In the early 16th century, Bohemia was in the forefront of new developments in fortification techniques. The monarchy played a less positive role in this period, the initiative being taken by the two great aristocratic families, the Pernštejns and the Rýzmbers. During the dramatic decades when the Turkish threat seemed most acute, extraordinary efforts were made by these magnates to create effective fortifications.

At the end of the 15th century, Pardubice in eastern Bohemia became the principal residence of William of Pernštejn, whom we have already encountered as the builder of Kunětická Hora. The site of this town, in the level country near the confluence of the River Labe and its tributary the Chrudimka, meant that specially designed fortifications were needed.

227
Rabí, Czechoslovakia. View of the castle. Its nucleus, with the big tower, dates from the 14th century, the reconstruction and extension from the 15th. The monumental outer defences were constructed from about the 1520s.

The castle of Pardubice, irregularly oblong in plan, was surrounded by massive earth ramparts with slanting scarps. In the four corners, U-shaped roundels were built, again of earth; at some 70 metres across, they were exceptionally large. The use of masonry was restricted to a low wall with loopholes which ran round the foot of the roundels and curtain walls. The earth fortifications rose only

228
Litoměřice, Czechoslovakia. Gun bastion of the 1513 city fortifications, in front of the Long Gate (no longer extant) with the late 14th century main wall in the background.

slightly above the level of the very large moat that encircled the entire castle; its narrowest part was in the south-east, on the city side, but to the west it attained a width of 60 metres. The low outer wall is known from the oldest picture of Pardubice, by Willenberg, which dates from 1602.

At Pardubice, the system applied to the large roundels at nearby Kunětická Hora was developed much further. In fact the compactly laid out castle was a unique fort at the time of its construction. Its fortification system, completed in 1511, heralds a new age in which the techniques of the Middle Ages were quickly to become obsolete. It was followed by the construction of outer fortifications for the small city of Pardubice; these were of similar design but diminutive by comparison with the castle. The castle was connected with the town by a trihedral outworks completed in 1515. The entire system, including the outworks, has been preserved to the present day.

William of Pernštejn also acquired the Tovačov estate in Moravia, and it was undoubtedly he who set on foot the new fortifications of the castle of Tovačov (Přerov district), which are identical with those of Pardubice. The irregular rhomboid of the castle is surrounded by earth ramparts with four bastions. The extensive bailey, narrowing to the west, was similarly fortified.

The two Pernštejn fortifications were based on the same principles as fortifications in the Netherlands. They developed in a similar environment, a flat terrain with an abundance of water. Constructing earth ramparts had significant advantages, since it was cheap as well as swiftly executed in times of danger (the advance of the Spanish against the Dutch, or the Turks against Bohemia or Moravia). However, the Pernštejn fortifications proved to be of European rather than local significance, representing an important preliminary stage in the emergence of the bastion system.

One of the visually most impressive Bohemian castles was Pernštejn (Žďár nad Sázavou district), the main seat of the great family. The complex outline of the castle, with a number of oriels, a parapet walk on corbels and the tower, makes a very picturesque impression. The main work of reconstruction was accomplished in the late 15th and early 16th centuries.

The entrance to the oblong, rather narrow north bailey was guarded by a barbican in the form of an asymmetrical bastion tower; its outer wall, of irregular curvature, is 5.5 metres thick. Beyond the ditch, towards the north, there is another bailey.

The Rýzmberk fortifications of southern Bohemia were always constructed of stone. The family's noblest project was the castle of Švihov, but the most monumental impression is created by Rabí (Klatovy district). This castle underwent an extremely complex development which began in the 14th century. The most intensive phase of construction was the last quarter of the 15th century, when the outer wall with mostly U-plan gun roundels was erected. The thickness of the walls varied considerably from a minimum of 2 metres to 5 metres on one of the roundels. The work was obviously carried out in haste, as a response to the Turkish victory at Mohacs, and was probably discontinued after the arrival of the news that the Turks had retreated from Vienna (1529); financial pressures were also important in bringing about this decision. The construction of the outer fortifications stopped on the east side of the castle with the big tower; the bailey there was only shielded by a wall. The splendid late Gothic fort was never completed.

The Moravian border castle of Mikulov (Břeclav district) occupies an extensive area on a rocky hill to the west of the town of Mikulov. Its defences were substantially improved in the second quarter of the

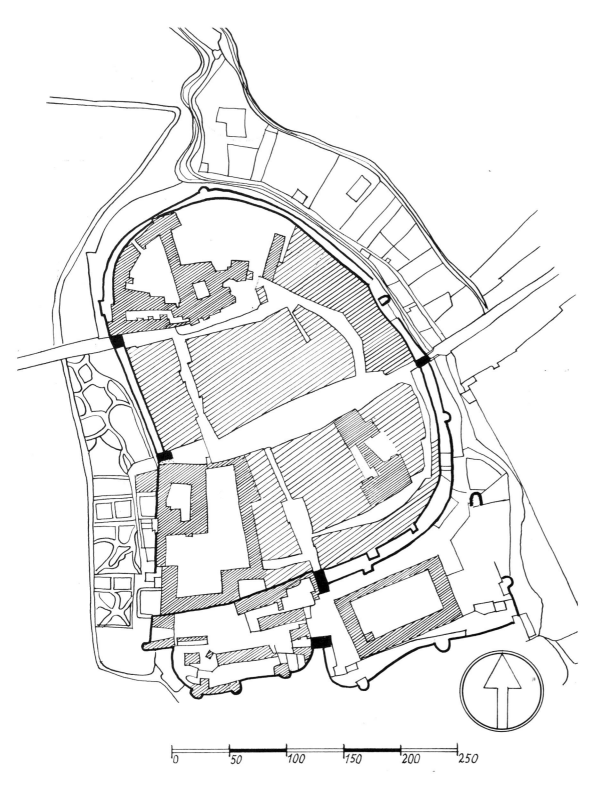

229
Třeboň, Czechoslovakia. Town plan, showing the fortifications according to a survey of 1827. The outer fortifications along the south side date from about 1525-27.

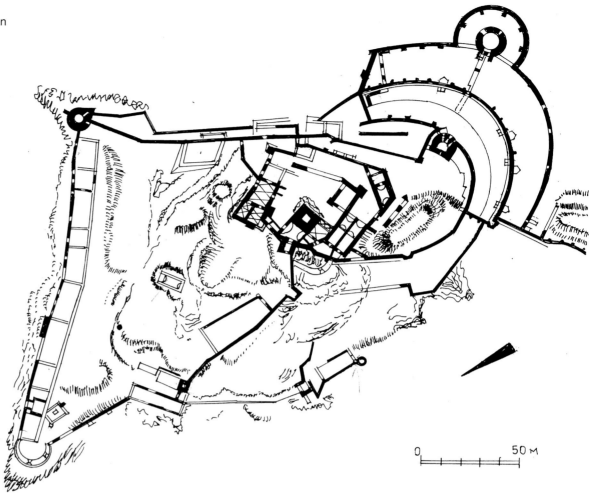

230
Trenčín, Czechoslovakia. Plan of the castle. Work on its defences culminated in the massive fortification of its south side in the 1510s and early 1520s. After Menclová.

0   50 M

231
Červený Kameň, Czechoslovakia. View of the castle from 1537.

16th century, when four sturdy, elongated gun bastions with circular ends were built.

At the beginning of the 16th century, the shift of defensive focus from the main wall to the outer wall was far from complete. Consequently several more important cities began to construct new walls, usually at a distance of some 30 metres from the original outer wall. As a rule this new wall was built on a rampart.

A good example of this development is the town of Litoměřice in northern Bohemia. In 1513 a new on the south side, some 70-100 metres in front of the existing walls. It consists of a wall of irregular trace which curves round towards the north, running as far as the somewhat recessed Nové Hrady Gate. The wall is reinforced by low, closely spaced semicircular gun bastion towers, reached from the town via vaulted passages in the rampart of the older fortification. In front of the wall there was a wide ditch, on the outside of which stood more bastion towers, later buried in a dyke.

In about 1530, construction of fortifications

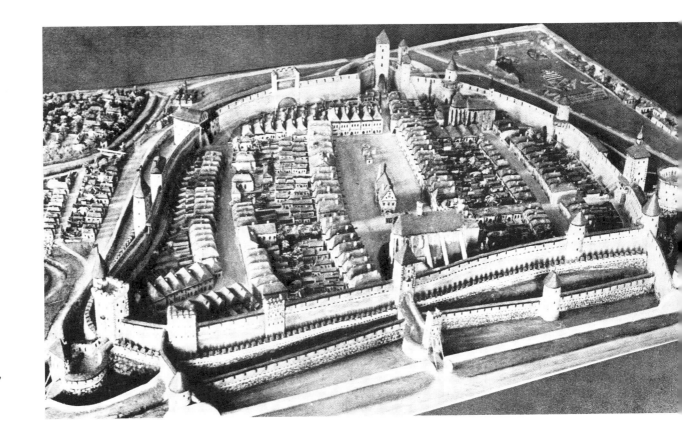

232
Bardejov, Czechoslovakia. Model of the Slovakian town, with its 14th-16th century fortifications, seen from the north.

outer wall was erected on the north and east sides of the city, which were not protected by the natural configuration of the ground. It was reinforced by semicircular bastion towers; higher, semicircular closed gun roundels were built only in a few angles of the wall that were particularly exposed to enemy attack. An outer ditch was dug in front of the wall. Comparable measures to bring forward the line of defence were undertaken in a number of other cities.

Třeboň, a charming small town in southern Bohemia, is fully enclosed by walls. It can be entered through only three gateways. In about 1525-27 Štěpánek Netolický built an outer defence system came to a temporary halt in Bohemia and Moravia. By this time castles had ceased to be viable as defensive structures, although they often retained important symbolic functions; and cities had ceased to be able to withstand artillery. Thus the era of Renaissance and Baroque forts began. However, these were not built in Bohemia and Moravia, but closer to the front line held against the Turks.

In Slovakia, the finest new fortification system was built on the southern, most vulnerable side of Trenčín Castle; even today, when it lies in ruins, its monumentality and originality of concept cannot fail to impress. In the exposed part of the newly modified south bailey, a U-shaped gun bastion was

233
Komárno, Czechoslovakia.
Contemporary engraving of
the Turks besieging the fort in
1594.

erected; on its north-eastern side there was a gun emplacement. Beyond the outer wall, with its emphatically concave trace, lay another bailey, surrounded by an inner ditch. This was separated from the deeper outer ditch (almost 20 metres wide) by a wall almost 18 metres high and 2.5 metres thick, with a firing gallery. Almost in the centre of its outer edge stood a circular tower surrounded by a shallower ditch whose trace was U-shaped; it was linked to the major outer ditch. The entire fortification system was organized in concave parallel lines. Built in the 1510s and early 1520s, Trenčín was unlike anything then known in Central Europe. Its construction was not inspired by any particular threat from the Turks, but was an act of political ambition.

The fortification system incorporating roundels developed widely in Slovakia. Later the roundels were to become non-functional, purely architectural features in late Renaissance and Baroque castles.

The fortifications of the former monastery at Bzovík (Zvolen district) were built after 1526. In the corners of the almost square plan are four large, vaulted U-plan gun roundels.

In 1537 the castle of Červený Kameň (near Bratislava) was built for the Fuggers of Augsburg, the international financiers whose dealings affected the course of European politics. Červený Kameň is an elongated rectangle in plan, its corners widening into four gun roundels; three are oval, one is U-

shaped. All round the castle ran a ditch and a high rampart which entirely concealed the buildings from view.

The best fortified of Slovak cities at the end of the Middle Ages was Bardejov. In the late 14th century it was protected by a main wall with a narrow bailey, an outer wall, a ditch and a rampart. In the 15th and early 16th centuries the defences were greatly strengthened by the addition of bastion towers to the main wall, and later by the construction of a new wall, with bastion towers on the north side, beyond the ditch. Barbicans were erected in front of the gateways.

Although much of the fabric has vanished, it is still possible to visualize Bardejov's fortifications. As well as several towers from earlier times, the monumental bastion towers of the final phase of construction are still partly extant, along with the round barbicans of the Upper and Lower Gates to the south and north-east of the town. Most of the bastion towers terminate in a semicircle. The Major Bastion on the south-east side of the city has an elongated form. A surprising feature is the addition of late Gothic bastion towers to the main wall, evidently because the narrow bailey had no great value as a fortification. The dating of the final phase of construction has not been determined with absolute certainty, but most of the work had probably been completed by the 1530s.

In response to the Turkish advance, intensive fortification work was undertaken in southern

Slovakia, where a number of leading Italian engineers were employed. Consequently Slovakia was among the few countries in which new Renaissance forts were built during the latter part of the 16th century. The fall of Buda (1541) made it urgently necessary to construct forts along the new frontier with the Turks. The fact that the Habsburgs ruled in Lombardy (Milan) facilitated the employment of Italian engineers, who were summoned to Vienna and instructed to design and forts in Slovakia.

Most attention was concentrated on Komárno, a town in an exposed position above the confluence of the Danube and the Váh. The Old Fort, built from 1543 and completed after 1550, stood right at the point where the rivers met; it was separated from the town by a deep ditch linking the two riverbeds. The plan of the fort was adapted to the terrain. It was rectangular, with two sharp tetrahedral bastions with orillons; one bastion was in the west, the other in the north corner. The west bastion housed the gateway. The south corner is reinforced with another bastion with orillons, of lesser depth and asymmetric plan. In the north-east the bastion is replaced by an irregular projecting platform. An elongated bihedral bastion with a sharp point completes the plan.

The identity of the engineer responsible for Komárno is not known; Decio, G. F. Testa and Castaldo have all been suggested. At Komárno a somewhat improved version of the Old Italian system of fortification was employed; the Old Fort, dating from the 1540s, was probably the first example of the employment of the pure bastion system outside the Mediterranean.

In 1578-88 the brothers Giulio and Ottavio Baldigara built the fort of Nové Zámky, which was demolished as early as 1724-25. Here the angles of a regular hexagon were reinforced by tetrahedral bastions with sharp points, connected to curtain walls by short necks with artillery casemates, so that all bastions were provided with orillons. Small observation turrets were attached to both the bastions and the curtains (in midspan).

The fort was entered by two gateways. It was surrounded by a moat 20 metres wide and 9 metres deep, as well as receiving partial extra protection from a surrounding bog.

The fort had neither ravelins nor a covered way; it belonged to the Old Italian school, with an improved, elongated bastion plan. By the 1580s its fortifications were already obsolete, so its speedy capture when the Turks attacked it in 1663 was hardly surprising.

★

In Hungary the increasing need for fortifications capable of resisting the Turks manifested itself in

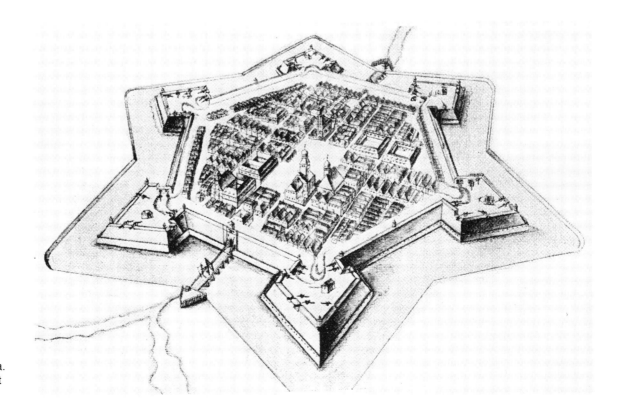

234
Nové Zámky, Czechoslovakia.
Drawing showing the fort as it
was in 1578-88. After Gerö.

189

improvements in the defences of medieval castles and cities and, on a far smaller scale, in the construction of new forts. The circular barbican of the castle of Siklós was built in the earlier part of the 16th century.

In 1537 Alessandro de Vedano began to modernize the fortifications of the castle above the town of Eger in northern Hungary; the town itself was subsequently fortified in 1573-83 by Ottavio Baldigara, who constructed a system of bastions.

The castle and the town of Sárospatak were fortified with a single wall; it was defended by bastions of various shapes (the majority tetrahedral) in the Old Italian style. The fortifications were constructed surprisingly early, between 1534 and 1541.

The fort of Szigetvár dates from 1543. At the four

235
Siklós, Hungary. The castle barbican, built in the early part of the 16th century; note the Baroque portal and the bridge across the ditch.

236
Sarvár, Hungary. Walls and bastions built around the castle at the end of the 16th century.

corners of its irregular trapezoidal layout were polygonal bastions, only one of them with a sharp point. The fortifications were surrounded by a ditch.

In 1562 the Italian engineer Pietro Ferrabosco prepared plans for new fortifications at the town of Györ, and in 1564-65 he personally directed their construction. The result was a fort right on the banks of the Danube. Curiously enough, Fer-

Hungarian fortifications of the 16th century, constructed under the eyes of Europe, represent a major effort designed to contain the Turks. It is interesting to note, however, that they remained faithful to the principles of the Old Italian school.

★

237
Gripsholm, Sweden. The castle was built from 1537.

rabosco used the Old Italian system at Györ. He mainly built shallow bastions with orillons, the bastion faces meeting at an obtuse angle; only two corner bastions meet at an acute angle. The fort was surrounded by a moat.

The pentagonal nucleus of the castle at Sarvár, with its massive rectangular entrance tower projecting from the wall face, dates from the 16th century. At the end of the century it was surrounded by an elongated pentagon of stone wall with a battered scarp and five tetrahedral bastions of equal height. The fortifications, built between 1588 and 1615, were designed by Donato Grazioli. The entire fort was protected by a ditch, originally filled with water.

In Poland, the town of Zamość was founded in 1580; the royal master builder, Bernardo Morando of Padua, saw to its construction. Only a few remains of his fortifications survive. The star-shaped layout, with shallow corner bastions of the Old Italian type with prominent orillons, was extended in the west by a large castle with corner bastions. The curtain walls between the bastions were of unequal length. The bastion on the northern boundary between the city and the castle has a very elongated, irregular shape. Everything about the fortifications of Zamość is characteristic of the Old Italian school.

★

191

In Scandinavia the rectangular castle type survived far into the 16th century. Torup Castle, near Malmö (Danish territory until 1658), dates from the first quarter of the 16th century. It has a square four-wing plan with an oblong inner courtyard. At two diagonally opposite corners there are strong circular gun towers.

In 1537 King Gustavus Vasa built the famous four-wing, four-tower castle of Gripsholm, above Lake Mälaren near Stockholm.

The most important Swedish fort was Kalmar, built on an island in Kalmarsund, opposite the island of Öland. In the 16th century the fortifications were improved. A low wall was built around the medieval castle, creating a trapezoidal bailey, and roundels, slightly higher than the wall, were raised in its four corners.

★

From the very beginning of the 16th century Italy assumed the creative initiative in developing the art of fortification in Europe. The wealth of innovatory ideas behind the new fortification system originated in the late 15th century, almost exclusively on Italian territory; Italians were chiefly responsible, although some outstanding contributions were made by Spanish engineers. (Established in Naples and later Milan, Spain was the dominant power in Italy.) Beyond the peninsula, everywhere in Europe, Italians were the sought-after master engineers, and the Italians also produced an extraordinarily rich theoretical literature. In the 16th century only two men outside Italy—both Germans—made really significant contributions to fortification theory; they were the artist Albrecht Dürer (1471-1528), whose ideas on the subject were still in some respects medieval, and the extremely forward-looking Daniel Speckle of Strasbourg (1536-89).

If we ask why it was that the new fortification system originated in Italy, the answer seems to be that the Italians possessed the optimum theoretical prerequisites while at the same time urgently needing to conceive new ideas and apply them at once in a strictly practical fashion. Existing Italian fortifications had failed signally to halt the triumphant progress of Charles VIII of France during his Italian campaign of 1494, and the threat of Valois and Habsburg intervention in Italian affairs existed alongside the even less palatable possibility of a Turkish invasion. Even if this failed to materialize, the Turks also imperilled the numerous Mediterranean possessions of Venice, the only Italian

state to remain a great power throughout the 16th century.

The fact that Italy was divided into several potentially hostile political units must also have stimulated the development of new fortification systems; and no doubt the Renaissance outlook, curious and wide-ranging, played a significant, if imponderable, role. However, a surprising feature of the decade during which the bastion system emerged was the time-lag between theory and practice. Theoretical works tended to appear after the event: they were not decisive factors in the conception of the system, but rather analysed and elaborated it.

It is therefore difficult to credit any individual with the invention of a particular fortification element, since in most cases where such an element is found, it is impossible to be certain that there had been no earlier practical employment of it.

Rome was the first important centre of the new fortification method. About 1500 the ancient Roman fortress of Castel San Angelo was incorporated into a square fortification with polygonal roundels in the corners. The parapet walk on corbels was supported by small arches. A particularly interesting feature was the circular tower in front of the bridge, serving as a kind of ravelin.

In 1501-03 Antonio da Sangallo the Elder built a castle by the sea at Nettuno for the Borgia Pope Alexander VI. It was still medieval in character, square in plan, with four bastions connected with the corners by means of short necks. Each bastion has a rounded leaf plan, without walls meeting to make a point. The lower part of Nettuno's walls are battered. On one side there is a low rectangular tower.

At about the same time Antonio da Sangallo the Elder also designed the fort at the west end of the town of Civita Castellana. It is somewhat irregular in plan. Three of the four corner bastions have a pointed drop-shaped plan, whereas the fourth is tetrahedral. The bastions are provided with brick revetment. Near the fifth, semicircular bastion there is an octagonal tower inside the fort.

As early as 1506, caponnières were used in Italy; these were covered passages designed to protect the lines of communication between various individual parts of fortifications.

In the early 16th century the fortifications of Crema, a Venetian town in Northern Italy, were reinforced by a chain of U-shaped bastion towers. The design of the polygonal citadel was similar. The material used was brick.

From 1508 onwards the new fort at Civitavec-

238
Civita Castellana, Italy. Plan of
the fort. After Monumenti.

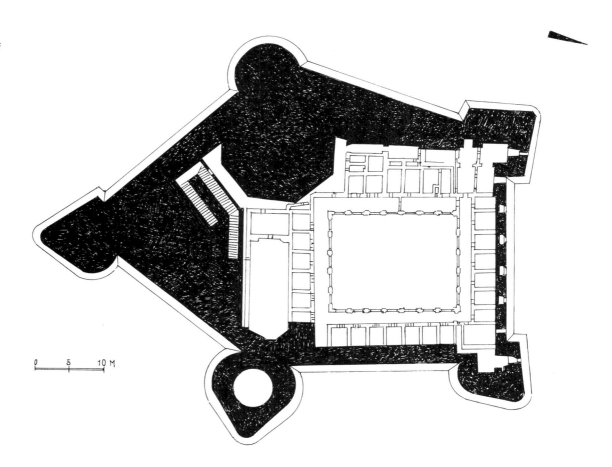

239
Civita Castellana, Italy. Aerial
view of the fort, showing the
octagonal tower. Beginning of
the 16th century.

chia, above the sea, was built to a design by the great Renaissance architect Donato Bramante (1444-1514). From 1515 construction continued under the supervision of the Florentine architect Antonio da Sangallo the Younger (1483-1546), who elaborated on the original design (a rectangular fort with four corner gun roundels), adding a hexagonal pointed bastion in the centre of the sea side; the wall and the roundels were the same height, but Antonio's bastion was much taller. The lower parts of the walls are provided with pronounced scarps. The fort was protected by a ditch.

The walls of Loreto, to the south-east of Ancona, terminate at both narrowed ends in low circular gun roundels dating from 1518-21.

In 1509-12 Giuliano da Sangallo (1445-1516), uncle of Antonio, built a rectangular citadel at Pisa; it stood near the River Arno, in the south-east corner of the left bank area of the city. Three corners were given rounded bastions, leaf-shaped in plan, similar to those of Nettuno. The walls with a lower scarp are clad with bricks.

The general appearance of the Old Stronghold in the port of Livorno is similar. Somewhat irregular in plan, it was built to a design by Antonio da Sangallo the Elder probably dating from 1506. The actual construction was completed much later.

Venice played a role of great importance in the 16th century changes in fortification techniques. At this time, of course, Venice was a powerful city state, controlling a large area in north-east Italy and a mercantile empire including Dalmatia and other Mediterranean outposts.

The system using pointed tetrahedral bastions was applied for the first time in history in the new fortifications constructed for the Venetian town of Verona. They were the work of the architect Michele Sanmicheli (1484-1559), and constitute the first integral work of the Old Italian school. The first to be built was Maddalena, the small bastion on the east side of the city; its faces meet at an obtuse angle. The new fortifications at Verona have not been precisely dated; it seems most likely that they were begun in 1527. The bastions are of various plans and sizes. Most are typical shallow Old Italian bastions with faces meeting at obtuse angles, orillons and lateral artillery casemates; but there are also almost right-angled and even acute angled bastions. The curtain walls, somewhat lower than the bastions, were rather long, between 220 and 300 metres. Beyond the walls there was a ditch. Sanmicheli also built two fine Renaissance gates, the Porta Nuova and the Porta del Palio.

There is an excellent example of a bastion fort at Aquila in the Abruzzi, which came under Spanish rule in 1529. Probably as early as 1530, the Spanish commander Pier Luigi Escriva di Valenza began to construct a castle, square in plan, with buildings on three sides and bastions in the corners; the long faces of the bastions, meeting at an acute angle, are joined to the curtain walls by double-curved orillons housing artillery casemates. The massive masonry of the bastions also contained listening galleries. The relatively low walls are protected by a ditch. In this fort, completed in 1549, the bastion system attained a high standard of technical perfection.

Escriva also built the Castel San Elmo at Naples on a six-pointed star plan from 1537; and from 1532 he worked on the reconstruction of the fortifications at Capua.

In 1534-35 the brothers Antonio and Giulio da Sangallo built the majestic Fortezza da Basso on the north side of their native Florence. The fort is designed as an elongated (east-west) pentagon with a dihedrally extended north side. At the corners stand bastions with faces meeting at acute angles in the east and near-right angles in the north. In the centre the bastion faces meet at a very obtuse angle without orillons. At the centre of the straight south side there is a piatta forma—a slightly projecting fortification, without pointed corners, which improved the defensive capability of the long curtains between bastions, otherwise one of the principal weaknesses of the Old Italian system. The fort was surrounded by a moat.

The covered way was the principal contribution of the Old Italian school to strengthening, and, in particular, deepening the fortifications system. About 11-16 metres wide, it ran along the outer side of the moat, protected by an earth rampart almost 3 metres high which sloped towards the enemy. The covered way was employed for the first time in the second quarter of the 16th century in the outer fortifications of the castle at Milan. At the corners of its trace the covered way extended to form places of arms with their points towards the glacis—the outer face of the rampart sloping down towards the enemy. These components are first mentioned in 1567.

At Barletta, on the Adriatic coast of Southern Italy, the four-wing castle dating from the reign of Charles V was superimposed on the early 13th century castle built by the Emperor Frederick II. The trapezoidal plan includes four corner bastions, their long faces meeting at a pronounced acute angle. Numerous loopholes open from the circular bastion area.

The Spanish were very active in building fortifications in the Italian peninsula. In 1543-44 the stronghold of Porto Ercole was erected on the Argentario peninsula in Tuscany. Its narrow plan terminated with the elements of hornworks on both short sides. The entire stronghold is surrounded by a ditch whose outer edge is adjoined by two simple ravelins; it is uncertain whether they were built at the same time as the fortifications or were added at a later date.

The Old Italian fortifications of Lucca are well preserved. The irregularly oval layout is enclosed by 12 metre high curtain walls punctuated by closely spaced orilloned bastions; most of these have faces meeting at obtuse angles and rounded inner cor-

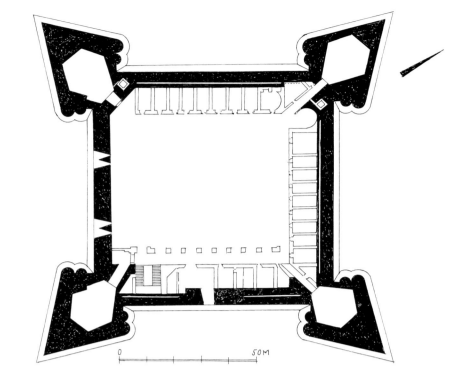

240
Aquila, Italy. Plan of the fort.
After Monumenti.

241
Aquila, Italy. Aerial view of the
fort, built in 1530-49, and the
surrounding ditch.

242
Lucca, Italy. Part of the wall with a bastion. Construction of the city's fortifications began in 1544.

244 ▶
Peschiera, Italy. View of one of the bastion towers and a curtain wall with gateway. The fort was built in 1553-56.

243
Porto Ercole, Italy. Aerial view of Forte Filippo, standing above the sea; it was built from 1557.

ners. The necks with casemates are very narrow. In the middle of the north side there was a shallow piatta forma instead of a bastion. The town was originally entered through three gateways. The fortifications were protected by a ditch; their construction began as early as 1544, but went on well into the 17th century. It was not until the final phase that the defences erected on the Old Italian system were strengthened by the incorporation of ravelins and a covered way.

In the 1540s, citadels on the five-pointed-star plan assumed their standard form; their construction in Italian cities was often not intended to serve any serious military purpose. One of the earliest was the now vanished citadel of Turin, built by one of the foremost representatives of the reformed Old Italian school, Francesco, Conte Paciotti of Urbino (1521-91). The citadel in Modena was strengthened by ravelins and a covered way, but it is not clear whether they formed part of the original fortifications.

In 1557 the construction of a second Spanish stronghold began above Porto Ercole; it was called Forte Filippo, after the reigning King of Spain,

Philip II. Its plan is highly original: it is a rectangular castle with four sharply pointed bastions containing a six-pointed star.

The pentagonal Venetian fort of Peschiera stands on the south bank of Lake Garda. It dates from 1553-56 and was probably designed by Gian Girolamo Sanmicheli (1513-58).

In 1561 work began on the fortifications of the Upper Town of Bergamo. The defences of this Venetian city, facilitated by its dominating position, were constructed in the pure Old Italian style. The walls were mainly protected by shallow bastions, only partly provided with orillons. At the easternmost point a kind of hornwork (a fortification with projecting corners) was constructed, and in several places the piatta forma was employed. The construction of the fortifications was completed in 1598.

The major Venetian town of Nicosia in Cyprus was newly fortified in 1567, shortly before the Turks attacked it. The work was executed in the Old Italian style, consisting of an almost circular peripheral wall reinforced by eleven shallow bastions with orillons.

In 1565 the epic siege of Malta thrilled the whole of Europe, which watched with bated breath as the Knights of St John successfuly withstood the besieging Turks. Only a year after the Turks retreated, the Grand Master of the Order, Jean Parisot de la Valletta, founded the city of Valletta, which was henceforth the main seat of the Knights of St John. The fortifications of the new city were constructed at the same time, the first phase being completed by about 1570. They were designed by the architect Francesco Laparelli and represented a high point in contemporary developments. Valletta's fortifications were examples of the New or Neo-Italian school, although naturally still including certain older elements; for example the piatta forma continued to be used instead of ravelins.

Valletta is situated on a tongue of land between two bays, the Grand and the Marsamuscetto Harbours. At the north-east point of the peninsula stands the fort of St Elmo, which was built in 1552 to the design of the Spanish engineer Pedro Pardo. It was the only part of the fortifications to be taken by the Turks in 1565, but in the new system it nonetheless assumed the functions of a citadel. In plan it is a four-pointed star. Towards the north-east, beyond a narrow ditch, there was a tetrahedral

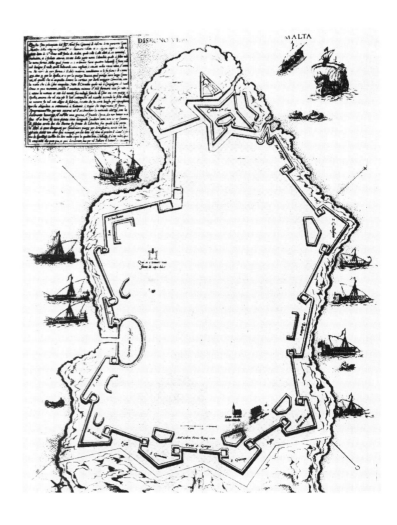

245
Valletta, Malta. The fortifications designed for the newly founded town by Francesco Laparelli; before 1570.

246
Valletta, Malta. View of part of the fortifications from the sea. They were constructed shortly after Malta was besieged by the Turks in 1565.

ravelin with a massive polygonal superstructure. The remaining area at the end of the peninsula was lined with low walls forming a kind of hornwork, an element not found in the original design. These are regarded as the earliest examples of this feature, which subsequently came into general use in fortifications.

St Elmo's was connected with the fortifications of the new city, whose walls were extremely thick. On the south-east side of the peninsula, the wall con-

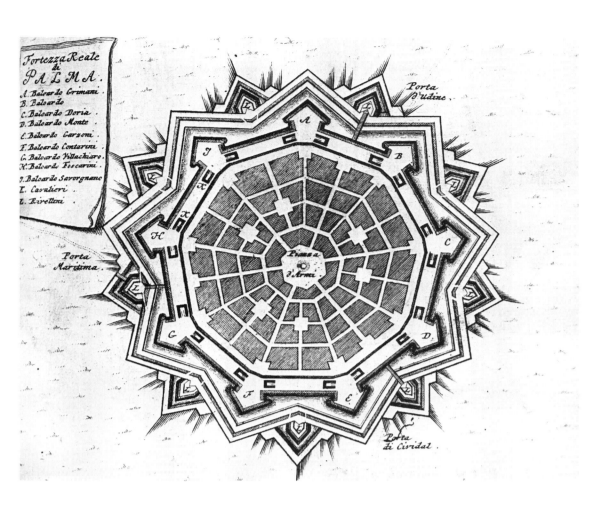

Fortezza Reale di PALMA.

A. Baloardo Grimani.
B. Baloardo
C. Baloardo Doria.
D. Baloardo Monte.
E. Baloardo Garzoni.
F. Baloardo Contarini.
G. Baloardo Villachiara.
H. Baloardo Foscarini.
J. Baloardo Savorgnano.
L. Cavalieri.
L. Rivellini.

Porta d'Udine.

Porta Maritima.

Piazza d'Armi.

Porta di Cividal.

247
Palmanova, Italy. Plan of the fort. After Fischer.

248
Palmanova, Italy. Aerial view of the fort, constructed in about 1593.

sisted of two slightly projecting piatta forma with a bastion between them, all with orillons and casemates. At once the most vulnerable and the shortest side, the south-west was protected by four closely spaced bastions, backed by mostly pentagonal cavaliers close to the inner face of the peripheral wall. The cavaliers increased the effectiveness of the bastions, enabling the defenders to fire artillery from an elevated position. The cavaliers of the Valletta fort were probably the first structures of this type in history. It is all the more surprising that no ravelins were used on the vulnerable south-west side to protect the curtain walls.

The north-west side of the fort was idiosyncratic in layout, being designed to save space for an arsenal and a harbour. The wall running from St Elmo's broke its trace twice at an obtuse angle. In the more distant corner of the citadel there were the loops of artillery casemates. The next corner consisted of a bastion with a cavalier on top. At the rear end of its north-west face there was a small rectangular break in which was placed another artillery casemate; this was protected by fortifications slightly overlapping the face of the bastion, giving rise to a sort of incomplete piatta forma. This projecting formation was twice repeated in the fur-

ther trace of the wall. The short curtain between two of them also incorporated the entrance to the harbour. The south-west piatta forma was connected with the south-west corner bastion. The entire fortification was surrounded by a ditch which followed the coastline around the two bays; beyond it was a covered way without places of arms.

Baldassare Lanci (1510-71) designed the fortifications of Grosseto, a city in the south of Tuscany; they were built in 1574-93. They are hexagonal in plan, with bastions with orillons in the corners; the bastion faces generally meet at a right angle or an acute angle. The ravelins and the covered way were probably added at a later date.

In 1590-95 the fortifications of the south side of Florence, beyond the Palazzo Pitti, were strengthened by the building of a fort, the Belvedere. In plan it consists of two three-pointed formations linked by a narrower central part.

The fortified Venetian city of Palmanova was founded in about 1593. It was remarkable not only for its fortifications, but also as one of the few Renaissance ideal cities that were actually built, having a completely regular radial plan with an octagonal piazza at its centre. The regular nine-sided periphery, with orilloned bastions in the corners and a

249
Kralyevitsa, Yugoslavia. Castle above the coastal town. 16th century.

ditch, is in complete harmony with this layout. The ditch has a covered way with minor places of arms linked to the bastions, whose faces meet at right angles. The layout of the fortified city was designed by the well-known architect Vincenzo Scamozzi (1552-1616).

It was evidently soon afterwards that the original fortification system was supplemented by tetrahedral ravelins inserted into the inner angles of the covered ways. The fortification system was completed by an outer covered way with places of arms.

Palmanova possessed all the elements characteristic of the Neo-Italian school, but it was not entirely representative, since the arrangement of individual features was untypical.

This survey of selected 16th century Italian forts has indicated that the distinction between Old Italian and Neo-Italian schools is less clearcut than has generally been assumed in scholarly studies. The transition between these widely different concepts of fortification was in fact gradual. This can best be observed in the changing shape, size and arrangements of the bastions. The bastions and curtain walls of the Old Italian school were about 9 metres high, exceeding the counterscarp in elevation by some 2 metres. Apart from the shallowness of the bastions, the principal drawback of Old Italian fortifications lay in the length of the curtains, which might be as much as 500 metres. The Neo-Italian school shortened the curtains to 250-200 metres and increased the curtain and bastion height to 12-15 metres, some 3-5 metres above the covered way. Essential features of the Neo-Italian school were the employment of ravelins to protect the curtains, and of a covered way with places of arms. The school also employed the hornwork, the fortification formation with corners projecting towards the enemy.

★

Thanks to Venetian dominance, developments on the opposite coast of the Adriatic were similar to those in Italy. An excellent example of Venetian acitivity is furnished by the fort of San Nicolo at Šibenik (now in Yugoslavia), which was built in 1540 by Michele Sanmicheli (1484-1559). The semioval roundel projecting seawards is linked to the obtuse point of the hornwork, which becomes much wider towards the rear. Its two demibastions with rounded inner corners are connected by a short curtain wall. Mention should also be made of the castle of Kralyevitsa in northern Dalmatia, which has circular corner towers.

★

Early 16th century Iberian fortifications are well represented by the Belem Tower, which stands near the north bank of the River Tagus, to the west of Lisbon. It was built in 1515-21 by Francisco de Arruda (active 1510-47). The massive rectangular tower with a receding top floor is richly architecturally articulated, giving it an apparently non-military character. It is surrounded by a hexagonal wall with gun embrasures. The corners are emphasized by small bastizans. The entire wall is battlemented.

★

Sixteenth century fortifications differed greatly from those of the preceding three centuries, with their essential medieval unity. The 16th century was a more fragmentary period. The medieval fortification style survived throughout the early part of the century in most countries, although the Pernštejn earth fortifications in Bohemia constituted an interesting exception. By contrast, in Italy the new bastion system had been developing from the very beginning of the century; it was then exported directly to Hungary and Slovakia on a large scale, whereas in other countries it was represented only by occasional examples. As we shall see, the bastion system became general in the course of the 17th century.

The Seventeenth Century

The 17th century was the most important period for the development of the bastion system. In retrospect it is inevitably dominated by the Marquis de Vauban, who so successfully implemented the expansionist policies of Louis XIV, but in fact there were also a great many other interesting developments in that turbulent century.

During its first half, Italian engineers continued to be in great demand abroad. This was especially true of Central Europe where, apart from the Ottoman threat, the Thirty Years' War of 1618-48 kept the region in turmoil.

The Neo-Italian school laid the basis for further developments, which for a time took place mainly in the Netherlands. The advances of the period can largely be attributed to a group of outstanding personalities. An engineer of Polish descent, Adam Freitag (1608-50), influenced the studies of Emil de Pagan (1604-65), a Frenchman who was the immediate predecessor of Vauban. Vauban's chief competitor was the leading figure of the Dutch fortification school, Menno van Coehorn (1641-1704).

In the course of the 17th century the bastion system became the universal norm, much as the medieval system had been in the 14th century. The culminating point of the bastion system was reached at the close of the 17the century.

★

Around 1600 the greatest fortifications engineer in France was Jean Errard (d. 1610), who served King Henri IV and is regarded as the founder of the French school of fortification. Errard applied the principles of the Neo-Italian school, as is most clearly apparent in the fortifications of Verdun (Meuse), constructed thirty years after his death. The layout of the walls and the citadel are influenced by Italian models, although the full Neo-Italian system was not employed.

Another outstanding member of the French school was Emile de Pagan, Comte de Merveilles, although the gradual loss of his eyesight prevented him from applying in practice his undoubtedly excellent theories. Pagan considered the conceptions of the Neo-Italian school insufficient, and devised considerable improvements in the bastion system, unquestionably basing his ideas on Freitag's work. He suggested that the bastions should be covered by a kind of advanced bastion tower placed in the ditch, a proposal which was to inspire the counter-guard introduced by Vauban. Pagan recommended that the firing power of the bastion should be increased by constructing three floors of artillery casemates instead of the customary two. He also proposed to establish tetrahedral retrenchments in the places of arms of the covered way.

From about the 1640s France seized the political initiative in Europe, and under Louis XIV (1643-1715) replaced Habsburg Spain as the predominant great power. These facts were reflected in contemporary fortifications. The outstanding figure, as both builder and conqueror of forts, was Sébastien le Prestre, Marquis de Vauban (1633-1707).

The number of Vauban's fortifications and re-fortifications, along with his active participation in sieges and campaigns, created a legendary aura around him that has obscured the reality of his achievement. By comparison with the theorists of the period, Vauban was a monumental builder, and the practical aspects of his extraordinary labours outweighed any theoretical considerations. In fact

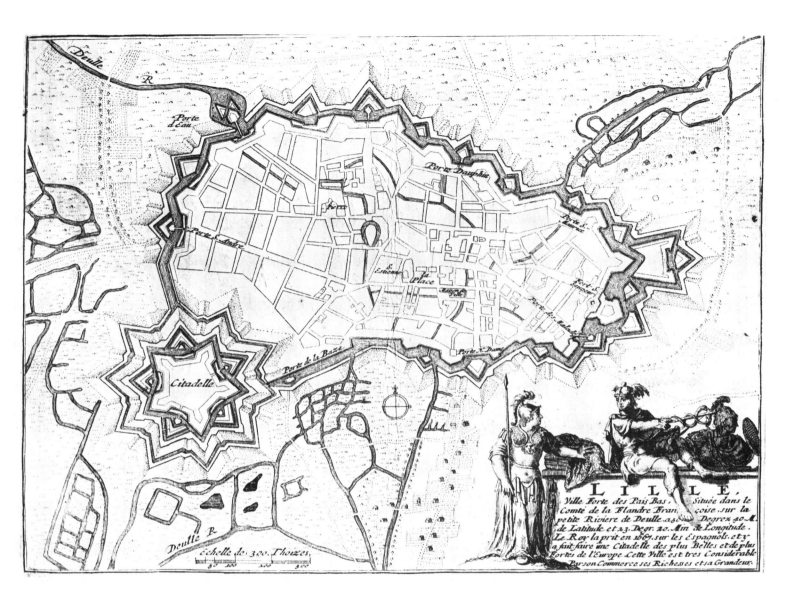

250
Lille, France. Plan (1695) of
the fortified town and its
citadel. The fortifications were
constructed after the French
captured Lille in 1667.

the characteristic feature of Vauban's fortifications is the way in which he synthesized his own conceptions with those which he had taken over from others.

The first of his major fortification projects was Dunkirk, purchased by Louis XIV in 1662 from Charles II of England. The work was completed in 1706. However, it did not survive Louis' reign: by the terms of the Peace of Utrecht (1713), which ended the long War of the Spanish Succession, France agreed to destroy the fortifications.

Vauban's activities developed on a far greater scale during the war of 1667-68 between France and Spain in the Spanish Netherlands, when it became his task to fortify the newly captured cities.

In 1667 the French took the important city of Lille. Shortly afterwards Vauban constructed the citadel there, which still exists; at the time it was considered the finest and strongest in Europe. It exhibits all the characteristics of Vauban's first manner. The pentagonal fortress is surrounded by tenailles, ravelins with separate reduits, and a covered way. (The reduit was a fortification to the rear of a ravelin and rising above it.) At the foot of the glacis there was a moat, in front of which there was another covered way.

The city of Ath (Hainaut, Belgium) was captured by the French in 1667. The fort was strengthened immediately under Vauban's direction, a model being prepared in 1668. In plan in was a regular octagon, with straight curtains and tetrahedral corner bastions, most of whose faces met at obtuse angles. The bastions were provided with retrenchments (in-

203

terior defence works) dividing their front parts. To protect the curtain walls, tenailles were positioned in front of them in the ditch, between the flanks of the bastions. In front of them, tetrahedral ravelins with small reduits rose from the bottom of the ditch. The ravelins were connected with the curtains by means of caponnières. In front of the gateways, two lunettes (small triangular outworks) supported the ravelin. There was a hornwork in front of the north-west bastion.

The whole fortification system was enclosed in a covered way with places of arms protected against flanking fire by traverses (minor elevations). The fortifications are representative of what is known as Vauban's first manner; they were demolished in 1830.

accounts for the construction of three pentagonal redoubts beyond the glacis. (Redoubts are independent outworks, not directly connected with the main defences of the fort.) In the south-west bend of the fort Vauban built a large hornwork. On the opposite, south bank of the River Sambre, there was a sizeable crownwork, a separate fortification with one or two complete bastions in the centre and deformed or half bastions in the corners. It was surrounded by a ditch and a covered way. The fortifications of Charleroi, too, disappeared in the course of time.

The city of Besançon (Doubs) only became indubitably French in 1674, upon which Vauban immediately began to fortify it. At Battant, the part of the city on the south-west bank of the River

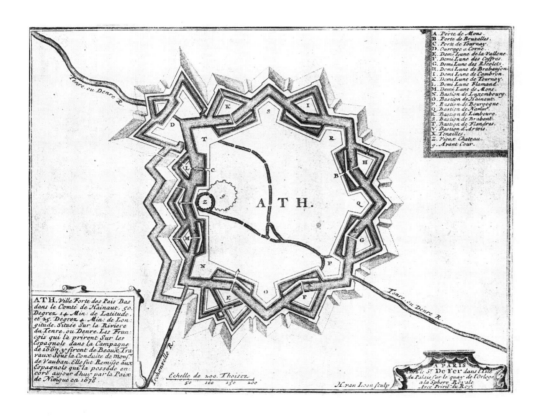

251
Ath, Belgium. Plan of the city fortified by the French after 1667.

252 ▶
Ath, Belgium. Model of the fortified city. Musée des Plans et Reliefs, Paris.

Another important example is Charleroi in Belgium, taken from Spain in 1667. It consisted of a hexagon with elongated, sharp-pointed bastions and cavaliers. The curtains were protected by tenailles; in front of them there were ravelins, some with reduits. On one side there was no ravelin, but only a small reduit.

The north and north-east bastions were protected by V-shaped counterguards (derived from Pagan's ideas) from which they were separated by a narrow ditch. This was the most vulnerable side, which

Doubs, he constructed a system comprising four bastions with orillons and cavaliers. The faces of the two front bastions meet at an obtuse angle. Ravelins without reduits were connected with the main system by means of caponnières. Lunettes stood in front of the covered way, which was punctuated by traverses; in effect, these lunettes, open at the rear, functioned as redoubts.

The city proper is enclosed by a double wall of medieval origin, strengthened with tetrahedral bastion towers.

In 1679 Vauban began to reconstruct the citadel on the site of the ancient city which dominates Besançon from the east. Here the oblong, relatively narrow site made it imposssible to employ the traditional polygonal plan.

The fortifications of Besançon have suffered remarkably little from the ravages of time. By contrast, almost nothing remains of the fort of Phalsbourg (Moselle), or Pfalzburg, on the border of Lorraine, which was built by Vauban in 1679-80. The fortification system was remarkably simple. In plan the main stronghold was an elongated hexagon with bastions at the corners. The bastion faces met at an acute angle. Some of the bastions were reinforced by cavaliers. The small orillons were linked with the curtain by short concave flanks. The other features of the fortifications were in the orthodox Neo-Italian manner. Two fort gateways still survive.

Saarlouis was founded by Louis XIV in 1680 as a fort at the crossing of the River Saar. The fortifications were built in 1680-86 by Thomas de Choisy with Vauban's help. The fortress, situated on the left bank, is hexagonal in plan. The bastions were designed in a similar fashion to those of Phalsbourg: some of them were provided with cavaliers. The tenailles were of a simple type. The reduits of most ravelins were separated from them by a narrow moat. The distinctive feature of the fortifications consisted of six projecting tetrahedral lunettes which were connected with the turns of the covered

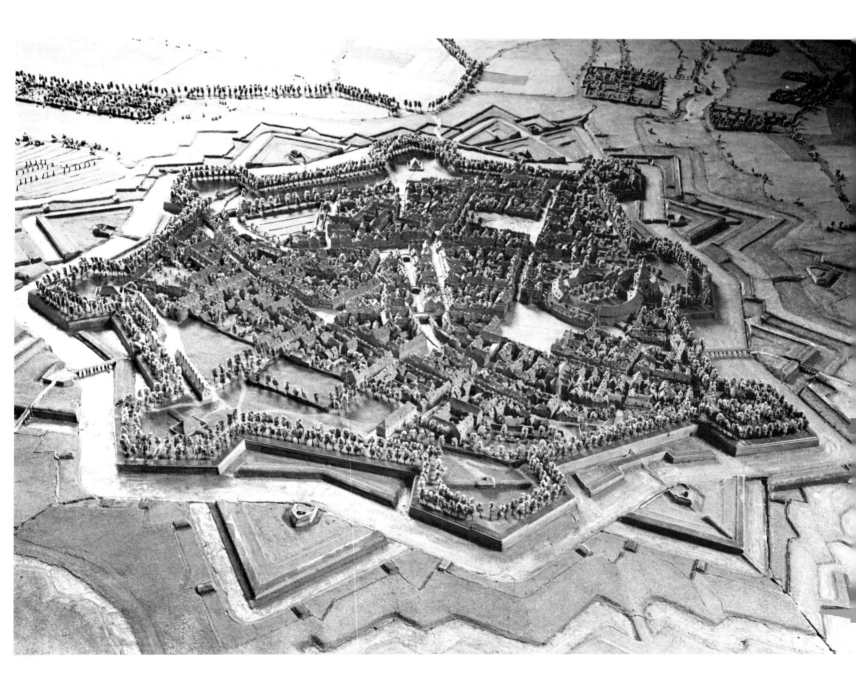

way. There was another covered way in front of them. The bridge-head on the north-east river bank was designed as a powerful hornwork, protected by a moat with a ravelin and a covered way with places of arms. The fortifications no longer exist.

The fort of Huningue (Haut Rhin) stands above the Rhine north of Basel, and was intended to protect the river crossing. Only one bastion now survives. It was constructed to Vauban's design in 1680-81, after his 'first system'. The basic plan was a five-pointed star with corner bastions with rounded orillons and cavaliers. In the ditch there were tenailles of complex design, repeating the shape of the bastion front. The curtains were protected by ravelins with prominent reduits. Above the ditch ran a covered way with places of arms and traverses. The west bastion was protected by a lunette in the moat. At the foot of the east ravelin, on the Rhine, there was a low tetrahedral bastion.

The entire fort was surrounded by an outer moat, irregular in outline. Hornworks protected its north and south sides. Two more hornworks protected the crossing; the one on the far (Baden) side of the river was a monumental feature with a ravelin and a pair of lateral lunettes. The fort was partly demolished in 1697, after the Peace of Rijswijk (Ryswick).

Another of Vauban's major projects was the reconstruction of the fortifications of Luxembourg, after the city was wrested from Spain in 1684. The result, in the eyes of Vauban's contemporaries, was to make the fort impregnable.

Luxembourg is well sited for defensive purposes, being protected by the deep valleys of the Alzette and the Pétrusse in the south and east. Consequently the fortifications on the west and north-west sides of the city are the principal points of interest to us. The bastions take a variety of forms, at least partly derived from the previous system. The curtains are protected by ravelins, the bastions by counterguards. The north-west ravelin was provided with a couvre face—a fortification structure protecting the ravelin in much the same fashion as counterguards protected bastions. Below the covered way, close to the places of arms, the slope of the glacis was broken to form a terrace on which there were seven redoubts, most of them five-sided. On the south, and even more so on the north and east sides, the fortifications were considerably simpler. The southern bluff of the city was the site of a citadel.

Vauban also built several outposts on the surrounding hills. The most important was on the high ground to the north, which was divided by a deep valley. There Vauban built a bastion front, protected by three ravelins, a ditch and a covered way. The narrow north-east projection of the fort, the Altmünster platform, was screened by a redoubt. On the Rham platform, directly opposite the citadel, Vauban built a more complex system of forti-

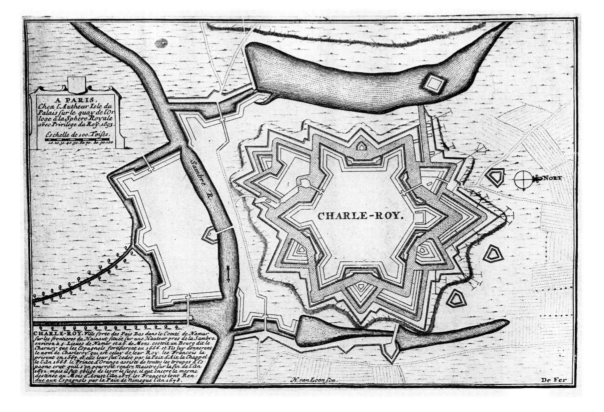

253
Charleroi, Belgium. The fort built by the French after 1667.

254 ▶
Besançon, France. Model (1772) of the fort, seen from the north-west. The fortifications were finished after 1674, the citadel was built in 1679, and the entire ensemble was completed in 1701.

206

fication comprising a redoubt and a lunette surrounded by a ditch. A hornwork was erected above the confluence of the Pétrusse and the Alzette, followed westwards by one redoubt and finally, south of the Pétrusse, a lunette with a reduit and a ditch. The plan of the city in 1695 illustrates the extraordinary extent of the fortifications after Vauban's reconstruction.

The fortified town of Blaye, on the east bank of the Gironde, protected the city of Bordeaux further inland. From 1685 Vauban converted Blaye into a Baroque fort closely linked with its medieval walls, working in his first fortification manner. Three new bastions with orillons were constructed. In the ditch, in front of the low curtains, there were ravelins with reduits; they were connected with the curtains by caponnières. Around the entire system ran a

covered way with places of arms. These fortifications have survived to the present day.

The city of Landau was fortified by Vauban in 1687-91. Its fortifications, which no longer exist, were examples of the great engineer's 'second system'. Characteristic features were the sharp-pointed tetrahedral bastions including tower-like features protected all round by massive counterguards. Simple tenailles and ravelins stood in front of the remaining sections of the curtain walls. Because of the River Queich, a more complex layout was necessary on the east side of the fort, where the ravelin was protected by a couvre face in front of it. North of the river a kind of small-scale hornwork was constructed. In the north-west Vauban erected a massive crownwork with three bastions, two ravelins and a covered way. Only two gateways survive. Vauban

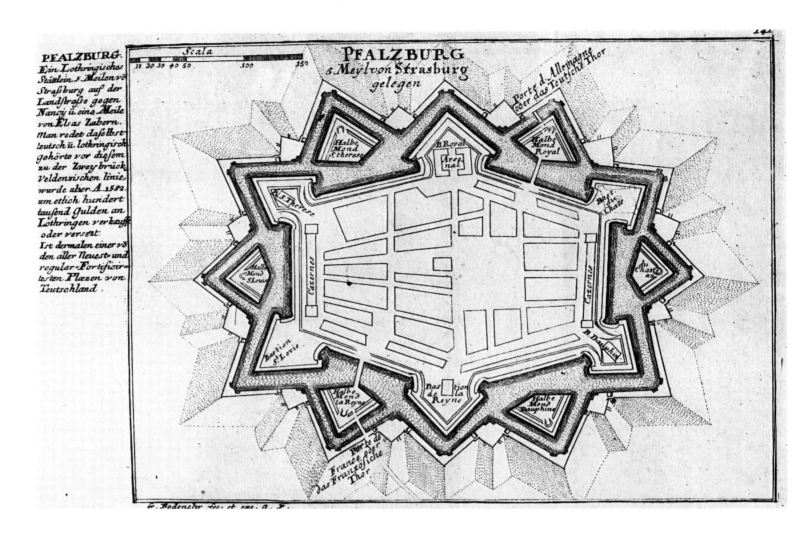

PFALZBURG
5 Meyl von Strasburg
gelegen

PEALZBURG.
Ein Lothringisches
Städlein 5 Meilen vö
Straßburg auf der
Landstraße gegen
Nancy u. eine Meile
von Elsas Zabern.
Man redet daselbst
teutsch ü. lothringisch
gehörte vor diesem
zu der Zweybrück.
Veldenzischen linie,
wurde aber A. 1582
um etlich hundert
taufend Gulden an
Lothringen verkaufft
oder versezt.
Ist dermalen einer vö
den aller Neuest-und
regular-Fortificir-
ten Plæzen von
Teutschland.

Scala

also applied his 'second system' to the fort of Belfort, built in 1686-91.

The fortifications of the city of Oléron (Charente Maritime), built from 1690 onwards, are interesting for their bastions with corner towers, a feature of Vauban's 'third system'. The fortifications have been preserved in good condition.

The fortified city of Neuf Brisach (Haut Rhin), built from 1699 onwards, is considered the finest example of Vauban's art. Although it suffered considerable damage during the Second World War, it retains an impressive military atmosphere, redolent of the 17th century. The regular chessboard pattern of the city, with a central square (literally square), is enclosed in an octagonal fortification scheme. Neuf Brisach was Vauban's last work, representing the culmination of his 'third system'. The city is enclosed in an inner bastion wall, the 'enceinte de sûreté', with short curtains interrupted by flat, slightly salient bastions with barely perceptible flanks; the faces of the bastions meet at an obtuse angle. From the bastion points project tetrahedral bastions, each with a tower at the highest point of

255
Pfalsbourg, France. Plan of the fort built in 1679-80. After Bodenehr.

256 ▶
Saarlouis, Germany. Plan of the fort built in 1680-86. After Bodenehr.

the whole deep system. Then comes the massive outer defence line, the 'enceinte de combat'. The curtains are protected by simple tenailles, uniform in design. The bastions were protected by massive tetrahedral counterguards, the faces of which met at a slightly obtuse angle. In front of the tenailles in the wide ditch there are tetrahedral ravelins with high reduits (also tetrahedral) in the background. A covered way of customary design completed the system. The fort was entered through four gateways placed at regular intervals. After Vauban's death in 1707 the construction was completed by Louis de Cormontaigne (1696-1752).

Vauban also strengthened the fortification system of the southern French city of Perpignan (Pyrénées Orientales); fortified by Philip II of Spain in 1556, it passed to France for good in 1659.

Construction of the fort at Auxonne (Côte d'Or) was started by Maréchal d'Apremont on the orders of Louis XIV, but completed by Vauban. On its south-west side the new fortification joined the existing castle with four round towers. In front of the curtains there are merely ravelins without tenailles or reduits. One bastion was surmounted by a cavalier, another was protected by a counterguard. The fortifications of Auxonne represent a rather simplified version of systems used elsewhere; the major parts are still in existence.

Of the long line of other forts that Vauban played some part in constructing or reconstructing, the following deserve to be mentioned: in France, Aire sur la Lys (Pas de Calais), Avesnes sur Helpe (Nord), Bayonne (Pyrénées Atlantiques), Belle-Île (Morbihan), Bergues (Nord), Bitche (Moselle), Briançon (Hautes Alpes), Gravelines (Nord), Landrecies (Nord), Longwy (Meurthe et Moselle), Maubeuge (Nord), Mont Dauphin (Hautes Alpes), St Martin de Ré (Charente Maritime), St Omer (Pas de Calais), Sedan (Meuse), Strasbourg (Bas Rhin), and the citadel in Toul (Meurthe et Moselle); and in Belgium, Bouillon, Menin, Nieuport, Tournai and Ypres.

In conclusion, a few general features of Vauban's 'systems' can be summarized in terms of measurements. Bastion faces met at an acute or right angle; the curtain walls did not exceed 300 metres; and neither they nor the bastions were less than 11 metres high. A few examples of Vauban's work, selected primarily because they are well documented, cannot do justice to his role in the development of European fortifications. Vauban's teacher, the outstanding French theorist Emile de Pagan, devised a number of fortification elements that were subsequently applied in practice by Vauban. But if Vauban's designs were notable for their adaptability to local conditions, they also improved over the years, a fact that can best be illustrated by a comparison between his first and third 'systems'. His critics and successors might improve on his work in certain aspects or details, but as a whole it survived until the very end of bastion fortification in the 19th century.

★

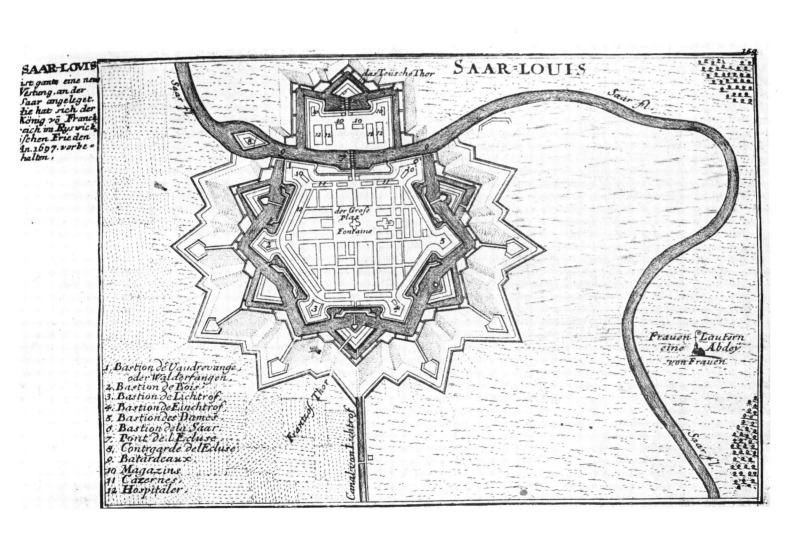

On British soil, protected by the sea and a powerful navy, the construction of forts was a relatively unimportant activity. Among the more interesting examples is the citadel of Plymouth harbour, construction of which began in 1666 under the direction of a Dutch engineer, Bernard de Gomme. Five bastions project from the irregular-shaped citadel; on the land side the curtains are protected by a pair of ravelins. A very remarkable architectural feature of the fort is the richly articulated gate of 1670, ascribed to Thomas Fitz.

At Tilbury (Essex), on the north bank of the Thames, there is a well preserved Baroque fort dating from 1671-83 and intended to shield London from an invader. Its pentagonal plan with corner bastions is protected by the river on the south side; elsewhere it is surrounded by a very wide moat with a ravelin covering the short north curtain. There is a low covered way protected by an outer ditch.

★

In the Netherlands, 17th century fortifications continued to be designed so as to make maximum use of the country's abundant water. As the prevailing building material was earth, used without stone or brick revetment, bastions and curtains were necessarily low, and ditches were relatively shallow (3 metres deep at most); this was compensated for by their great breadth. The endeavour to increase the strength of earth walls brought about the necessity for the fausse braye, a low advance rampart at the foot of bastions and curtains. Freitag designed a type of ravelin, also intended to stand in the moat in front of the bastion point; these were used for the first time in the fort at Nijmegen.

The Dutch school of fortification culminated in the work of Baron Menno van Coehorn (1641-1704), 'the Prince of Engineers'. Coehorn required categorically that the fort should be invisible to the enemy. The covered way and the bottom of the outer dry ditch should have been dug down to the water level, so that, at the first stroke of the pick, the enemy would get wet. The bastions and ravelins were provided with orillons. Coehorn's fortifications were constructed in depth, even the ravelins being provided with fausses brayes. There were reduits on top of the ravelins, which protected not only the curtains but also the bastion points; however, these outer ravelins were not provided with orillons. Minor retrenchments were also constructed in the places of arms. Using these methods

Coehorn fortified the strategically important city of Bergen op Zoom, to the north of Antwerp.

A remarkable example of a surviving 17th century Dutch fortified city is Naarden, to the southwest of Amsterdam, not far from the Zuider Zee. Its basic plan is hexagonal, with sharp or near-rectangular bastions which have very short flanks in the corners necessitated by the orillons. On top of the bastions there were cavaliers. The main fortified area apears to float in the wide moat, surrounded by regularly spaced ravelin 'islands'. Beyond these, a covered way with places of arms follows the line of the moat. The entire fortification system is enclosed by an outer moat.

The small town of Veere (Zeeland), on the north coast of the island of Walcheren, has a system of fortifications that seems out of keeping with its small size. On the land side the town is protected by a series of tetrahedral bastions whose faces meet at a near-right angle. Beyond them, at some distance, there was another bastion system with curtains, not fully integrated with the inner fortifications. This outer line of defence included a moat, on the outside of which a covered way obviously once stood. The general appearance of Veere's fortifications suggests that they were built in the middle decades of the 17th century.

The Dutch fortification school arose in direct response to military and geographical conditions in the Netherlands. Nevertheless it exercised considerable influence abroad in the late 17th century.

★

In Germany, once so rich in fortifications, the 17th century was a period of relative inactivity, probably because of the general disorder that prevailed throughout the Empire. A proper survey is difficult because so much has been destroyed in subsequent wars.

Mannheim, which became a city in 1606, was fortified in a remarkable fashion. Its citadel, a seven-pointed star in plan with tetrahedral bastions and ravelins, adjoined the city—fortified similarly—on the north-east side. Designed by the Dutch engineer Barthel Janson, its plan represented a splendid early application of the Dutch fortification system. After being destroyed by the French the fortifications were reconstructed from 1698 by the famous Menno van Coehorn. Nothing now survives, however.

Breisach was once known as the key fortress

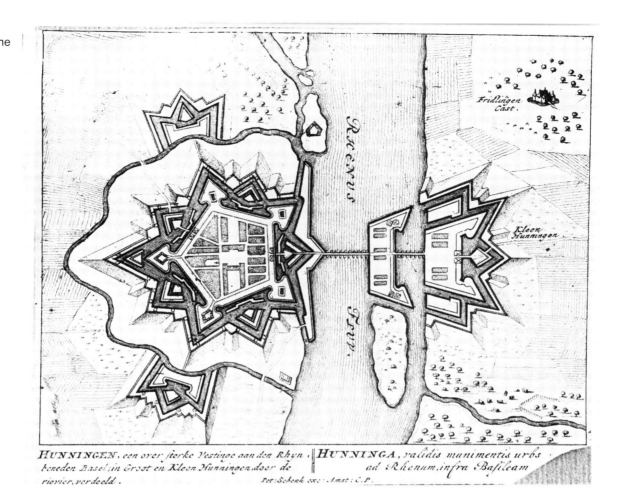

257
Huningue, France. Plan of the fort, engraved by Schenk. It was built in 1680-81.

HUNNINGEN, een over sterke Vestinge aan den Rhyn, beneden Basel; in Groot en Kleen Hunningen, door de rievier, verdeeld. ǁ *HUNNINGA, validis munimentis urbs ad Rhenum, infra Basileam*

Pet: Schenk exc. Amst: C.P.

★

protecting the Holy Roman Empire; now the only relic of its fortifications is the Rhine Gate, built during a French occupation in 1670. A similar fate befell the Baden fort of Philippsburg to the north-west of Bruchsal, founded in 1615 and occupied by the French between 1640 and 1698.

However, it is possible to find a good example, still extant, of fortifications constructed in the period following the Thirty Years' War (1618-48). This is the fort of Rosenberg, to the north-east of the small town of Kronach in upper Franconia. Construction of the stronghold, a regular five-pointed star in plan, began in the 1650s under the direction of Antonio Petrini (1624-1701).

At Stolpen in Saxony, to the east of Dresden, the medieval castle fortifications were strengthened with tetrahedral bastions from 1675 onwards.

Construction of a fort at Berlin began in 1658, using the Dutch fortification method. At the foot of the bastions and curtains stood a continuous fausse braye, and beyond it a moat with a covered way around it.

The fort of Stade, south of the Elbe and west of Hamburg, was built by the Swedes after the Thirty Years' War. Traces of it are still visible in the surrounding greenery.

In East-Central Europe the Turkish threat continued to be acute, culminating in the second siege of Vienna in 1683 which represented the Turks' final, unsuccessful effort to advance further into Europe. The significance of the easternmost part of Austria, the Burgenland, increased greatly during this period.

The castle of Forchtenstein, standing in a dominant position on a rocky hill, was converted into a strong fort during the middle years of the 17th century. Its medieval origins are recalled by a circular tower at the highest point of the castle area, dating from the end of the 13th century. Tetrahedral bastions were built in both east corners of the castle. These also strengthened the east corners of the bailey, which was accessible through a massive second gateway, entered via the first gateway across a wide west ditch controlled by two bastion towers and another bastion tower on the corner of the upper castle.

On the side of two older castles near the town of Feldbach in eastern Styria, the mighty fort of Riegersburg was built in the 17th century to hold back the Turks. Here, evidence of its medieval or-

211

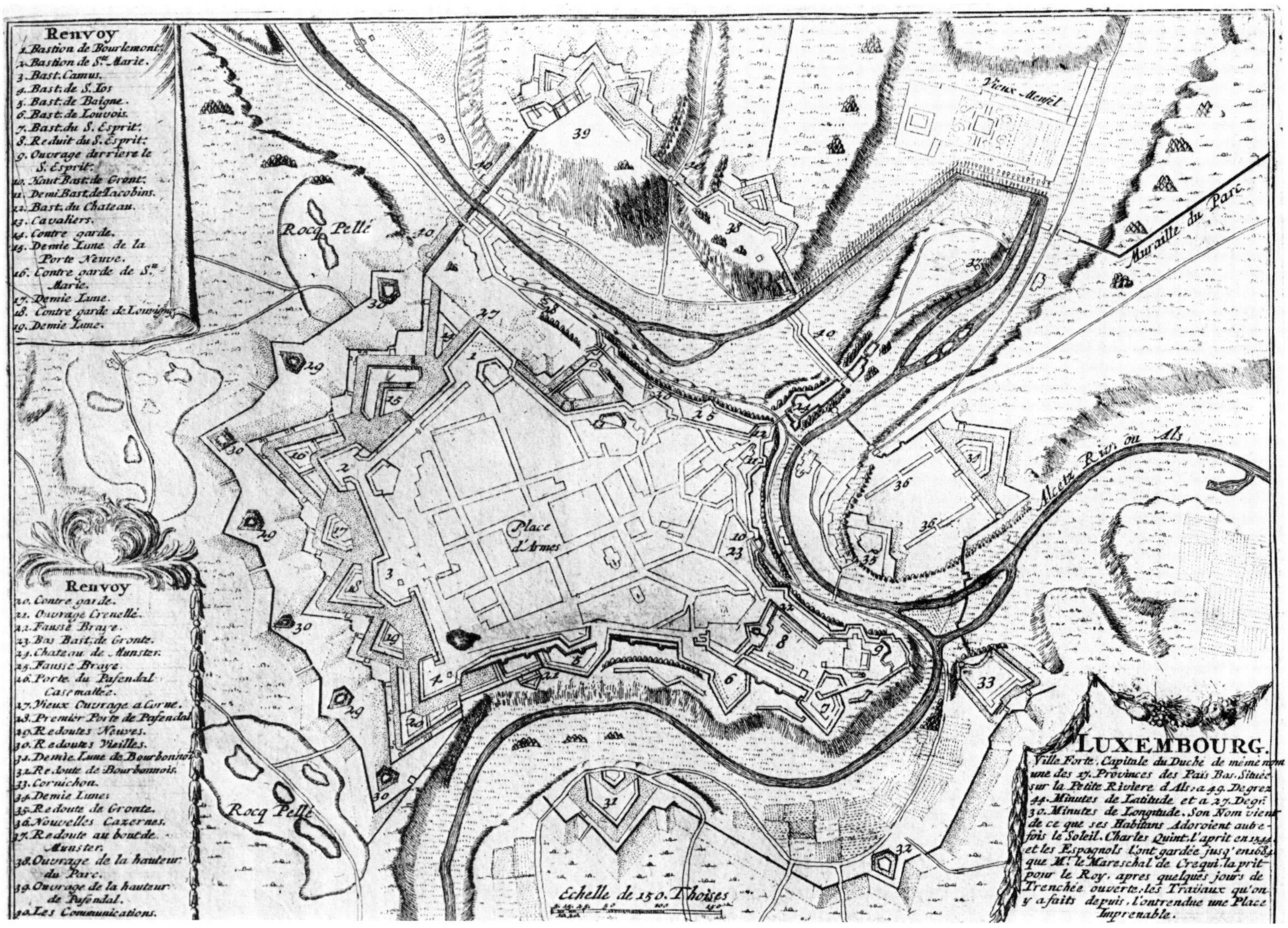
Renvoy
1. Bastion de Bourlemont.
2. Bastion de Ste. Marie.
3. Bast. Camus.
4. Bast. de S. Ios
5. Bast. de Baigne.
6. Bast. de Louvois.
7. Bast. du S. Esprit.
8. Reduit du S. Esprit.
9. Ouvrage derriere le S. Esprit.
10. Haut Bast. de Gront.
11. Demi Bast. de Iacobins.
12. Bast. du Chateau.
13. Cavaliers.
14. Contre garde.
15. Demie Lune de la Porte Neuve.
16. Contre garde de Ste. Marie.
17. Demie Lune.
18. Contre garde de Louvigny.
19. Demie Lune.
Renvoy
20. Contre garde.
21. Ouvrage Crenellé.
22. Fausse Braye.
23. Bas Bast. de Gronte.
24. Chateau de Munster.
25. Fausse Braye.
26. Porte du Pafendal Casematée.
27. Vieux Ouvrage a Corne.
28. Premier Porte de Pafendal
29. Redoutes Neuves.
30. Redoutes Vieilles.
31. Demie Lune de Bourbonnois
32. Redoute de Bourbonnois.
33. Cornichon.
34. Demie Lune.
35. Redoute de Gronte.
36. Nouvelles Cazernes.
37. Redoute au bout de Munster.
38. Ouvrage de la hauteur du Parc.
39. Ouvrage de la hauteur de Pafendal.
40. Les Communications.
Rocq Pellé
Place d'Armes
Vieux Mensel
Muraille du Parc
Rivier ou Als
Echelle de 150. Thoises
LUXEMBOURG.
Ville Forte, Capitale du Duche de même nom une des 17. Provinces des Pais Bas. Située sur la Petite Riviere d'Als, a 49. Degrez 44. Minutes de Latitude et a 27. Degr. 30. Minutes de Longitude. Son Nom vient de ce que ses Habitans Adoroient autrefois le Soleil. Charles Quint l'aprit en 1544 et les Espagnols l'ont gardée jusq' en 1684 que Mr. le Mareschal de Crequi la prit pour le Roy, apres quelques jours de Trenchée ouverte. les Travaux qu'on y a faits depuis, l'ont rendue une Place Imprenable.

258
Luxembourg. Plan (1695) of the fortified city. The fortifications were completed after 1684.

igin is apparent in its extremely large area and the dispersed character of its defences. It is entered through the first gateway from the south. The second, Zeiler Gate leads to the south-west bailey, fortified by a wall with a pair of tetrahedral bastions. From there the visitor climbs to Anne's Gate, which formed part of the complex fortifications of what was once the Lichtenegg castle. Each of its south corners is reinforced with a tetrahedral bastion whose faces meet at a near-right angle. At the south-east foot of the castle there is another gateway leading to the bailey of the lower castle, guarded by the Pyramid Gate in the north. The long road between the lower and upper castle areas proceeds to the Wenceslas Gate below the lower corner of the upper castle of Kronegg, protected by a ditch in the south and east. Beyond the wall of the upper castle there is another east ditch. The area between the two castles is protected by a wall, linked to the outer fortification of the upper castle, with a shallow projecting bastion tower. This wall proceeds as far

259 ►
Luxembourg. Model (1805) of the city and fort, seen from the south-east.

as the north-west corner of the entire fort, which is reinforced by another bastion tower.

The south-east bastion tower of the lower castle joins the eastern section of the peripheral wall, which is also protected by bastion towers. The wall encompasses a vast area on the north-east and east sides of the fort.

The new fortifications of the upper castle were built as early as the Thirty Years' War period (the outer ditch with the Wenceslas Gate). The construction of the fort took place shortly before the last major Turkish onslaught in 1683. As a whole Riegersburg represents a peculiar mixture of the medieval and early Baroque—one that was probably not very effective in military terms.

In the course of the 17th and the 18th centuries the Tirolian border fort of Kufstein was gradually extended southwards and provided with bastions with casemates.

★

The Thirty Years' War greatly increased the importance of Bohemia, while demonstrating the inadequacy of its fortifications. Shortly after the war, in 1653, Joseph, Baron Priami of Roverat, prepared a scheme to fortify Prague; construction began immediately and went on until 1721. However, the fortifications are impressive only in their scope, not militarily. The tetrahedral bastions took a variety of different forms. Initially they rose from the bottom of a ditch which lacked almost all the basic advance elements used in contemporary fortification: the ravelins were restricted more or less to the gateways; the only tenaille and counterguard probably formed part of a later modification of the defence; and there was no glacis.

The citadel of Prague was built on top of the Vyšehrad hill; it was protected by five major bastions, and on the south-west side, a hornwork. The curtains were 79-144 metres long (around the New Town as much as 227 metres long); the ditch was on average 44 metres wide and 5 metres deep; the bastions and curtains were 9-12 metres high.

Impressive though this sounds, in developmental terms the late 17th century fortifications of Prague are without significance. Even at the time of their construction they were ineffective and obsolete.

Similar, extremely simplified designs were used for the forts at Brno (built at the foot of the still extant medieval castle of Špilberk) and at Cheb (formerly Eger) in western Bohemia. Equally ineffective was the bastion fort of Uherské Hradiště in eastern Moravia.

In southern Slovakia the New Fort was of somewhat higher quality. It was added in 1663-73 to the fortress at Komárno; Francis Wymes directed the operation. The New Fort has a hornwork form

supplemented by a central tetrahedral bastion.

The growing menace from the Turks prompted the foundation and, in 1665-69, the speedy construction of the small Slovakian fort of Leopoldov (Trnava district). It is hexagonal in plan, with corner bastions and three-sided ravelins in the moat. It is the purest (albeit belated) manifestation of Neo-Italian fortification in the territory of Czechoslovakia.

A large scale effort to strengthen the key Hungarian fort of Györ was made at the same time. On three sides of the original Old Italian fortifications, the moat was made much wider and crammed with new structures. The ravelins in front of the curtains functioned alongside the counterguards of the bastions, protected by tetrahedral lunettes. The whole extremely complex system was supplemented with a hornwork and further lunettes of the most varied form. A covered way ran around the periphery.

In late 17th century Poland, the most significant development was the fort built near the estuary of the Vistula, in the immediate vicinity of the city of Gdańsk (formerly Danzig). In 1673 the original fort with four corner bastion towers was protected by a system consisting of five bastions connected by curtains with three small ravelins in front of them. Around the ditch ran a covered way with places of arms. On the opposite river bank stood a hornwork with lateral bastions, a continuous fausse braye and one axially sited ravelin. The covered way was very large in area.

The attractive castles with bastions in southern Poland no longer had the character of true forts. Remarkable exceptions are the five-sided bastion fortifications at Wisnicz, east of Cracow, which date from 1615-21, and the similar castle of Krzyztopór at Uyazd (1621-44).

In Denmark the reigns of Christian IV (1588-1648) and Frederick III (1648-70) witnessed the most intensive fortification works, represented by the fivepointed, star-shaped citadel of Frederikshavn in Copenhagen and the castle of Kronborg in Helsingör in the Sound.

The hexagonal Old Italian citadel at Casale Mon-ferrato on the River Po, fortified with tetrahedral bastions, was reconstructed at great expense by Vauban after it was taken by the French. Its reconstruction consistently employed such standard features as tenailles, major ravelins with reduits, counterguards, a lunette in the ditch and a covered way with places of arms.

Although still a force to be reckoned with, Spain went into a long, slow decline during the 17th century.

The coastal fort of Rosas, below the French border, has a five-pointed star plan with corner bastions. On four sides there are three-sided ravelins in front of the curtains. Three bastion towers were protected by large lunettes. The whole fortification was surrounded by a covered way. The fort was completed in the second half of the 17th century.

An example of an Italianized Spanish fort is Badajoz, near the Portuguese border. Its northwest, south and east sides are fortified by a bastion system; some of the bastions are provided with orillons. The faces of the tetrahedral bastions meet at a right or an obtuse angle. The curtains are protected by ravelins in the ditch. The fortification is encircled by a covered way with places of arms. The fort was probably completed in the mid-17th century.

To sum up, European fortifications of the 17th century have many distinctive features. Significant technical advances were concentrated in two countries, France and the Netherlands; other countries copied but did not improve on their methods. The cheaper and less time-consuming Dutch techniques had many more imitators than the far more costly and protracted methods of Vauban. In some places, especially in Central Europe, the older Italian school remained influential, although fortifications of this type were often constructed in simplified forms.

The Eighteenth Century to the Mid-Nineteenth Century

The death of Vauban in 1707 was followed by a period in which his successors made various improvements on his technique. To their contemporaries these were of considerable significance, but from a late 20th century retrospect, the finer distinctions between various theorists no longer seem of great moment.

Vauban's principal follower, Louis de Cormontaigne (1696-1752), considered himself as merely a corrector of Vauban's first system. In 1750 an engineering school at Mézières in eastern France was founded; subsequently very influential, it became a centre from which Cormontaigne's doctrines were propagated.

A more original personality was Marc René, Marquis de Montalambert (1714-1800), the creator of tenaille fortifications; his conclusions entirely destroyed the traditional bastion system. But although Montalambert's ideas influenced the theory of fortification construction, they actually came too late, since the old forts were doomed by the rapid development of siege artillery. It is a nice irony that the aristocratic Marquis de Montalambert lived, wrote and published his theoretical works in Paris, quite unaffected by the events of the French Revolution.

With a few exceptions, our survey of the final century of historical forts will concentrate on Bohemia and Moravia, where the biggest and most interesting new projects were undertaken until forts became completely obsolete. As it happens, it is in Czechoslovakia that many 18th and 19th century forts have survived more or less intact, and have been preserved as cultural monuments.

At Alba-Julia in Transylvania (Romania), a seven-sided citadel, still extant, was built in 1714-39. Its orilloned corner bastions follow Vauban's manner, and it has simplified tenailles, ravelins with reduits and a covered way. The entrance to its eastern part was guarded by a lunette projecting beyond the covered way.

In Scotland, Fort George, about 8 miles from Inverness, was built (c. 1744-63) on a neck of land surrounded by the waters of the Moray Firth. The fort has a symmetrical oblong plan narrowing to the south-east. On the land side there is a hornwork; in the corners of both long sides there are wide, shallow tetrahedral bastions; and in the south-west the fort terminates in a two-faced bastion with large orillons. The ravelin and the covered way with retrenchment were sited to the north-east, on the land side. Both east curtains were protected by projecting, two-faced casemates.

★

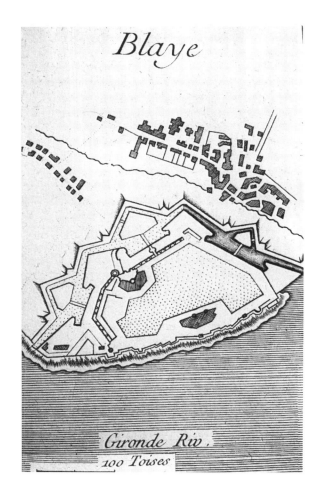

The large Moravian fort of Olomouc was reconstructed during the reign of Maria Theresa (1740-80). The new work was carried out in 1742-56 after designs by the French architect Pierre Philippe Bechade de Rochepine, linking up with earlier fortifications erected after the Thirty Years' War. However, only scattered fragments of these fortifications now survive.

The impressive fortifications of Hradec Králové in eastern Bohemia have also disappeared, virtually without trace. They were built between 1776 and 1782, and their chief designer was a Czech military engineer, Václav Pavlovský, who was mainly influenced by the work of Vauban. In plan the fortifications comprised an eight-pointed star with eight bastions, most of whose faces met at an obtuse angle. Only four bastions were provided with cavaliers,

260.
Blaye, France. Plan (1789) of the fort.

261
Blaye, France. Model (1703) of the fort, built from 1685 onwards. View from the south-west, from the River Gironde.

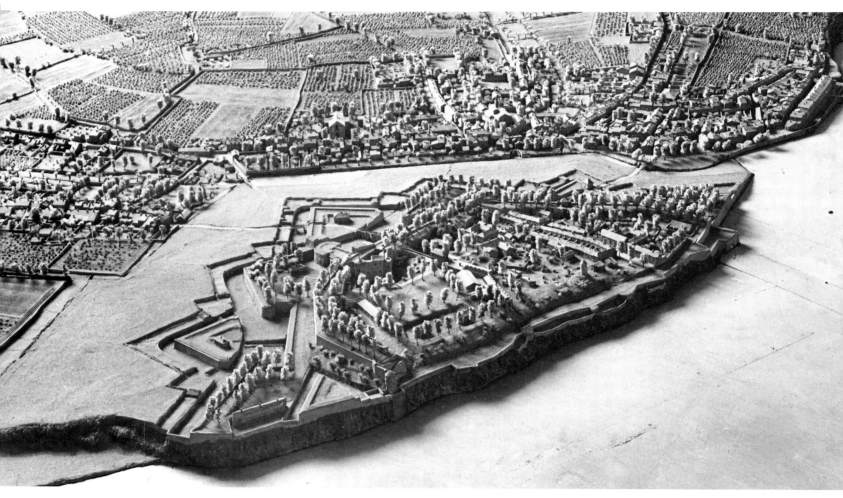

216

262
Blaye, France. Part of the
fortifications in front of the
forts, with a gate in the curtain,
a ditch and a ravelin.

and tenailles were only constructed in front of
two gateways. All the curtains were protected by
two-sided ravelins, accompanied by retrenchments
along the covered way above the ditch, either
with small lunettes or small arsenals. The curtains
were connected with the ravelins by means of caponnières.

Following a war between Austria and Prussia in
1778, intensive construction began on two forts,
Terezín and Josefov. Both of them survive, and they
now represent the best examples of the art of fortification before the demise of the bastion system.

Terezín in northern Bohemia was constructed in
1780-90 to a design by Carlo Pellegrini, and consists of three parts. The Major Fort stands on the
west bank of the River Ohře; the Minor Fort is
further to the east. The two are connected by upper
and lower retrenchments.

The Main Fort is heptagonal in plan, with a long
east side. Eight tetrahedral bastions, varying in
shape and layout, defend the corners and the centre
of the east wall. Only four of the bastions are
provided with cavaliers. The two bastions at the
west corners are closed by retrenchment structures.
With the exception of the east side, the curtains are
protected by tenailles. The ravelins are of two types:
two of them comprise the retrenchment structures,
four the reduits. A road passes through two ravelins.
Both west corner bastions are covered by a counterguard.

The main ditch runs along the bastions, while
secondary ditches, linked by caponnières, surround
the ravelins and counterguards. Except on the east
side, the fort is surrounded by a covered way. The
places of arms are of two types, the more complex
being provided with retrenchments. The fort was
entered through four gateways and four posterns.
All of the fortifications are clad with bricks.

The far side of the bridge crossing the River Ohře
was guarded by a lunette with short bastion fronts

217

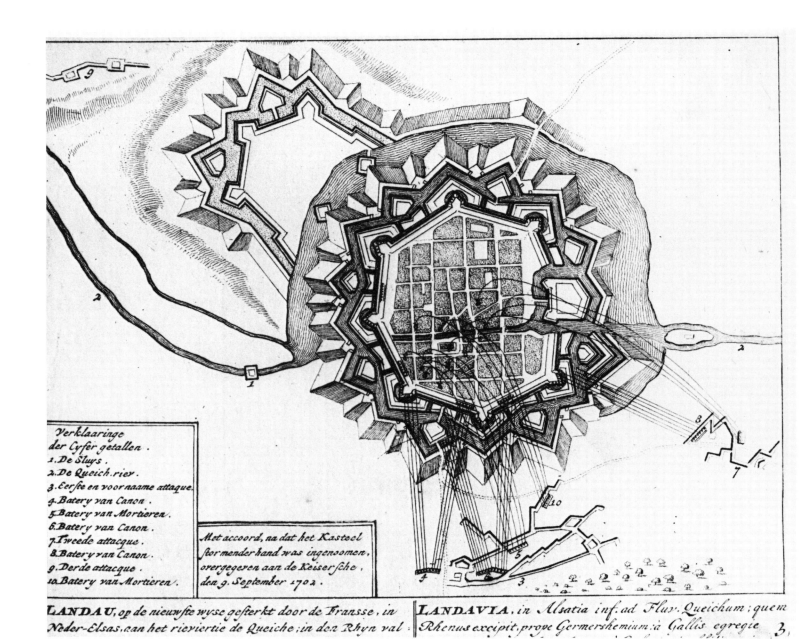

Verklaaringe
der Cyfer getallen.
1. De Sluys.
2. De Queich. rier.
3. Eerste en voor naame attaque.
4. Batery van Canon.
5. Batery van Mortieren.
6. Batery van Canon.
7. Tweede attacque.
8. Batery van Canon.
9. Derde attacque.
10. Batery van Mortieren.

Met accoord, na dat het Kasteel
stormender hand was ingenomen,
overgegeven aan de Keisersche,
den 9. September 1702.

LANDAU, op de nieuwste wyse gesterkt door de Fransse, in
Neder-Elsas, aan het rieviertie de Queiche; in den Rhyn val.

LANDAVIA, in Alsatia inf. ad Fluv. Queichum; quem
Rhenus excipit, prope Germershemium: a Gallis egregie

on either side, linking with the north and south
fortifications of the area between the Major and
Minor Forts; these, enclosed on both sides by
bastion fronts with a major tetrahedral bastion in the
centre, comprise the so-called upper and lower
retrenchments.

The Minor Fort has the character of a citadel,
with a pair of tetrahedral (east) bastions and two
(west) demibastions. Only the east curtain is protected by a tenaille and, in front of it, a ravelin with a
reduit. The north ravelin is a simple structure, and
instead of a south ravelin, a reduit was built, along
which ran the road to Prague. The places of arms
of the covered way are partly supplemented by
retrenchments.

263
Landau, Germany. Plan of
the fort at the time of its
siege in 1702. Engraved by
Schenk. The fortification was
built in 1667-91.

264 ▶
Landau, Germany. The French
Gate, built c. 1687-91.

218

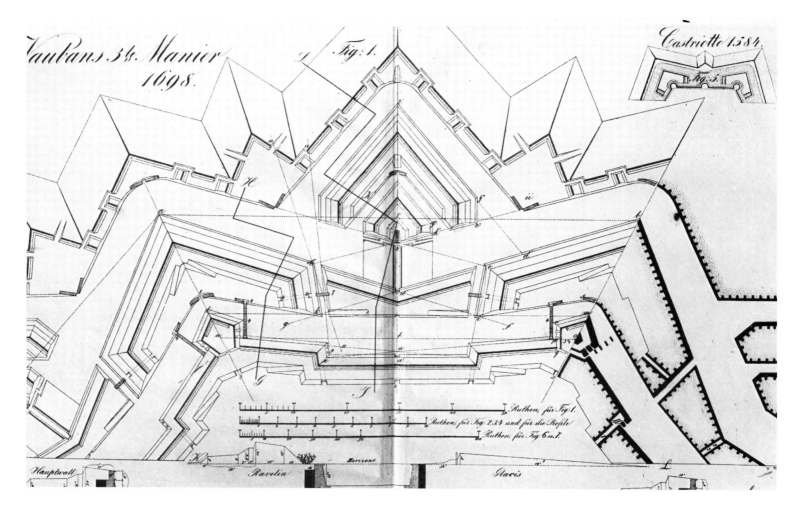

Vaubans 3ᵉ Manier
1698.   Fig. 1.   Castriette 1584.
Fig. 5.

Ruthen, für Fig. 1.
Ruthen, für Fig. 2.3.4. und für die Reste.
Ruthen, für Fig 6 u. 7.

Hauptwall   Ravelin   Horizont   Glacis

◀ 265
Plan of fortifications built according to Vauban's third system or manner. After von Zastrow.

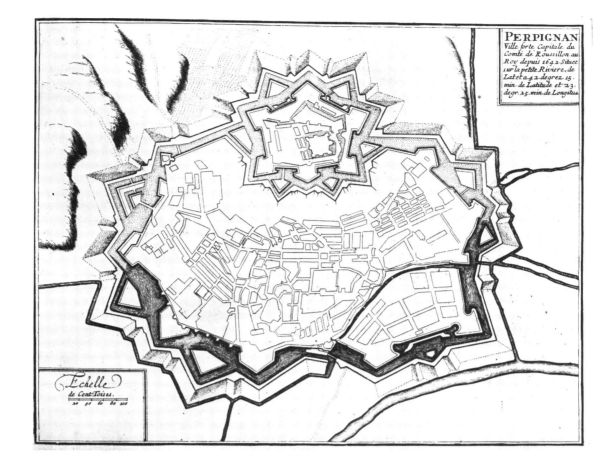

267
Perpignan, France. Plan of the fortified city of 1695. The fortifications were strengthened in the late 17th century.

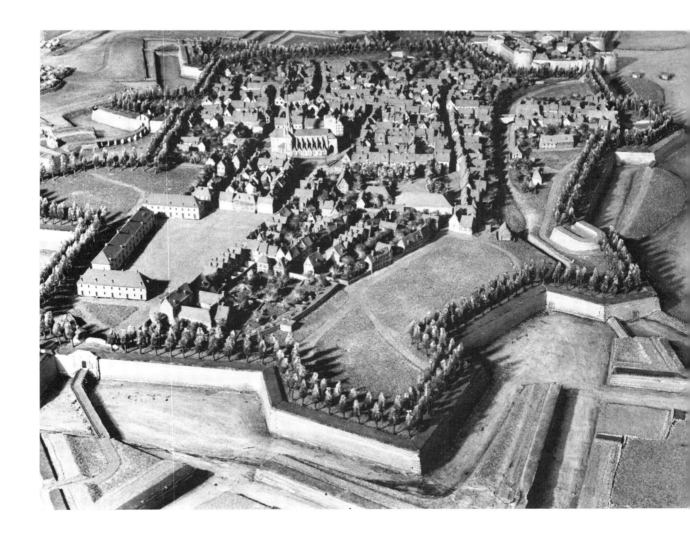

◀ 266
Neuf Brisach, France. Model (1706) of the fort, which was begun in 1698.

268
Auxonne, France. Model of the fort of 1677.

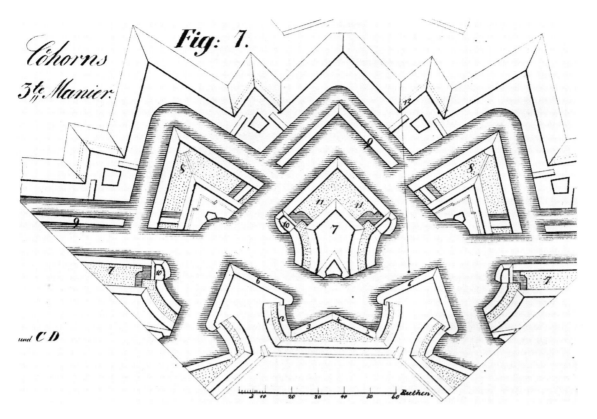

Fig: 7.

Cohorns 3te Manier.

und C D

Ruthen.

269
Plan of fortifications built according to van Coehorn's mature manner. After von Zastrow.

To the south-east of the Minor Fort there are tetrahedral lunettes surrounded by a ditch and connected with the fort by a covered way.

Josefov in eastern Bohemia was constructed between 1781 and 1787 to a design by Louis Querlonde du Hamel. The Upper Fort, on a hilltop above the south bank of the River Metuje, is one of the most attractive fortifications of the period. The fort proper comprises a somewhat irregular octagon with eight tetrahedral bastions, widely different in plan, without cavaliers.

The north side of the fort, protected by a crownwork, was simpler in design than the other sides; the traditional tenailles, caponnières and ravelins were all employed. The fortification system on the other sides was supplemented by massive counterguards which covered the adjacent sections of the curtains as well as the bastions. The ravelins were strengthened by reduits. The covered way was particularly well protected. Between the ravelin were small lunettes or retrenchments separated from the covered way proper by a narrow ditch.

Beyond the covered way, above the confluence of the River Metuje and Elbe, stood a hornwork. North of the Upper Fort, between the Metuje and the Elbe, there was a fortified island.

The Lower Fort, actually a crownwork with a couple of bastions, is situated to the north of the Upper Fort. Its north gate was protected by a tenaille and a ravelin, and the entire fort was surrounded by a covered way. A large redoubt was erected between the rivers.

During the 18th century the Turks were pushed far back into south-eastern Europe, but Komárno retained its importance. From the beginning of the 19th century it was gradually converted into a large military base with fortifications extending to the south bank of the Danube. Construction went on into the third quarter of the 19th century.

In 1815-32 the fort of Ehrenbreitstein was built in a remarkable position above the Rhine, opposite Coblenz.

Montalambert's doctrines, at first underestimated by the French, were used by the Prussians in building their forts. However, it soon became necessary to take new measures to prolong the life of the 17th and 18th century forts. Immediately after the end of the Napoleonic wars, advanced forts or outposts began to be constructed. In Olomouc they were built from 1829 onwards, at first some 800-1200 metres from the covered way. Eventually these outworks were situated at a distance of 4-6 kilometres from the main fort. From the mid-19th century, 'Neo-Prussian' detached strongpoints

222

were usually circular in plan. Nevertheless, with the dawn of the age of modern warfare the bastion system was doomed.

★

In retrospect, historic permanent fortifications can be seen to have passed through two great cycles, from classical times to the late Middle Ages and from the Renaissance to the 19th century. Techni-

270
Naarden, Netherlands. Aerial view of the fortified city from the south. 17th century.

271
Stolpen, Germany. The medieval nucleus of the fortress dates mainly from the 15th to 16th centuries, the Baroque fortifications from 1675 onwards.

272
Forchtenstein, Austria. Medieval castle converted to a Baroque fort in the middle years of the 17th century. The bastions were built in 1652. The circular tower with a projecting edge in the foreground dates from the end of the 13th century.

273
Riegersburg, Austria. View from the west of the fort, built on the site of two older castles. There is a bailey of complex layout on the right; the older Kronegg Castle stands on the left. The fort dates from the later 17th century.

274
Riegersburg, Austria. The Wenceslas Gate, dating from 1637-53.

225

275
Prague, Czechoslovakia. The Leopold Gate of Prague's citadel on Vyšehrad, built from 1676-78 after a design by Carlo Lurago.

276
Györ, Hungary. Part of the Baroque fortifications built in the 1660s.

cally, development proceeded by sudden spurts, the impulse coming from countries that were not necessarily large and populous (medieval Bohemia, the early modern Netherlands). The intentions underlying different systems also changed over time. In the fortifications of the classical world, a conceptual unity prevailed. The Middle Ages, on the other hand, were characterized by strong diversifying tendencies, suppressed from time to time in the interests of uniformity (as imposed, for example, by monarchs or by the Order of Teutonic Knights). Finally, with the coming of the bastion system, individualism disappeared, if only for economic reasons: only the state could afford to build such powerful, complex fortresses.

With the passing of these extraordinary monuments to human inventiveness—now, ironically, treasured cultural artefacts—we bring to an end our survey of a millennium of European fortifications.

277
Casale Monferrato, Italy. Plan of the fort (1727). It was reconstructed in the last quarter of the 17th century. After Fischer.

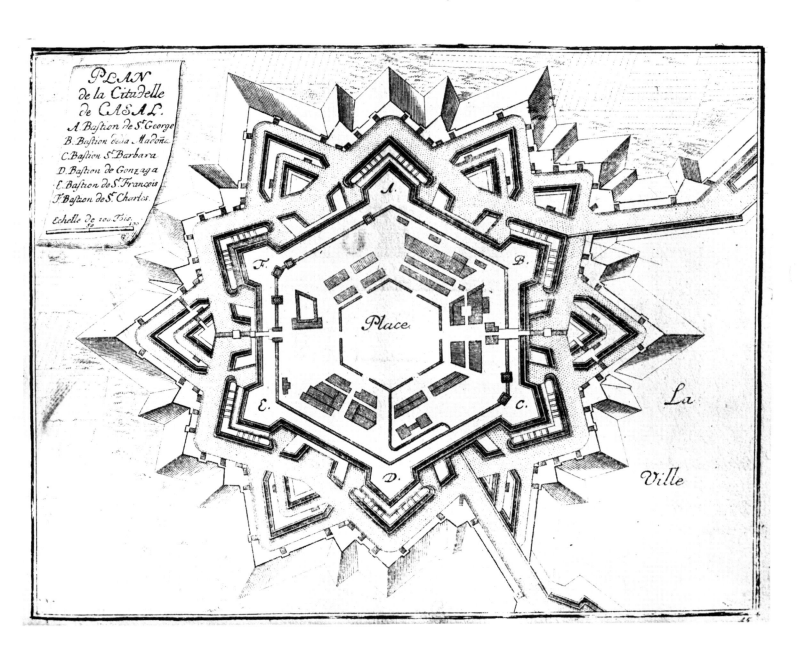

278
Hradec Králové,
Czechoslovakia. Model of the
town and fort as it was in
1865, seen from the north-
west. The fort was built in
1766-82.

279
Terezín, Czechoslovakia. The
Minor Fort, part of the more
extensive fort built in 1780-90.

280
Josefov, Czechoslovakia.
Plan of the fort, built between
1781 and 1787.

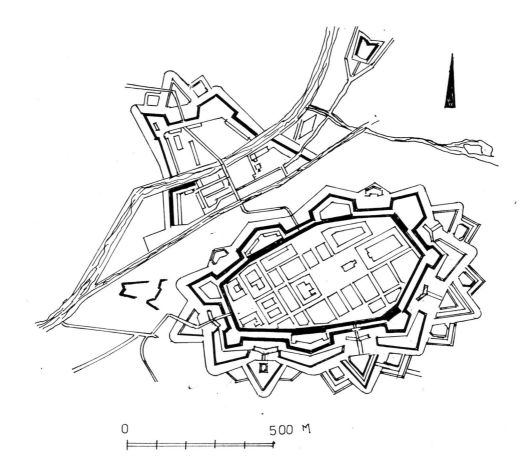

281
Ehrenbreitstein, Germany.
A fort above the Rhine, built
1815-32, with
a bulky gun bastion in the
foreground.

0   500 M

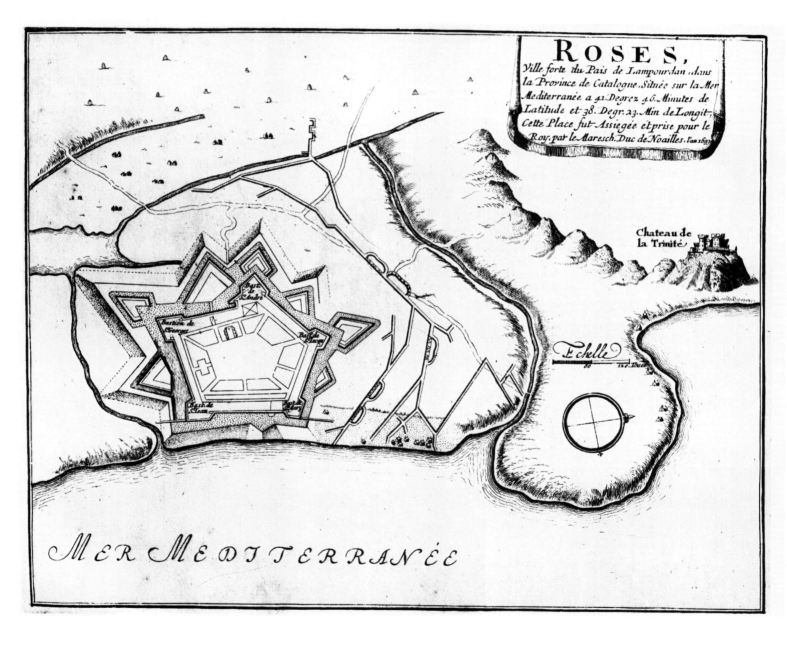

ROSES,
Ville forte du Païs de Lampourdan, dans
la Province de Catalogne, Situé sur la Mer
Mediterranée a 41. Degrez 46. Minutes de
Latitude et 38. Degr. 23. Min de Longit.
Cette Place fut Assiegée et prise pour le
Roy, par le Maresch. Duc de Noailles, l'an 1693.

Chateau de la Trinité

Echelle

MER MEDITERRANÉE

282
Rosas, Spain. Plan of the fort
(1695). It was built in the late
17th century.

Glossary

BARBICAN	Advanced fortification work protecting the gateway of a city or castle.
BARTIZAN	Projecting corner turret.
BASTION	Fortification work, usually four-sided (tetrahedral) and situated in the corners of the wall, with a sharp point, making possible active defence and flanking fire.
BASTION TOWER	Tower projecting from the wall face and functioning as a BASTION.
BATTER	The outward slope of a revetment.
BRATTICE	Temporary wooden gallery for use in a siege.
CAPONNIÈRE	Covered passage across a ditch to an outer fortification structure such as a RAVELIN.
CASEMATE	Covered chamber for musketry or artillery.
CAVALIER	Superstructure containing a battery, usually sited above the centre of a bastion.
CITADEL	Heavily fortified, independent defensive structure within city walls, dominating an ancient or a medieval town; in the bastion system, the strongest part of the fort.
CORBEL	Stone support projecting from the wall face.
COUNTERGUARD	Detached structure protecting a BASTION.
COUNTERSCARP	Outer face of a ditch.
COUVRE FACE	Low rampart in the ditch protecting the face of a RAVELIN; analogous in function to the COUNTERGUARD and FAUSSE BRAYE.
COVERED WAY	Passage along the outer edge of a ditch, protected by a rampart forming the GLACIS; it is usually some 10 metres wide.
CROWNWORK	Advanced fortification structure screening the entrance to a bastion fort.
CURTAIN, CURTAIN WALL	Stretch of wall between two towers, BASTION TOWERS or BASTIONS.
DONJON	Monumental main building of a medieval castle; a residential great tower. KEEP is an alternative term for donjons, particularly widely used down to the 12th century.
FAUSSE BRAYE	Low rampart in the ditch, in front of the main fortification.
GLACIS	Rampart of the covered way, sloping away towards the enemy.

283
Barbican of the Prague Gate,
Slaný, completed in 1472
(demolished 1841). From an
old drawing.

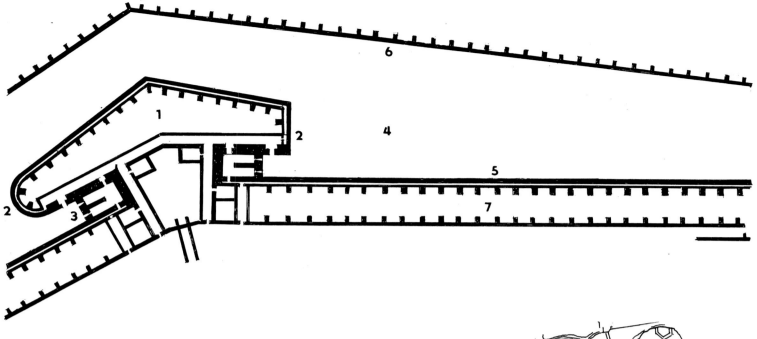

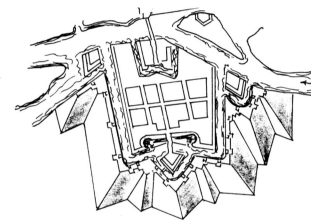

284
The bastion system as developed by the Old Italian school of fortification (after von Zastrow).
1 — bastion; 2 — orillons;
3 — casemates; 4 — ditch;
5 — scarp; 6 — counterscarp;
7 — part of the curtain wall.

285
Hornwork of the French fort of Mézières, on the south bank of the River Maas. Late 17th century.

286
Crownwork. Schematic representation after E. Wagner's *Trecht, Wehr und Waffen im Dreissigjährigen Krieg,* Hanau, 1980.

HORNWORK	'Horned' structure consisting of two demibastions, one at each end of a curtain.
KEEP	See DONJON.
LUNETTE	Triangular (originally crescent shaped) defensive structure, open at the rear, often flanking a RAVELIN.
MACHICOLATION	Permanent masonry gallery supported by corbels and provided with openings through which missiles etc. could be dropped on to the enemy below.
MERLON	The solid upright part of a parapet, alternating with voids (crenels).

MOTTE	Artificial mound.
NECK DITCH	Ditch cutting across a neck of land to hinder an enemy's advance.
ORILLONS	Round or squared-off extensions of a bastion's faces, designed to protect its recessed flanks.
PIATTA FORMA	Fortification structure protecting the curtain between two bastions; it is square or rectangular in plan, or takes the form of a small tetrahedral bastion.
PILASTER	Vertical strip slightly projecting from the wall face.
PLACE OF ARMS	Enlarged area in a COVERED WAY where troops could assemble.
POSTERN	Small gateway in a castle or fort from which the besieged could sally out.
RAVELIN	Fortified structure, more or less triangular in plan, sited in the ditch to defend the curtain.
REDOUBT	Detached, independent outwork.
REDUIT	Defensive structure to the rear of, and higher than, a RAVELIN.
RETRENCHMENT	Interior defence works, usually consisting of a trench and parapet.
REVETMENT	Retaining wall; that is, a wall supporting a weight of earth or water.
ROUNDEL	Low, circular, semicircular or U-shaped tower for artillery, projecting from the wall face.

287
Fortifications built to Vauban's first system (after von Zastrow).
1 — bastion; 2 — cavallier;
3 — curtain; 4 — tenaille;
5 — ditch; 6 — caponnière;
7 — ravelin; 8 — reduit;
9 — covered way; 10 — place of arms; 11 — traverse;
12 — small lunette;
13 — glacis.

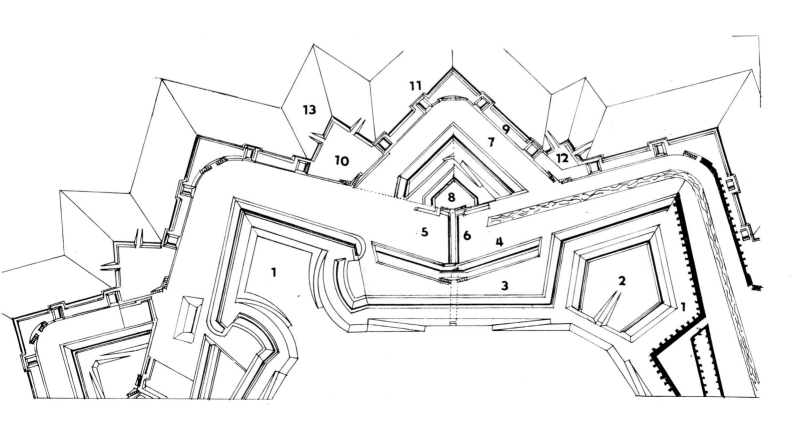

233

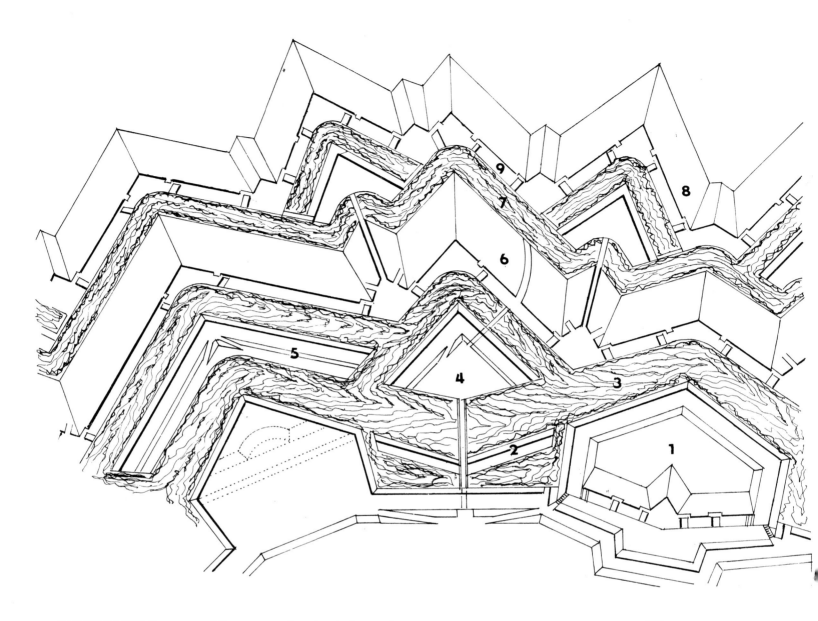

RUSTICATION	Masonry made of cut stone whose outer face is only roughly dressed; also known as *en bosse*.
SCARP	Inner face of a ditch.
SHELL KEEP	Castle consisting of a high, strong ring wall with residential buildings adjacent to its inner face.
SHIELD WALL	Exceptionally thick wall, protecting the castle on its most vulnerable side.
TENAILLE	Low earth or masonry structure, built in the ditch to protect the CURTAIN.
TRACE	Circuit or fortified perimeter, also known as the enceinte.
TRAVERSE	Small bank or wall that cuts across the line of a COVERED WAY.

288
Fortifications built to Vauban's improved first system (after von Zastrow).
1 — bastion; 2 — tenailles; 3 — main ditch; 4 — ravelin; 5 — counterguard; 6 — covered way with place of arms; 7 — outer ditch; 8 — flèche; 9 — outer covered way.

Bibliography

Androuet du Cerceau, J., *Des plus excellents bâtiments de France,* Paris 1868-1870

Baillie Reynolds, P. K., *Kenilworth Castle,* London 1956

Beritić, L., *Les remparts de Dubrovnik,* Dubrovnik 1982

Bochenek, R., *Od palisád k podzemním pevnostem* (From palisades to underground forts), Prague 1972

Bornheim, S. W. von, *Rheinische Höhenburgen,* Vol. 3, Neuss 1964

Brisac, C., *Le Musée des plans et reliefs,* Paris 1981

Bruns, L., *Hohenstaufensschlösser,* Königstein 1941

Citadelles et villes fortes, Paris 1978

Clasen, K. H., *Die mittelalterliche Kunst im Gebiete des Deutschordenstaates,* Preussen 1, Königsberg i. Pr. 1927

Dehio, G., *Handbuch der deutschen Kunstdenkmäler, Österreich II.,* Vienna-Berlin 1935

Dehio, G., *Handbuch der deutschen Kunstdenkmäler, Der Bezirk Halle,* Berlin 1976

Dehio, G., *Handbuch der deutschen Kunstdenkmäler, Bayern I.,* Franken 1979

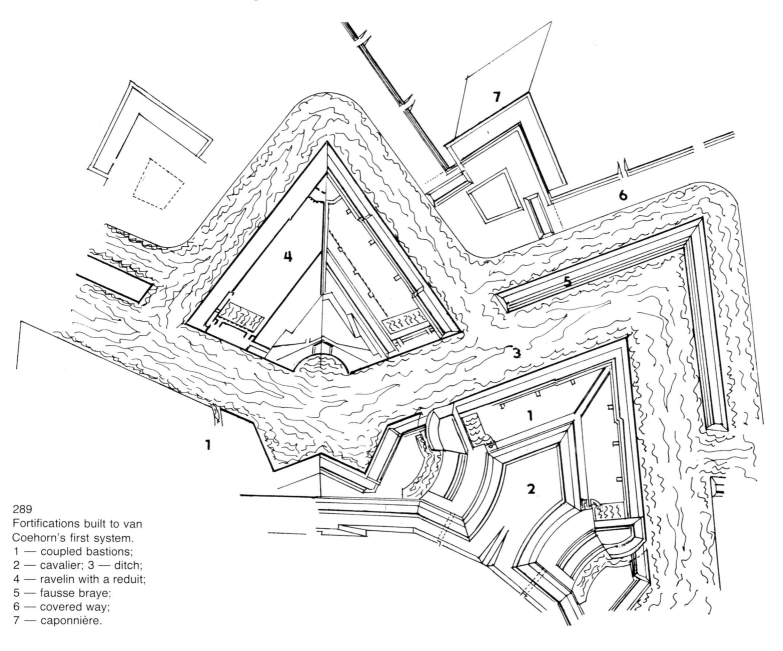

289
Fortifications built to van Coehorn's first system.
1 — coupled bastions;
2 — cavalier; 3 — ditch;
4 — ravelin with a reduit;
5 — fausse braye;
6 — covered way;
7 — caponnière.

Dehio, G., Gall, E., *Handbuch der deutschen Kunstdenkmäler, Rheinfranken*, Berlin 1943

Dehio-Handbuch. Die Kunstdenkmäler Österreich, Salzburg-Vienna-Munich 1963

Dunan, M. E., 'Les châteaux forts du comté de Luxembourg', in: *Publications de la section historique de l'Institut Grand-Ducal de Luxembourg* LXX, 1950

Durdík, T., 'Vývoj hradů 13. století v Čechách' (The development of 13th century castles in Bohemia), in: *Folia historica bohemica* 1, 1974, p. 177 ff.

Durdík, T., 'Nástin vývoje českých hradů 12.-13. století' (Outline of development of Bohemian castles in the 12th and 13th centuries), in: *Archaeologia historica* 3, 1978, p. 41 ff.

Durdík, T., *Hrady kastelového typu v Čechách* (Castles of rectangular French type in Bohemia), Prague 1982

Durdík, T., *České hrady* (Bohemian castles), Prague 1984

Durdík, T., 'Archeologické poznatky památek 6.—15. století v Čechách 1975-1985' (Archaeological discoveries of the 6th-15th century monuments in Bohemia 1975-1985), in: *The Fifth Congress of the International Union of Slavonic Archaeology*, Kiev 1985, pp 261-267

Ebersolt, J., *Monuments d'architecture byzantine*, Paris 1934

Ebhardt, B., *Deutsche Burgen*, Berlin 1898-1907

Ebhardt, B., *Die Burgen Italiens*, Berlin 1909-27

Ebhardt, B., *Der Wehrbau Europas in Mittelalter*, Frankfurt am Main 1978

Enaud, F., *Les châteaux-forts en France*, Paris 1958

Enlart, C., and Verrier, J., *Manuel d'archéologie française 2, Architecture civile et militaire*, II, *Architecture militaire et navale*, 2nd ed., Paris 1932

Fialová, H., and Fiala, A., *Hrady na Slovensku* (Castles in Slovakia), Martin 1966

Gerö, L., *Magyarországi Várepitészet* (Hungarian castles), Budapest 1955

Gerö, L., *Ungarische Burgen*, Budapest 1969

Gilyard-Beer, R., 'Artillery fortification in Britain', in: *Bulletin IBI* 29, 1971, pp. 28-31

Glossarium Artis, Burgen und Feste Plätze, Tübingen 1977

Gruszecki, A., *Bastionowe zamki w Malopolsce* (Bastion castles in Little Poland), Warsaw 1962

Guerquin, B., *Zamki Sląskie* (Castles in Silesia), Warsaw 1957

Guerquin, B., *Zamki w Polsce* (Castles in Poland), Warsaw 1974

Hogg, I., *A History of Fortification*, London 1981

Hotz, W., *Elsass-Lothringen, Handbuch der Kunstdenkmäler München*, Berlin 1976

Hotz, W., *Pfalzen und Burgen der Stauferzeit*, Darmstadt 1981

Jenny, H., *Kunstführer der Schweiz*, Bern, undated

Kašička, F., 'Státní zámek Konopiště a jeho nejstarší proměny' (State castle of Konopiště and its earliest metamorphoses), in: *Archaeologia historica* 3, 1976

Klaar, A., *Beiträge zur Planaufnahmen Österreichischer Burgen* II, Niederösterreich 2, Vienna 1974

Les forces de l'Europe I-VIII, Paris 1694-97

Líbal, D., *Stálá opevnění doby poděbradské a jagellonské v díle O. Frankenberga 'Husitské válečnictví po Lipanech'* (Permanent fortifications of the Poděbrad and Jagiello period in O. Frankenberg's work 'Hussite Warfare after the Battle of Lipany'), Prague 1960

Líbal, D., *Starobylá města* (Ancient cities), Prague 1970

Líbal, D., 'Umění románské, gotické, architektura' (Romanesque and Gothic art, architecture), in: *Praha středověká* (Medieval Prague), Prague 1983

MacIvor, I., *The Fortifications of Berwick-upon-Tweed*, HMSO, Edinburgh 1967

Menclová, D., *Hrad Bratislava* (The Castle of Bratislava), Bratislava 1936

Menclová, D., 'O středověkém opevnění našich měst' (On medieval fortifications of our cities), in: *Zprávy památkové péče* X, 1952, p. 193 ff.

Menclová, D., 'Vliv husitských válek na pozdně gotickou fortifikační architekturu' (Influence of the Hussite Wars on Late Gothic fortification architecture), in: *Umění* IX, 1961, p. 433 ff.

Menclová, D., *České hrady* (Bohemian castles), Vols. I—II, Prague 1972

Monumenti d'Italia, Castelli, Novara 1978

Morel, P., *Carcassonne, La cité*, Paris 1965

Mrusek, H. J., *Burgen in Europa*, Leipzig 1973

Nitschen, J., plan in the publication *Tower of London*, London 1976

O'Neil, B. H. St J., *Deal Castle*, HMSO 1956

Oprescu, G., *Die Wehrkirchen in Siebenbürgen*, Dresden 1961

Peers, Ch., *Pevensey Castle*, London 1957

Piper, O., *Burgenkunde*, Munich 1912

Pisoň, Š., *Hrady, zámky a kaštiele na Slovensku* (Castles in Slovakia), Martin 1973

Ramelli, A. C., 'Venticinque schede per una storia del fronte bastionato', in: *Castellum* 1971, p. 69 ff.

Romaňák, A., 'Obranný systém pražskej bastionovej fortifikácie' (Defence system of Prague bastion fortification), in: *Historie a vojenství* 6, 1964, p. 939 ff.

Romaňák, A., *Pevnost Terezín* (The fort of Terezín), Prague 1972

Romaňák, A., and Picková, V., 'Z dejín novodobého pevnostného stavitelstva' (From the history of modern fortification construction), in: *Historie a vojenství* 8, 1966, p. 1061 ff.

Ross, A., *The Castles of Scotland*, London 1973

Salch, C. L., *Dictionnaire des châteaux et des fortifications du moyen âge en France*, Strasbourg 1979

Schellart, A. I. J. M., *Kastellen*, Deventer 1974

Schuchhardt, C., *Die Burg im Wandel der Weltgeschichte*, Potsdam 1931

Simpson, W. D., *Bodiam Castle*, London 1954

Stankiewicz, J., 'Nadmorska twierdza w Woslonjśiu' (The coastal stronghold on the Vistula), in: *Kwartalnik architektury i urbanistiki* I, 1956, p. 115 ff.

Tower of London, HMSO, London 1967

Traux, M. de, *Die beständige Befestigungskunst*, Wiener Neustadt 1817

Trost, H., *Norddeutsche Stadttore zwischen Elbe und Oder*, Berlin 1959

Tuulse, A., *Die Burgen in Estland und Lettland*, Tartu 1942

Tuulse, A., *Burgen des Abendlandes*, Vienna-Munich 1958

Volpe, G., *Rocche e fortificazioni del Ducato di Urbino*, Urbino 1982

Wäscher, H., *Die Burgen Mitteldeutschlands*, Halle 1955

Weingartner, J., *Bozner Burgen*, Innsbruck 1922

Weingartner, J., and Hörmann, M., *Die Burgen Tirols*, Innsbruck, Bozen 1981

Willemsen, C. A., *Apulien, Kathedralen und Kastelle*, Cologne 1971

Winnig, A., *Der deutsche Ritterorden und seine Burgen*, Königstein im Taunus, 1943

Zastrow, A. von, *Geschichte der beständigen Befestigung*, Leipzig 1939

Index

Roman numbers indicate pages, numbers in italic refer to captions to the illustrations.

Abbreviations: arch. = architect; bd. = builder; dpt. = department; eng. = engineer; env. = environs; form. = formerly; prov. = province; reg. = region; s. = see; s.a. = see also

239

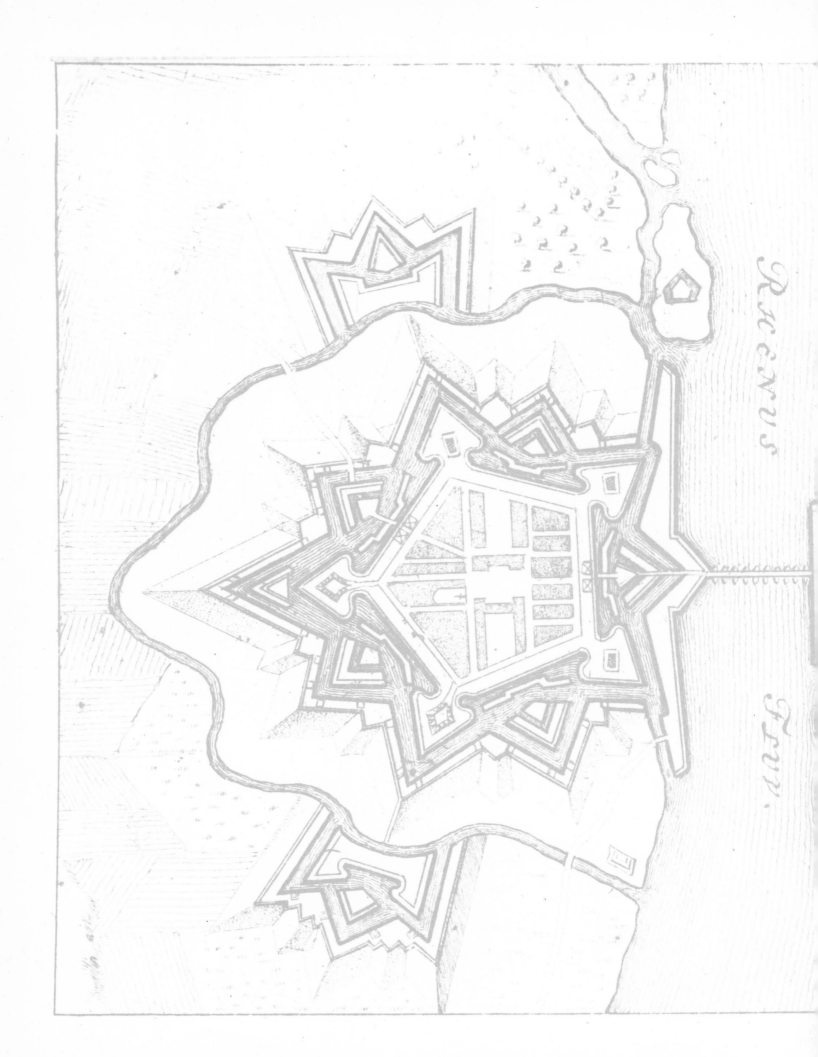

CHARLE-ROY.

NORT

H. van Loon fec.

De Fer